Publications of the
National Bureau of Economic Research, Inc.

Number 46

National Product since 1869

National Bureau of Economic Research, Inc.

OFFICERS

SHEPARD MORGAN, Chairman
C. REINOLD NOYES, President
BORIS SHISHKIN, Vice-President
GEORGE B. ROBERTS, Treasurer
W. J. CARSON, Executive Director
MARTHA ANDERSON, Editor

DIRECTORS AT LARGE

CHESTER I. BARNARD, *President, New Jersey Bell Telephone Company*
OSWALD W. KNAUTH, *New York City*
H. W. LAIDLER, *Executive Director, League for Industrial Democracy*
SHEPARD MORGAN, *Vice-President, Chase National Bank*
C. REINOLD NOYES, *New York City*
GEORGE B. ROBERTS, *Vice-President, National City Bank*
BEARDSLEY RUML, *Chairman, Board of Directors, R. H. Macy & Company*
HARRY SCHERMAN, *President, Book-of-the-Month Club*
GEORGE SOULE, *Director, The Labor Bureau, Inc.*
N. I. STONE, *Consulting Economist*
J. RAYMOND WALSH, *Economist, Congress of Industrial Organizations*
LEO WOLMAN, *Columbia University*

DIRECTORS BY UNIVERSITY APPOINTMENT

E. WIGHT BAKKE, *Yale*
C. C. BALDERSTON, *Pennsylvania*
W. L. CRUM, *Harvard*
GUY STANTON FORD, *Minnesota*
H. M. GROVES, *Wisconsin*
CLARENCE HEER, *North Carolina*
WESLEY C. MITCHELL, *Columbia*
PAUL M. O'LEARY, *Cornell*
W. W. RIEFLER, *Institute for Advanced Study*
T. O. YNTEMA, *Chicago*

DIRECTORS APPOINTED BY OTHER ORGANIZATIONS

PERCIVAL F. BRUNDAGE, *American Institute of Accountants*
FREDERICK C. MILLS, *American Statistical Association*
BORIS SHISHKIN, *American Federation of Labor*
WARREN C. WAITE, *American Farm Economic Association*
DONALD H. WALLACE, *American Economic Association*

RESEARCH STAFF

ARTHUR F. BURNS, *Director of Research*

MOSES ABRAMOVITZ
MORRIS A. COPELAND
SOLOMON FABRICANT
W. BRADDOCK HICKMAN
F. F. HILL
THOR HULTGREN
SIMON KUZNETS
CLARENCE D. LONG
RUTH P. MACK
FREDERICK C. MILLS
WESLEY C. MITCHELL
GEOFFREY H. MOORE
RAYMOND J. SAULNIER
GEORGE J. STIGLER
LEO WOLMAN

Relation of the Directors to the Work and Publications of the National Bureau of Economic Research

1. The object of the National Bureau of Economic Research is to ascertain and to present to the public important economic facts and their interpretation in a scientific and impartial manner. The Board of Directors is charged with the responsibility of ensuring that the work of the Bureau is carried on in strict conformity with this object.

2. To this end the Board of Directors shall appoint one or more Directors of Research.

3. The Director or Directors of Research shall submit to the members of the Board, or to its Executive Committee, for their formal adoption, all specific proposals concerning researches to be instituted.

4. No report shall be published until the Director or Directors of Research shall have submitted to the Board a summary drawing attention to the character of the data and their utilization in the report, the nature and treatment of the problems involved, the main conclusions and such other information as in their opinion would serve to determine the suitability of the report for publication in accordance with the principles of the Bureau.

5. A copy of any manuscript proposed for publication shall also be submitted to each member of the Board. For each manuscript to be so submitted a special committee shall be appointed by the President, or at his designation by the Executive Director, consisting of three Directors selected as nearly as may be one from each general division of the Board. The names of the special manuscript committee shall be stated to each Director when the summary and report described in paragraph (4) are sent to him. It shall be the duty of each member of the committee to read the manuscript. If each member of the special committee signifies his approval within thirty days, the manuscript may be published. If each member of the special committee has not signified his approval within thirty days of the transmittal of the report and manuscript, the Director of Research shall then notify each member of the Board, requesting approval or disapproval of publication, and thirty additional days shall be granted for this purpose. The manuscript shall then not be published unless at least a majority of the entire Board and a two-thirds majority of those members of the Board who shall have voted on the proposal within the time fixed for the receipt of votes on the publication proposed shall have approved.

6. No manuscript may be published, though approved by each member of the special committee, until forty-five days have elapsed from the transmittal of the summary and report. The interval is allowed for the receipt of any memorandum of dissent or reservation, together with a brief statement of his reasons, that any member may wish to express; and such memorandum of dissent or reservation shall be published with the manuscript if he so desires. Publication does not, however, imply that each member of the Board has read the manuscript, or that either members of the Board in general, or of the special committee, have passed upon its validity in every detail.

7. A copy of this resolution shall, unless otherwise determined by the Board, be printed in each copy of every National Bureau book.

(Resolution adopted October 25, 1926 and revised February 6, 1933 and February 24, 1941)

National Product since 1869

Simon Kuznets
University of Pennsylvania

Assisted by
Lillian Epstein
and
Elizabeth Jenks

NATIONAL BUREAU OF ECONOMIC RESEARCH, INC.

New York 1946

Copyright, 1946, by

National Bureau of Economic Research, Inc.

1819 Broadway, New York 23

All Rights Reserved

Manufactured in the U. S. A. by

H. Wolff, New York

Contents

Preface   xv

PART I
ANNUAL ESTIMATES, 1919-1943

A   Character of the Estimates   3
    1   Flow of Commodities to Consumers   3
    2   Flow of Services to Consumers   7
    3   Flow of Goods to Consumers   12
    4   Capital Formation   13
    5   National Product   18
B   Basic Tables   24

PART II
DECADE ESTIMATES, 1869-1938

A   Character of the Estimates   59
    1   Commodity Flow   59
      a   Coverage of Basic Series   59
      b   Passing from Output at Manufacturers' Prices to Flow at Final Cost   62
      c   Adjustment for Business Use of Passenger Cars and Related Products   73
    2   Flow of Goods to Consumers   76
    3   Capital Formation   79
    4   National Product   85
B   Basic Tables   90

PART III
THE SHARE OF SERVICES IN THE FLOW OF GOODS TO CONSUMERS

A   Share of Total Outlay Expended for Services, Low Income Urban Consumers, 1870-1914   123
    1   Character of the Data   123
      a   Consumer Groups Covered   123

	b Deriving Total Outlay	124
	c Variations in the Coverage of Components	125
	d The Percentage Distribution	126
	e Assignment to Commodities and Services	127
	2 Summary of Evidence	127
	a Per Year Change in the Total Service Share for Sample States	127
	b Median and Arithmetic Mean Changes in the Total Service Share for State Samples	129
	c Median Total Service Share for State Samples	129
	d Movement of Service Share Components	131
B	Expenditure Patterns for Low Income Urban Consumers and for All Urban, Rural Nonfarm, and Rural Farm Consumers, 1935/1936 and 1941, and the Relation Assumed for 1870-1914	134
	1 Major Differences between the Source Material for the Early and Later Years	135
	a Consumer Income Group Covered	135
	b Inclusion of Imputed Values	135
	c Detail of Presentation	135
	2 Relative Size of the Service Shares for Urban, Rural Nonfarm, and Rural Farm Consumers	136
	3 Changes in the Relative Size of the Service Shares for Urban, Rural Nonfarm, and Rural Farm Consumers	137
	4 Service Shares for All Consumers, 1870-1914	138
C	Movement of the Total Service Share for All Consumers, 1869-78 to 1929-38	140
	1 The Final Series	140
	2 An Over-all Check	141

Appendix

A	United States Reports on Consumers' Expenditures for Years before 1919	150
	1 Tabular Summary of Sources and Characteristics of United States Sample Data for Years before 1919	150
	2 Extrapolation to 1914 of the BLS Sample Data for 1918	155
	3 Adjustment of the Extrapolation to 1914	156

    4 Apportioning the Undistributed Sundry Item in the State Samples between Services and Commodities by the 1890/91 and 1918 United States Samples   158
B State Reports on Urban Consumers' Expenditures   160
C Appraisal of the Sample Data and of the Comparisons   169
D United States Reports on Consumers' Expenditures since 1919   180

Part IV

REPRODUCIBLE WEALTH—ITS GROWTH AND INDUSTRIAL DISTRIBUTION, 1880-1939

A Character of the Estimates   185
  1 Scope   185
    Omissions   187
    Excesses   188
  2 Allocation by Type   189
  3 Allocation by Industry   190
  4 Valuation   191
  5 Gross or Net   192
  6 Comparison with Capital Formation   193

B Basic Tables   200

Index   235

Tables

I	a	Commodity Flow to Consumers, Earlier NBER and Present Estimates Compared, 1919-1938	5
I	b	Commodity Flow to Consumers, Present and Other Current Estimates Compared, 1929-1942	6
I	c	Flow of Services to Consumers, Present Residual Estimates Compared with Earlier NBER, Other Current, and Alternative Estimates, 1919-1943	10
I	d	Flow of Goods to Consumers, Present and Other Estimates Compared, 1919-1943	12
I	e	Gross and Net Capital Formation, Present and Other Estimates Compared, 1919-1943	16
I	f	Gross and Net National Product, Peacetime Concept, Present and Earlier NBER Estimates Compared, 1919-1938	20
I	g	Gross and Net National Product, Present and Department of Commerce Estimates Compared, 1939-1943	22
I	1	Flow of Perishable Commodities, at Cost to Consumers, Current and 1929 Prices, 1919-1943	24
I	2	Flow of Semidurable Commodities, at Cost to Consumers, Current and 1929 Prices, 1919-1943	27
I	3	Flow of Consumer Durable Commodities, at Cost to Consumers, Current and 1929 Prices, 1919-1943	28
I	4A	Flow of Services Not Embodied in New Commodities, at Cost to Consumers, Current and 1929 Prices, 1919-1943	32
I	4B	Alternative Estimate of Services Not Embodied in New Commodities, at Cost to Consumers, Current and 1929 Prices, 1919-1943	34
I	5	Flow of Goods to Consumers, Current and 1929 Prices, 1919-1943	35
I	6	Flow of Producer Durable Commodities, at Cost to Purchasers, Current and 1929 Prices, 1919-1943	36
I	7	New Construction by Type, Current Prices, 1919-1943	40
I	8	New Construction by Type, 1929 Prices, 1919-1943	41
I	9	War Output, Gross and Net, Current Prices, 1919-1943	42
I	10	War Output, Gross and Net, 1929 Prices, 1919-1943	44

TABLES

I	11	Net Changes in Inventories and in Claims against Foreign Countries, Current and 1929 Prices, 1919-1939	46
I	12	Net Changes in Inventories and in Claims against Foreign Countries, Current and 1929 Prices, 1939-1943	50
I	13	Gross Capital Formation, Total and Nonwar, Current and 1929 Prices, 1919-1943	50
I	14	Gross National Product, Peacetime and Wartime Concepts, Current Prices, 1919-1943	51
I	15	Gross National Product, Peacetime and Wartime Concepts, 1929 Prices, 1919-1943	52
I	16	Capital Consumption, Current and 1929 Prices, 1919-1943	53
I	17	Net Capital Formation, Total and Nonwar, Current and 1929 Prices, 1919-1943	54
I	18	Net National Product, Peacetime and Wartime Concepts, Current Prices, 1919-1943	55
I	19	Net National Product, Peacetime and Wartime Concepts, 1929 Prices, 1919-1943	56
II	a	Steps in Estimating Gross Commodity Flow and Construction, Average Value per Year, 1869-1918	64
II	b	Ratios of Income Originating in Transportation and Trade to National Income and to Income Originating in Commodity Production, 1869-1928	66
II	c	Comparison of Allowance for Construction Costs other than Materials with Income Originating in Contract Construction, 1869-1928	69
II	d	Ratio of Allowance for Repairs and Maintenance Construction to Total Value of Real Estate Improvements, 1880-1922	71
II	e	Gross Commodity Flow and Construction, Decade Estimates and Averages of Annual Estimates, 1919-1938	74
II	f	Share of Services in the Flow of Goods to Consumers, 1869-1938	79
II	g	Consumption of Construction and Producer Durable Commodities Compared with Gross Flow, 1869-1938	81
II	h	Net Changes in Inventories and in Claims Against Foreign Countries Compared with Total Capital Formation, 1869-1938	84
II	i	Net National Product Derived from Commodity Flow	

		Data Compared with Martin's Estimates of Realized National Income, 1869-1938	86
II	j	Rates of Growth, Successive Overlapping Decades, Gross National Product in 1929 Prices and Two Indexes of 'Total' Production, 1869-1938	88
II	1	Perishable Commodities, Averages per Year by Decades, 1869-1938	90
II	2	Semidurable Commodities, Averages per Year by Decades, 1869-1938	93
II	3	Consumer Durable Commodities, Averages per Year by Decades, 1869-1938	95
II	4	Producer Durable Commodities, Averages per Year by Decades, 1869-1938	97
II	5	Construction, Averages per Year by Decades, 1869-1938	99
II	6	Calculation of Flow of Consumer and Producer Durable Commodities Adjusted for Business Use of Passenger Cars, 1899-1923	102
II	7	Services Not Embodied in New Commodities, Averages per Year by Decades, 1869-1938	104
II	8	Flow of Goods to Consumers, Averages per Year by Decades, 1869-1938	106
II	9	Flow of Goods to Consumers, Per Capita and Per Consuming Unit, Averages per Year by Decades, 1929 Prices, 1869-1938	107
II	10	Net Changes in Inventories, Averages per Year by Decades, 1929 Prices, 1869-1938	108
II	11	Net Changes in Inventories, Averages per Year by Decades, 1869-1938	111
II	12	Net Changes in Claims Against Foreign Countries, Averages per Year by Decades, 1869-1938	113
II	13	Gross Capital Formation, Averages per Year by Decades, 1869-1938	115
II	14	Consumption and Net Production, Producer Durable Commodities and Construction, Averages per Year by Decades, 1869-1938	116
II	15	Net Capital Formation, Averages per Year by Decades, 1869-1938	118
II	16	Gross and Net National Product, Averages per Year by Decades, 1869-1938	119
II	17	Gross and Net National Product, Per Capita and Per Gainfully Occupied, Averages per Year by Decades, 1929 Prices, 1869-1938	120

TABLES

III	1	Total Service Share for State Samples, Low Income Urban Consumers, Various Dates, 1870-1914	128
III	2	Medians and Arithmetic Means of Per Year Changes in Total Service Share, Low Income Urban Consumers, Fifteen-year Periods	129
III	3	Median Total Service Share, Low Income Urban Consumers, Ten- and Fifteen-year Periods	130
III	4	Positional Means of Total Service Shares, Low Income Urban Consumers, Ten- and Fifteen-year Periods	131
III	5	Components of Total Service Share for State Samples, Low Income Urban Consumers, Various Dates, 1870-1914	132
III	6	Positional Means of Service Shares, Low Income Urban Consumers, Fifteen-year Periods	133
III	7	Service Shares for Urban, Rural Nonfarm, and Rural Farm Consumers, Income Groups up to $1,500 and All Income Groups, 1935/36	136
III	8	Service Shares for All Consumer Groups, 1870-1914	139
III	9	Service Shares for All Consumers, 1869-1938	142
III	10	Total Outlay on Services, Current and 1929 Prices, 1869-1938	144
III	11	Two Estimates of the Flow of Food and Clothing to Consumers, 1869-1928	146
A	1	Extrapolation to 1914 of the United States Sample for 1918	155
A	2	Changes from 1935-39 to 1942 in the Percentage Shares of Total Expenditures, Based on Extrapolated and on Observed Values	157
A	3	Estimated Changes from 1914 to 1918 in Service Shares Computed from Urban Sample Data Compared with Changes from 1914 to 1919 Computed from Comprehensive Totals	158
IV	a	Increase in Wealth Compared with Net Capital Formation, Census Dates, 1880-1922, 1929 Prices	194
IV	1	Value of Land, Census Dates, 1880-1922, Based on Reported Valuation	201
IV	2	Value of Real Estate Improvements, Census Dates, 1880-1922, Based on Reported Valuation	202
IV	3	Value of Equipment, Census Dates, 1880-1922, Based on Reported Valuation	213
IV	4	Price Indexes (1929 : 100), Census Dates, 1880-1922	216

IV	5	Value of Real Estate Improvements, Census Dates, 1880-1922, 1929 Prices	218
IV	6	Value of Equipment, Census Dates, 1880-1922, 1929 Prices	219
IV	7	Value of Improvements and Equipment, January 1, 1919	220
IV	8	Value of Additions to Improvements and Equipment, Gross and Net, Current Prices, 1919-1938	224
IV	9	Value of Additions to Improvements and Equipment, Gross and Net, 1929 Prices, 1919-1938	226
IV	10	Growth of Reproducible Wealth other than Household, Selected Dates, 1880-1939, 1929 Prices	228
IV	11	Value of Real Estate Improvements and Equipment, Selected Dates, 1880-1939, 1929 Prices	230
IV	12	Value of Real Estate Improvements and Equipment, by Industry, Selected Dates, 1880-1938, 1929 Prices	231
IV	13	Increase in Value of Real Estate Improvements and Equipment, by Industry, Selected Dates, 1880-1939, 1929 Prices	233

Preface

This report, largely a collection of statistical tables with notes describing the sources of data and the procedures, is chiefly for reference by students and technical users. The brief text in each of the four parts describes the characteristics of the estimates; indicates in the few instances where choice was possible the reasons why certain procedures were selected; and compares the estimates with others.

Most of the estimates are for national product or income, either net or gross of the consumption of durable capital; and for components by final use, i.e., flow of goods to consumers and capital formation, each in turn apportioned by major categories. Part I assembles the annual estimates of national product and final use components, 1919-43. Part II provides decade series of the same totals and categories, 1869-1938, the decades overlapping by five years. In Part III the derivation of the proportion of the flow of goods to consumers accounted for by services not embodied in new commodities is discussed in detail. In Part IV national wealth estimates since 1880 are analyzed and recalculated, primarily in order to allocate capital formation by categories of users.

The series utilize the past work of the National Bureau on annual estimates of national income and capital formation, as well as the more recent work by the Department of Commerce; W. H. Shaw's study of the flow of finished commodities; sample data on the structure of consumers' budgets; and the successive estimates of national wealth. The data being far from adequate in coverage and consistency, particularly for years before 1919, the series are reliable only as far as ingenuity can make them.

Because data are not fully adequate and statistical expedients had often to be resorted to, we present both the final estimates and the underlying data in detail. Technical students and users are thus given an opportunity to examine the estimates critically; select the parts they deem both relevant to their purposes and sufficiently accurate to be used; and modify or discard others as they see fit.

This volume stems from the studies of national income, one of the first undertakings of the National Bureau of Economic Research; and of capital formation, initiated in 1933 at the request of the Committee on Credit and Banking of the Social Science Research Council. It draws heavily upon the past and current work of the National Income Unit of the Department of Commerce. The staff of the latter has, as always, been helpful and cooperative in giving us access to the original worksheets and in checking upon our interpretation of the coverage and derivation of the series.

In preparing this volume, I was assisted throughout by Lillian Epstein and Elizabeth Jenks. Their contribution to it is even more extensive than to preceding reports published in this field by the National Bureau. Miss Jenks participated most actively in the preparation of Parts II and III, and is responsible for most of the text discussion in Part III. Miss Epstein participated most actively in the preparation of Parts I and IV, and is responsible for most of the text discussion in Part IV.

In the review of the report by the Research Staff and the Board of Directors of the National Bureau valuable comments were received from Thor Hultgren and Solomon Fabricant. Most of their suggestions were adopted in revising the manuscript for publication.

Martha Anderson edited the report and helped in seeing it through the press.

I am glad to record my appreciation of the assistance rendered me by these colleagues and friends.

SIMON KUZNETS

Director's Comment

I think it should be emphasized in addition to the many warnings throughout the text which the author has so carefully given, that the findings rest on statistical data less solid than the author's income studies and most other work of the National Bureau. The findings therefore should be used only by persons who have studied the text, so that they are aware of the scantiness of the data and the nature of the assumptions. Two examples will suffice to illustrate this general warning: (1) The assumption is made that the distributive mark-on was the same in the decades 1869 to 1919 as in the period 1919-35 on which considerable data are obtainable. My observations would lead to a guess that distributive mark-on increased in the later decades as compared to the earlier. (2) The trend towards a larger percentage of consumer expenditure in services throughout the decades rests on data covering only the lowest urban income classes, and even then requires certain interpretation. Whether or not this is typical of all income classes cannot be resolved owing to lack of comparable data.

The careful and scholarly handling of the material is no recompense for the inadequacy of the data, if the results are uncritically accepted.

OSWALD W. KNAUTH

PART I

Annual Estimates, 1919-1943

A Character of the Estimates

The annual estimates of national product follow the concepts formulated in *National Product in Wartime* (National Bureau of Economic Research, 1945); but from the detailed data presented here, several other totals can be derived.

Tables I 1-I 19 set forth the estimates, component by component, and indicate sources of the data and the mode of derivation, sometimes in the table proper but more often in the notes. The estimates rest upon those already published by the National Bureau, particularly on commodity flow and capital formation, 1919-33, and on national income, 1919-38; and exploit the Department of Commerce's work for recent years, both on the flow of finished goods and on gross national product and its components. But changes in our original estimates had to be made, to take advantage of new data and to establish greater consistency with the Department of Commerce totals used as extrapolation bases for recent years.

1 *Flow of Commodities to Consumers*

The value of commodities—perishable, semidurable, and durable —flowing to consumers at cost to them, was originally estimated for 1919-33 on the basis of Census and other data—the description and results being given in detail in *Commodity Flow and Capital Formation,* Vol. One (National Bureau of Economic Research, 1938); and was extrapolated through 1938 by various sample series (*ibid.,* and *Bulletin 74,* National Bureau, June 1939).

Two major adjustments were made in these earlier estimates of the flow of commodities to consumers, in current prices. The first was to allow for business use of passenger cars and related products. In the original estimates no allowance was made, largely for lack of a basis upon which to calculate the share of the current output of passenger cars, parts, tires, gasoline, etc. purchased for and used by individuals in pursuit of their business. In preparing the Department of Commerce current series on the flow of finished goods to consumers W. H. Shaw estimated this share to be 30 percent, and we applied this percentage uniformly throughout the period to the totals for passenger cars, parts, tires, and other related products. This adjustment affected the estimates for all years from 1919 on.

The second adjustment applied to the years after 1933 alone: for the old bases for extrapolation beyond 1933, then current series on retail sales, were substituted Shaw's more comprehensive and reliable estimates, prepared at the Department of Commerce. The latter were based upon full consideration of Census data for 1939 as well as upon intensive utilization of all current annual samples.

For the values in 1929, as distinct from current prices, additional adjustments were made. An error in the procedure used originally in converting consumer durable (and producer durable) commodities to 1929 prices necessitated one of these adjustments. The other was called for by the availability of more comprehensive, and hence, more suitable price indexes for the years after 1933 than were at hand when our original estimates for 1934-38 were adjusted for price changes.

The resulting differences between the present estimates of commodity flow to consumers and those originally published by the National Bureau, both in current prices, are summarized in Table I a. As should have been expected, the allowance for business use of passenger cars and related products reduced the commodity flow to consumers. Since passenger cars and related products appear in all three commodity groups—gasoline and oil in the perishable, tires in the semidurable, and the cars and parts in the durable—the estimates for each group are smaller. However, the reduction is negligible, both absolutely and relatively, in the perishable and semidurable categories; and is substantial only in the durable, of which passenger cars and parts constitute a large proportion. The additional adjustment for 1934-38 has served to augment the proportional reduction due to the allowance for business use of passenger cars and related products. For the semidurable and durable groups, but not for the perishable, the absolute and proportional reduction from the original to the present estimates was larger for 1934-38 than for 1919-33.

The procedures by which we originally estimated commodity flow to consumers and those Shaw used in his work at the Department of Commerce differ mainly in the treatment of passenger cars and related products. Consequently, after the former had been adjusted for business use our present estimates and Shaw's

TABLE I a
Commodity Flow to Consumers
Earlier NBER and Present Estimates Compared, 1919-1938
(averages per year, dollar figures in billions, current prices)

	PRESENT ESTIMATES (1)	EARLIER NBER ESTIMATES (2)	AVERAGE DIFFERENCE (1 - 2) (3)	PERCENTAGE DIFFERENCE (% OF 2) (4)
1919-1933				
1 Perishable	23.7	24.1	−0.4	−1.5
2 Semidurable	10.2	10.5	−0.3	−2.7
3 Durable	6.4	7.2	−0.8	−10.9
4 All commodities (1 + 2 + 3)	40.3	41.8	−1.4	−3.4
1934-1938				
5 Perishable	24.3	24.3	0.0	0.0
6 Semidurable	8.1	8.7	−0.6	−6.9
7 Durable	5.4	6.2	−0.8	−12.9
8 All commodities (5 + 6 + 7)	37.9	39.2	−1.3	−3.3

COLUMN 1
LINE
1-3,
5-7 Col. 2 of Tables I 1, I 2, and I 3.

COLUMN 2
1-3 Col. 1 of Tables I 1, I 2, and I 3.
5-7 National Bureau *Bulletin* 74 (June 1939), Table 1.

agree closely (Table I b, lines 1-4). The differences, minor for each commodity group, are due to slight changes Shaw made in the apportionment of total output between finished and unfinished on the basis of new data in the Census of 1939 and other sources not available when the original estimates for 1919-33 were prepared; minor changes in classification; and more precise adjustments for exports and imports. This close agreement made the use of Shaw's series for extrapolation of our totals beyond 1933 all the more justifiable.

In contrast, the present estimates of commodity flow to consumers differ considerably from the Department of Commerce's corresponding component of gross national product (Department of Commerce definition). On the average they are almost $4 billion per year larger (Table I b, lines 5-7). The excess is concentrated in the nondurable group (a combination of perishable and semidurable), that in consumer durables being negligible. Shaw's series on commodity flow to consumers, likewise

TABLE I b

Commodity Flow to Consumers

Present and Other Current Estimates Compared, 1929-1942

(averages per year, dollar figures in billions, current prices)

	PRESENT ESTIMATES (1)	OTHER ESTIMATES (2)	AVERAGE DIFFERENCE (1 - 2) (3)	PERCENTAGE DIFFERENCE (% OF 2) (4)
COMPARISON WITH SHAW'S ESTIMATES, 1929-1942				
1 Perishable	25.6	25.8	−0.2	−0.8
2 Semidurable	9.2	8.7	+0.5	+5.4
3 Durable	6.0	6.1	−0.1	−1.7
4 All commodities (1 + 2 + 3)	40.8	40.6	+0.2	+0.4
COMPARISON WITH DEPARTMENT OF COMMERCE NATIONAL PRODUCT COMPONENTS, 1939-1942				
5 Nondurable	42.4	38.8	+3.6	+9.3
6 Durable	7.4	7.3	+0.1	+0.7
7 All commodities (5 + 6)	49.8	46.1	+3.7	+8.0
COMPARISON OF TWO DEPARTMENT OF COMMERCE ESTIMATES: SHAW'S (COL. 1) AND NATIONAL PRODUCT COMPONENTS, 1939-1942				
8 Nondurable	42.1	38.8	+3.3	+8.5
9 Durable	7.5	7.3	+0.2	+2.6
10 All commodities (8 + 9)	49.6	46.1	+3.5	+7.5

COLUMN 1

LINE
1-3,
5 & 6 See notes to Table I a, col. 1.

8 & 9 Col. 3 of Tables I 1, I 2, and I 3.

COLUMN 2

1-3 See notes to col. 1, lines 8 and 9.

5, 6,
8 & 9 *Survey of Current Business,* April 1944, p. 13, Table 10.

prepared at the Department of Commerce, is $3.5 billion per year larger than the Department's second series, derived as part of gross national product, the excess again being concentrated in nondurables (Table I b, lines 8-10).

The differences are due largely to the way in which the Department of Commerce estimates commodity flow to consumers in its series on gross national product: from total gross national product—the sum of national income and other items (depreciation and depletion, business taxes, etc.)—it subtracts government expenditures, private gross capital formation, and an independently calculated flow of services to consumers. In general, national product totals calculated by the flow of income method fall somewhat short of totals that are sums of separate estimates of the flow of goods to consumers and capital formation (i.e., final product categories). Hence, any final product category derived as a residual, i.e., by subtracting, from a total based on income flows, other final product categories calculated directly, would be smaller than an estimate derived independently. The concentration of this shortage in nondurables in the Department of Commerce residual estimate of the flow of commodities to consumers is due to the peculiarities of the apportionment of the total between the two subgroups, and is in large degree fortuitous.

For reasons given below, in our present estimates this residual approach is applied to the category of services flowing to consumers. Having decided to do this, we had to estimate the flow of *commodities* to consumers directly instead of as a residual. Hence the present estimates, closely agreeing with Shaw's but larger than those calculated by the Department of Commerce as a component of gross national product, have been retained.

2 *Flow of Services to Consumers*

Like the series published earlier by the National Bureau, the present estimates of the flow of services to consumers are derived as a residual: by subtracting from national income net capital formation and commodity flow to consumers, both subtrahend and diminuend being calculated directly and independently from diverse sources. Choice of this residual procedure involves a twofold decision: (a) to use, as a controlling total, national income estimated as the sum of income payments and undistributed profits originating in the various industries; (b) in combining this controlling total with estimates of final product categories, to derive as a residual the flow of services to consumers rather than any other final product category.

The first decision would have no effect upon the residual estimates were national income totals derived as the sum of income flows identical with those derived as the sum of final product categories, each computed directly and independently. But national income calculated by the income flow approach is consistently less than the sum of independently approximated final product categories, as indicated by the estimates of Clark Warburton, Harold Barger, and Shaw.[1] The decision, therefore, involves a choice between two totals that differ significantly, though the percentage difference does not exceed 5 percent; and the difference affects the category estimated as a residual.

It is easy to point out omissions in any national income total based upon the income flow procedure; several are listed and their magnitudes approximated in *National Income and Its Composition* (National Bureau of Economic Research, 1941) II, 419-35. One is, therefore, inclined at first to consider the larger of any two national income totals as the more comprehensive and hence the more reliable; and this would lead to choosing the larger total, calculated as the sum of independently derived estimates of final product components. But further reflection casts serious doubt upon the assumption that the larger total, calculated by the final product approach, covers net income yielding activities in the economy more adequately. It is easy to underestimate the extent to which commodities that are in their final physical shape and services that by their character are not necessarily confined to final consumers are used by individuals in their business capacity and, therefore, represent unfinished rather than final goods. Thus, in any area covered, it is easy to suspect an inherent upward bias in a national income total estimated by the final product method.

As both approaches have potential and sometimes clearly recognizable imperfections, the choice of one as a controlling total is a matter of judgment. In earlier National Bureau publications the total estimated by the flow of income method was favored on the ground that even in estimates of *commodity* flow, lack of adequate data compel a greater use of approximations than was necessary in the flow-of-income estimates; and that for services in particular, an independent estimate of flow to consumers would be difficult and subject to a wide margin of error. While two independent estimates of services have since been made, and while undoubtedly more data made for better direct estimates of final

[1] See *Studies in Income and Wealth* (National Bureau of Economic Research), Vol. Three, 1939, pp. 319-80; Vol. Four, 1942, particularly pp. 66-87; and a comparison of Shaw's estimates of the flow of goods to consumers with that derived as a residual by the Department of Commerce, Table I d, below.

commodity flows, it seems to us that the advantage of greater accuracy combined with adequately comprehensive coverage still lies with national income totals based on the flow of payments and of undistributed net gains. Moreover, they can be allocated by industrial origin, type of payment, and for some years by size among various groups of income recipients. And it is of distinct advantage to associate the final product divisions with totals subject to these other apportionments and distributions.

The decision is a temporary expedient. It might have been avoided had we scrutinized both the flow of income and final product estimates closely all the way back to 1919, and effected a reconciliation between them. While preferable to the embarrassment of having to choose between two over-all totals, both somewhat out of line, such reconciliation, for lack of adequate data, would still necessitate many forced judgments. Furthermore, as most of the additional information is for recent years and the Department of Commerce is working intensively on both approaches, it did not seem advisable to try to get a solution that could not be more than a makeshift. Until the Department achieves the reconciliation needed a choice must be made; and here it is in favor of using as a controlling total national income derived by the flow of incomes approach.

Once this first decision has been made, the second—to derive as a residual the flow of services to consumers rather than any other final product category—reflected the judgment that it is for this sizable category that data are least adequate. As compared with the other large components (the three groups of commodity flow to consumers, producer durables, and construction) the estimate of the service flow to consumers is based upon the scantiest data, and involves decisions concerning apportionment between business and final use that are least controlled by adequate information. Our production censuses are primarily for commodities; our current samples cover chiefly commodity production and handling; and the large flow of services, because of their intangible and heterogeneous character, is still a quantity whose estimate by the direct approach, based upon independent data, is hazardous. Here again the decision is forced by gaps in the present information, and may be different when further work in the field has been done.

TABLE I c

Flow of Services to Consumers
Present Residual Estimates Compared with Earlier NBER,
Other Current, and Alternative Estimates, 1919-1943
(all include imputed rent and direct taxes; averages per year, dollar figures in billions, current prices)

	PRESENT RESIDUAL ESTIMATES (1)	OTHER ESTIMATES (2)	AVERAGE DIFFERENCE (1 - 2) (3)	PERCENTAGE DIFFERENCE (% OF 2) (4)
COMPARISON WITH EARLIER NBER ESTIMATES				
1 1919-1933	22.8	21.4	+1.4	+6.6
2 1934-1938	21.4	18.8	+2.6	+14.0
COMPARISON WITH BARGER'S ESTIMATES				
3 1921-1928	23.5	25.6	−2.1	−8.2
4 1929-1938	22.8	24.3	−1.5	−6.2
5 1921-1938	23.1	24.9	−1.8	−7.1
COMPARISON WITH SHAW'S ESTIMATES				
6 1929-1938	22.8	26.3	−3.5	−13.2
COMPARISON WITH SHAW'S AND DEPARTMENT OF COMMERCE NATIONAL PRODUCT COMPONENT ESTIMATES, 1939-1942				
7 With Shaw's	28.1	30.2	−2.1	−6.9
8 With national product component	28.1	29.7	−1.6	−5.5
COMPARISON WITH ALTERNATIVE ESTIMATE DERIVED BY EXTRAPOLATION (NOT AS RESIDUAL)				
9 1919-1943	23.7	27.8	−4.1	−14.6

COLUMN 1

LINE
Table I 4A, col. 2.

COLUMN 2

1 & 2 Data underlying estimates in *National Income and Its Composition*, I, 285, Table 41.

3-5 *Outlay and Income in the United States* (National Bureau of Economic Research, 1942), Table 22, p. 228, plus direct taxes (Table I 4A, col. 7).

6 & 7 *Survey of Current Business*, June 1944, p. 11, Table 2, plus direct taxes (Table I 4A, col. 7).

8 *Survey*, April 1944, p. 13, Table 10, line 19, plus direct taxes (Table I 4A, col. 7), plus *net* imputed rent (Shaw's gross, *Survey*, June 1944, p. 9, multiplied by 40 percent, the NBER ratio of net to gross in 1938).

9 Table I 4B, col. 3.

The present estimates of the flow of services to consumers are larger than the earlier, derived by the same method and published by the National Bureau (Table I c, lines 1 and 2), because the original estimates of national income were retained; the adjustments in the net capital formation totals, though minor before 1934, were downward; and the estimates of commodity flow to consumers were reduced by an allowance for the business use of passenger cars and related products. As the diminuend was unaffected and the subtrahend reduced, the residual—the flow of services to consumers—is larger than in the original series.

However, though the present estimates are larger on the average than the original, the total is still smaller than that derived directly from independent data. They average somewhat less than $2 billion short of Barger's (lines 3-5). Since Shaw's estimates are even larger than Barger's, owing chiefly to more comprehensive coverage, our totals are short of Shaw's by an annual average of $3.5 billion (line 6). Finally, the Department of Commerce estimate of services as part of gross national product, while computed directly rather than as a residual, is somewhat smaller than Shaw's, but still exceeds the present estimate by an average of $1.6 billion per year (line 8).[2]

From the several independent estimates of the flow of services an approximation can be made for this category that would parallel the present residual series for 1919 through 1943, but would be based upon an extrapolation of the most recent independent estimate, that by Shaw, through the years prior to 1929. This alternative series is on the average some $4 billion per year larger than the residual series, or about 15 percent of the former (Table I c, line 9). There is little question that this alternative series gives a more reliable picture of *year to year* variations in the flow of services to consumers than the present or the old residual series: for several reasons short term fluctuations in a service total derived as a residual are erratic.[3] But the main question, whether the average level of the residual series is a better approximation to the average service flow to consumers; or, if somewhat too low, tends to offset any possible exaggerations in the other final product components, cannot be answered definitively.

The twofold decision, discussed above, means that we use the

---

[2] The service component of the gross national product total in the Department of Commerce estimate excludes imputed rents. Were the latter included, the Department of Commerce estimate of services would exceed the present by a substantially greater amount than is indicated in Table I c. For 1938 our estimate of individuals' net imputed rent is $1.4 billion (*National Income and Its Composition*, II, Table F 5, p. 735).
[3] *Ibid.*, I, 283 ff.

present residual estimate in deriving any larger totals. But naturally, students more concerned with the flow of services itself than with it as part of a larger total, may prefer the series given in detail in Table I 4B or some other alternative based upon a different approach.

3 Flow of Goods to Consumers

The total flow of goods to consumers is a sum of commodities and services. The several adjustments, discussed above, in its components yield a series fairly close both to those published earlier by the National Bureau and to the two current Department of Commerce series (Table I d).

TABLE I d
Flow of Goods to Consumers
Present and Other Estimates Compared, 1919-1943
(all include imputed rent and direct taxes; averages per year, dollar figures in billions, current prices)

	PRESENT ESTIMATES (1)	OTHER ESTIMATES (2)	AVERAGE DIFFERENCE (1 - 2) (3)	PERCENTAGE DIFFERENCE (% OF 2) (4)
COMPARISON WITH EARLIER NBER ESTIMATES				
1 1919-1933	63.1	63.1	0.0	0.0
2 1934-1938	59.3	58.0	+1.3	+2.3
COMPARISON WITH SHAW'S ESTIMATES				
3 1929-1938	60.0	63.4	−3.3	−5.3
COMPARISON WITH DEPARTMENT OF COMMERCE NATIONAL PRODUCT COMPONENT				
4 1939-1943	82.2	79.8	+2.3	+2.9
COMPARISON OF SHAW'S (COL. 1) AND DEPARTMENT OF COMMERCE NATIONAL PRODUCT COMPONENT				
5 1939-1942	79.7	75.8	+3.9	+5.2

COLUMN 1
LINE
1-4 Table I 5, col. 5.
  5 *Survey of Current Business,* June 1944, p. 11, Table 2, plus direct taxes (Table I 4A, col. 7).

COLUMN 2
1 & 2 *National Income and Its Composition,* I, 137, Table 1, col. 4.
  3 See note to col. 1, line 5.
4 & 5 *Survey of Current Business,* April 1944, p. 13, Table 10, line 16, plus direct taxes plus net imputed rent (see note to Table I c, col. 2, line 8; imputed rent assumed the same in 1943 as in 1942).

In both the present and the earlier derivation, the flow of goods to consumers is in essence the difference between national income (measured by the flow of incomes approach) and net capital formation (measured independently). Since we have retained the original estimates of national income for 1919-38 and since for 1919-33 revisions in capital formation canceled over the period, the average of the residual—flow of goods to consumers, in current prices—is identical in the present and earlier published estimates (line 1). For 1934-38, however, more recent data led to a smaller estimate of net capital formation, and to a correspondingly larger flow of goods to consumers (line 2)—on the average slightly more than 2 percent larger than the earlier published totals for 1934-38.

The present estimate of the flow of goods to consumers is lower than Shaw's, in which all components are derived independently (line 3). Yet the difference is only slightly more than 5 percent of Shaw's total because the excess in his service component is offset in part by the shortages in his commodity components; and, of course, constitutes a much lower percentage of the flow of goods to consumers than of any of its components.

While the present estimates are somewhat smaller than Shaw's, they are larger than the Department of Commerce second series, calculated as part of gross national product by the residual method (line 4). They are thus between the two Department of Commerce estimates. If the prospective reconciliation of the two approaches gives a final total between the two, it will closely approximate the present estimates; although its distribution between commodities and services might still differ somewhat from that in the present estimates.[4]

4 *Capital Formation*

In the peacetime concept of national product, war goods are treated as a species of capital whose use is to help sustain or increase the flow of goods to the country's population. Hence,

---

[4] The analysis in *National Product in Wartime,* Part II, uses the Department of Commerce estimates of the flow of commodities to consumers, i.e., similar to that in col. 2, line 4 (excluding imputed rent). The reason for not using the present estimates was a desire to retain consistency with the Department of Commerce estimates for 1939-43 except for the all-important problems of pricing war production and defining net national product in wartime. See also note 6.

the corresponding *net* national product total excludes consumption of war goods and includes only net additions to the stock of war goods (finished, unfinished, or war plants); and the corresponding *gross* national product total is, in addition, gross of the current consumption of war plants. In the wartime concept of national product, the aims of the armed conflict are considered as being on a par with the satisfaction of consumer wants, and therefore a final purpose. All finished war goods ready for use in armed conflict are then final goods—like the finished commodities and services that flow to consumers. Hence, the corresponding *net* national product total includes all finished war goods, durable and nondurable, as well as net additions to the inventory of unfinished war goods and to the stock of war plants; and the corresponding *gross* national product is, in addition, gross of the current consumption of war plants.

The difference between the peace- and wartime concepts is in the treatment of capital formation; the flow of goods to consumers is measured the same way in both. As a component of national product, peacetime concept, capital formation is the sum of new construction, whether for war or other purposes (both excluding maintenance repairs); flow of producer durable equipment to final users, including war types; net flow into all inventories, except final consumers'; net changes in claims against foreign countries, no matter how originated in the production process. In deriving national product in accordance with the wartime concept, it is more practicable to confine capital formation to nonwar, i.e., exclude from construction, durable equipment, inventory change, and claims against foreign countries everything covered under war output; and attempt to measure whatever *war* capital formation enters the broader category of war output. It is capital formation as a component of peacetime national product that is most comparable with the earlier estimates of capital formation; consequently, the present estimates of capital formation, peacetime concept, are compared with the earlier published estimates.

For two of the four components—net flow to inventories and net changes in claims against foreign countries—the earlier published estimates have been retained. The former item should have been expanded since the earlier estimates did not cover government inventories. But no such revision was feasible. Limitations of data confined revisions to the two quantitatively important components—construction and producer durable equipment.

In the original estimates of construction, two approaches were tried: one based upon the flow of construction materials, the other upon direct data on new construction in various sectors (residential, farm, public utility, government, etc.). The second was chosen in estimating capital formation, for it alone yields a total exclusive of maintenance and minor repairs. The series can more easily be kept up to date, and gives an estimate of new construction in which user categories can be distinguished.

The reason for revising these earlier estimates of new construction, based upon diverse data for the several user categories, lay in the accretion of new information and the availability of new comprehensive estimates—primarily the work of Lowell J. Chawner, but continued and revised at the Department of Commerce. It seemed better to adopt these new estimates since the definitions and methods were quite similar to those by which our original series were prepared. Likewise, more recent information was used in adjusting the current dollar value series for changes in prices.

For 1919-33 the revision did not cause any material change in average construction (Table I e, line 1). For 1934-38, however, the new data give an average about 12 percent lower than the earlier level (line 6).

In producer durables the main adjustment was the allowance for business use of passenger cars and related products, already discussed in connection with the estimates of commodity flow to consumers. This allowance tended to make the gross flow of producer durable equipment to final users larger than in the original estimates, by the value of passenger cars and related *durable* products estimated as purchased by business and other enterprises. And for 1919-33 indeed, the present estimates exceed the earlier by an annual average of $0.7 billion, or almost 15 percent of the original totals (Table I e, line 2).

However, for 1934-38 the second adjustment, the use of new data to extrapolate the earlier detailed estimates beyond 1933, reduced the estimated flow of producer equipment enough to more than offset the allowance for the business use of passenger

TABLE I e

Gross and Net Capital Formation
Present and Other Estimates Compared, 1919-1943
(averages per year, dollar figures in billions, current prices)

	PRESENT ESTIMATES (1)	OTHER ESTIMATES (2)	AVERAGE DIFFERENCE (1 - 2) (3)	PERCENTAGE DIFFERENCE (% OF 2) (4)
PEACETIME CONCEPT, PRESENT AND EARLIER NBER ESTIMATES				
1919-1933				
1 Construction, gross	7.7	7.8	a	−0.5
2 Producer durable, gross	5.2	4.5	+0.7	+14.5
3 Gross capital formation	14.6	14.0	+0.6	+4.4
4 Capital consumption	8.9	8.3	+0.6	+7.1
5 Net capital formation (3 − 4)	5.7	5.6	b	+0.5
1934-1938				
6 Construction, gross	4.4	5.0	−0.6	−12.5
7 Producer durable, gross	4.5	4.7	−0.3	−5.4
8 Gross capital formation	9.9	10.7	−0.9	−8.2
9 Capital consumption	8.6	8.2	+0.4	+5.4
10 Net capital formation (8 − 9)	1.2	2.5	−1.3	−52.2
PRIVATE CAPITAL FORMATION, PRESENT AND DEPARTMENT OF COMMERCE, 1939-1943				
11 Gross	11.0	10.9	+0.1	+0.9
12 Consumption	9.1	8.2	+0.9	+11.0
13 Net	1.9	2.7	−0.8	−29.6

a Less than −$50 million.
b Less than $50 million.

COLUMN 1

LINE
1 & 6 Table I 7, col. 7.
2 & 7 Table I 6, col. 2.
3 & 8 Table I 13, col. 1.
4 & 9 Table I 16, col. 4.

LINE
11 Col. 5 of Table I 14 minus col. 6 of Table I 7.
12 Line 11 minus line 13.
13 Table I 17, col. 1.

COLUMN 2
1-4, Data underlying the estimates in 'Uses of National Income in Peace and War',
6-9 National Bureau *Occasional Paper 6,* March 1942, p. 37, Table 8.

11 *Survey of Current Business,* April 1944, p. 13, Table 10, line 8.

12 *Ibid.,* p. 14, Table 13, line 3, plus depreciation on owner-occupied residences (carried at $1.1 billion for 1939-43).

13 Line 11 minus line 12.

cars. The present estimate of producer durable goods is on the average $0.3 billion per year smaller than the earlier (line 7).

The effects of these revisions in the construction and the producer durable categories upon gross capital formation (lines 3 and 8) are naturally different for the two periods 1919-33 and 1934-38. The present estimates of gross capital formation exceed the earlier for 1919-33 by an average of $0.6 billion per year, largely because of the allowance for the business use of passenger cars. For 1934-38 they are on the average $0.9 billion per year less than the earlier estimates, owing to downward adjustments in both construction and producer durable equipment. These revisions indicate that the recovery during 1934-38 in gross capital formation must have been smaller than suggested by the earlier estimates—an observation true of the totals in 1929 prices as well.

The allowance for the consumption of durable capital, needed to pass from gross to net capital formation, is based upon Solomon Fabricant's work. As for the earlier estimates, his original series were used. But the allowance for the business use of passenger cars meant that the original estimate of the consumption of durable capital, which excluded the annual depreciation on passenger cars owned and used by business enterprises, had to be expanded to include it. A second adjustment was made to allow for the consumption of war construction, since Fabricant's estimates of depreciation on government construction apparently do not allow for war installations (see Table I 16). Because of these upward adjustments, the present estimate of durable capital consumption, still based primarily upon Fabricant's series, is somewhat larger than the earlier (Table I e, lines 4 and 9).

Subtraction of this revised allowance for capital consumption from the revised estimate of gross capital formation yields the present series on net capital formation (peacetime concept). For 1919-33 the effects of the adjustment upon the diminuend, gross capital formation, and upon the subtrahend, capital consumption, almost cancel, so that the average difference between the present and the earlier series of net capital formation is insignificant. In contrast, for 1934-38 the downward adjustment of gross capital formation is augmented by an upward adjustment of the deduction, i.e., capital consumption. Consequently, the new residuals for 1934-38, viz., the present estimates of net capital formation, are much lower than the earlier (line 10): the total is cut in half, again suggesting that the recovery in the levels of net capital formation during these years was much less than the earlier estimates indicated.

No basic work on national product or capital formation estimates has been done at the National Bureau for years beginning with 1939. Hence, the Department of Commerce estimates of the components of gross capital formation were used to extend our estimates beyond 1938. The close agreement for 1939 between our estimates of the two dominant components—construction and producer durables—and the Department of Commerce totals justified this procedure. Supplementary estimates had to be made only for components that differed by definition from those of the Department of Commerce (e.g., nonwar public construction, needed to derive nonwar capital formation).

The present and Department of Commerce estimates of *private* capital formation alone may properly be compared for 1939-43.[5] The gross totals agree closely (line 11), in small part because the present estimates take over estimates of some minor components from the Department of Commerce series.

However, the present estimate of capital consumption for 1939-43 is larger than the Department's (line 12), because we use Fabricant's economic measures of depreciation, i.e., estimates adjusted for the difference between the cost and replacement bases of valuation of durable capital, and the Department uses accounting measures, resting essentially upon cost. As a consequence, the present estimates of private net capital formation for 1939-43 are smaller than those of the Department of Commerce.[6]

5 National Product

In the earlier estimates of national income and gross national product war production was practically ignored. But its rapid rise in recent years has forced careful consideration. Consequently

---

[5] A Department of Commerce series for total capital formation back to 1929 was published in May 1942. Recent issues of the *Survey of Current Business* carry data on private capital formation since 1939 alone.

[6] In *National Product in Wartime*, Part II, the estimate of capital consumption used to pass from gross to net nonwar capital formation is an accounting rather than an economic measure; and hence identical with the Department of Commerce's rather than with the present estimate. The reason was an attempt to retain consistency with the Department of Commerce estimates of national product in current prices, except on the all-important ground of the basic concept. Since economic measures of capital consumption are used in association with a national income total adjusted for the difference in depreciation charges between cost and reproduction bases of valuation, they had to be used also for 1939-43.

the earlier totals, on a purely conceptual basis, do not correspond closely with those of either the peace- or wartime gross and net national product as formulated in *National Product in Wartime*. National income, as earlier defined and measured by the income flow approach, would approximate the peacetime concept of net national product if government net savings took into account changes in government assets of a war character (in the calculation of changes in assets as offsets to changes in debt). The earlier estimate of gross national product would approximate the peacetime total of gross national product if it included, in addition, depreciation on war construction. For both net and gross totals the approximation to the *wartime* concept would require, in addition to the adjustments just suggested, treating the production of all finished war goods gross of current consumption.

The earlier estimates of both national income and gross national product, while not identical with, are close to the peacetime concepts of net and gross national product, as recently formulated. The quantitative differences are of such relatively minor proportions that even if no adjustments are made, the earlier totals can for practical purposes be treated as tolerable approximations to national product, peacetime concept.

This is particularly true of national income, as earlier defined and measured. As already indicated, to bring these earlier estimates into correspondence with the peacetime concept of net national product, the only adjustment called for is to include changes in war facilities and goods in the hands of government. These changes, whether calculated by applying a straight line depreciation on 'investment in peace' or depreciation on various categories of war product based on their average life (see *National Product in Wartime,* Part I), are minor through most years of peace, but we do not know exactly how small. In our earlier calculation of national income, particularly of government savings, account was taken of changes in the net value of government construction, *including* war construction, with the minor error of somewhat too low a figure for the depreciation charge on government construction (see Sec. 4 and Table I 16). Changes in government-held inventories of war goods of other description could not have been great from 1920 through 1941. Hence the practical expedient of assuming that the earlier de-

TABLE I f
Gross and Net National Product, Peacetime Concept
Present and Earlier NBER Estimates Compared, 1919-1938
(averages per year, dollar figures in billions)

	PRESENT ESTIMATES (1)	EARLIER NBER ESTIMATES (2)	AVERAGE DIFFERENCE (1 - 2) (3)	PERCENTAGE DIFFERENCE (% OF 2) (4)
NET NATIONAL PRODUCT (NATIONAL INCOME)				
1919-1933				
1 In current prices	68.8	68.8	0.0	0.0
2 In 1929 prices	69.2	69.1	a	+0.1
1934-1938				
3 In current prices	60.6	60.6	0.0	0.0
4 In 1929 prices	74.6	72.5	+2.1	+2.9
GROSS NATIONAL PRODUCT				
1919-1933				
5 In current prices	77.7	77.1	+0.6	+0.8
6 In 1929 prices	78.3	77.7	+0.6	+0.8
1934-1938				
7 In current prices	69.2	68.8	+0.4	+0.6
8 In 1929 prices	84.2	81.6	+2.6	+3.1

a Less than $50 million.

COLUMN 1

LINE		LINE	
1 & 3	Table I 18, col. 3.	5 & 7	Table I 14, col. 3.
2 & 4	Table I 19, col. 3.	6 & 8	Table I 15, col. 3.

COLUMN 2
1 & 3 *National Income and Its Composition,* I, 137, Table 1, col. 1.
2 & 4 *Ibid.,* I, 147, Table 5, col. 1.
5 & 7 National Bureau *Occasional Paper 6,* p. 37, Table 8.
6 & 8 Data comparable with estimates in *ibid.*

tailed estimates of national income in current prices, as developed in *National Income and Its Composition,* are identical with estimates of net national product, peacetime concept, does not involve a significant error. Such identification was held justifiable; and the use of the earlier estimate of national income in current prices for 1919-38 as a controlling total descriptive of net national product, peacetime concept, explains the identity in Table I f of the present and earlier estimates of national income (net national product, peacetime concept) for both 1919-33 and 1934-38 (lines 1 and 3).

In 1929 prices, however, the net totals are not identical—for two reasons. First, the apportionment of national income or net national product by final product categories is changed by adjustments that raised the relative proportions of the service flow to consumers throughout the period; and also raised the relative proportion of the flow of goods to consumers and diminished the relative proportion of net capital formation during 1934-38. Second, for these more recent years, the earlier and somewhat less comprehensive 'deflation' indexes were replaced by more carefully compiled indexes. The difference between the present and the earlier national income series in 1929 prices is, on the average, negligible for 1919-33, but significant for 1934-38. For this later period, the present estimates in 1929 prices are somewhat larger.

From national income or net national product we pass to gross national product by adding an allowance for the current consumption of durable capital. In approximating the peacetime concept of gross national product, we added to the allowance for the current consumption of durable capital the consumption of war construction (Table I 16). Moreover, the new allowance for the business use of passenger cars and parts meant also a larger total for the consumption of durable business capital. As a result, the present estimates of gross national product, peacetime concept, are larger than the earlier estimates, even in current prices (Table I f, lines 5 and 7). The excess is identical, as it must be, with that of the present over the earlier estimate of capital consumption (Table I e, lines 4 and 9). The differences in the totals in current prices naturally carry over to the comparison in 1929 prices (Table I f, lines 6 and 8); except that we have here in addition the effects of a different adjustment for price changes, for reasons already discussed in connection with the national income-net national product totals.

The comparison of the present estimates of gross and net national product, either peace- or wartime concepts, with those of the Department of Commerce for 1939-43 is complicated by conceptual differences, for which it is impossible to correct so as to bring out similarities or disparities in the statistical results proper. Any attempt to adjust for differences in definition would

TABLE I g

Gross and Net National Product, Present and Department of Commerce Estimates Compared, 1939-1943

(include imputed rent; averages per year, dollar figures in billions, current prices)

	PRESENT ESTIMATES (1)	DEPARTMENT OF COMMERCE ESTIMATES (2)	AVERAGE DIFFERENCE (1-2) (3)	PERCENTAGE DIFFERENCE (% OF 2) (4)
GROSS NATIONAL PRODUCT				
1 Present peacetime & Department of Commerce gross national product at market prices	116.8	130.5	−13.7	−10.5
2 Present wartime & Department of Commerce gross national product at market prices	124.6	130.5	−5.9	−4.5
NET NATIONAL PRODUCT				
3 Present peacetime & Department of Commerce national income	102.3	104.7	−2.4	−2.3
4 Present wartime & Department of Commerce national income	112.8	104.7	+8.1	+7.7

COLUMN 1

LINE
1 Table I 14, col. 3.
2 Ibid., col. 7.

LINE
3 Table I 18, col. 3.
4 Ibid., col. 7.

COLUMN 2

1 & 2 *Survey of Current Business*, April 1944, p. 13, Table 10, line 1.
3 & 4 *Ibid.*, p.14, Table 13, line 1, plus net imputed rent (see note to Table I d, col. 2, line 4).

necessitate somewhat arbitrary assumptions, which would render a purely statistical check highly dubious.

But since it is the basic conceptual differences that are largely responsible for disparities in magnitudes, we juxtapose the present and the Department totals for these recent years, with just one correction for coverage (imputed rent). The present *peacetime gross* national product total is smaller than gross national product as defined by the Department of Commerce (Table I g, line 1). The difference, averaging close to $14 billion per year or about 10 percent of the Department of Commerce total, is due, in addition to purely statistical discrepancies (likely to be minor), to the following differences in concept: our peacetime gross national product total omits (a) all nondurable war output, i.e., services of the armed forces, etc.; and (b) nonwar expenditures of governments, except those representing final products (as measured by direct taxes of individuals, kept at the prewar level) or gross additions to government construction. The Department of Commerce gross national product total, which includes fully all expenditures of governments on commodities and services, is obviously swelled by both items.

Our *wartime gross* national product is still about $6 billion short of the Department of Commerce gross national product, a shortage somewhat less than 5 percent of the latter (line 2). This difference is due, in addition to minor statistical discrepancies, to the exclusion from our wartime gross national product total of item (b) as defined above (i.e., a substantial part of the nonwar outlay of governments).

Our *peacetime* concept of *national income* excludes the part of war output that is financed by wartime increases in direct taxes of individuals; the Department of Commerce national income includes all direct taxes paid by individuals. The statistical discrepancy due to this conceptual difference, unlike the others, can be calculated: averaging $4 billion per year, it more than accounts for the shortage of the present estimates in line 3. In contrast, our *wartime* concept of *net national product* includes all war output, except the minor deduction of depreciation on war construction; and the Department of Commerce national income total includes only such part of war output as is represented by direct taxes of individuals. Thus, the rather substantial excess of the present estimates of wartime net national product over those of the Department of Commerce national income is easily explained.

The difficulties in devising truly comparable bases for measuring national product in times of peace and of major war suggest caution in comparing estimates for 1942 and 1943 with estimates for earlier years. Particular note should be made of the adjustments for changes in prices of war goods (discussed in detail in *National Product in Wartime,* Part II), which attempted to take into account not only movements over time but differences in level as compared with prices of peacetime goods.

B BASIC TABLES

TABLE I 1
Flow of Perishable Commodities, at Cost to Consumers
Current and 1929 Prices, 1919-1943
(dollar totals in billions)

	Original Estimate in *Commodity Flow and Capital Formation* (1)	Adj. for Business Use of Passenger Cars (2)	Department of Commerce Estimate (Shaw) (3)	Price Index 1929 : 100 (4)	Total 1929 Prices (5)
1919	24.6	24.4		122.8	19.9
1920	27.3	26.9		128.4	21.0
1921	22.0	21.8		99.6	21.8
1922	21.4	21.1		93.2	22.6
1923	23.0	22.7		96.5	23.5
1924	23.8	23.4		92.6	25.3
1925	25.4	25.0		99.6	25.1
1926	27.1	26.6		101.4	26.3
1927	26.7	26.3		98.1	26.8
1928	27.3	26.9		100.7	26.7
1929	28.6	28.0	27.8	100.2*	28.0
1930	26.4	25.9	25.9	94.5	27.5
1931	21.5	21.2	22.1	80.7	26.2
1932	18.1	17.8	18.1	68.8	25.9
1933	18.1	17.8	17.7	66.3	26.9
1934		20.7	20.9	72.3	28.6
1935		22.8	23.0	77.0	29.6
1936		25.3	25.5	76.8	32.9
1937		27.2	27.4	79.5	34.2
1938		25.7	25.9	75.1	34.2
1939		26.6	26.8	73.7	36.1
1940		28.2	28.4	74.8	37.7
1941		32.6	32.9	80.7	40.4
1942		38.9	39.2	97.3	40.0
1943		44.3		109.3	40.5

* The price index to the base 1929 : 100 is for the flow of goods destined for domestic consumption *before* account is taken of inventory changes. The price index shown is that implicit in the flow of goods to consumers at cost to them, i.e., *after* account is taken of inventory changes. The difference between the two for 1929 is due to the use of changes in inventories in current valuations for the current price series (i.e., distributive inventories at the beginning and end of 1929, without conversion of either to 1929 prices) and of changes in inventories in 1929 prices for the 1929 price series. The former, rather than the latter approach, had to be used in estimating the current price series (even in 1929) since for all other years samples of distributive margins reflected changes on the assumption that inventories were used at current valuation (see *Commodity Flow and Capital Formation,* Vol. One, p. 271).

COLUMN

1 *Commodity Flow and Capital Formation,* Vol. One, p. 324, Table V-10, line A 1.

2 *1919-33:* col. 1 minus the flow of gasoline and lubricating oils and greases for business use of passenger cars. The Bureau of Foreign and Domestic Commerce

ANNUAL ESTIMATES, 1919-1943

COLUMN

in its October 1942 release, *Output of Manufactured Commodities, 1929-1939* (mimeo.), allocates 30 percent of passenger car output to the producer durable category on the basis of relevant studies by the Public Roads Administration and other agencies. A similar adjustment was made for gasoline, lubricating oils and greases, 30 percent of the finished output being transferred to the unfinished category as representing current business use. It was assumed that the distributions of the final flow of these items and of the output are identical.

The flow is computed as the sum of output for domestic consumption and spread, minus net changes in inventories (i.e., total difference between manufacturers' value and cost to final buyers). Output, shown for the odd years 1919-33 in *Commodity Flow and Capital Formation*, Vol. One, Table I-4, is interpolated for the even years by the total for the minor group of which it is a part (*ibid.*, Table II-3). Output for domestic consumption is estimated by multiplying output by the minor group ratio of output for domestic consumption to output of finished products as derived from *ibid.*, Tables II-5 and II-3. The spread is assumed to be the same as that for the minor group of which the commodity is part. For 1929 it is shown in *ibid.*, Table III-5. Extrapolation to 1919 and 1933 is by the spread for the major group as estimated from *ibid.*, Tables II-5 and V-6. The adjustment for inventories is derived from the same source.

1934-42: estimated on the basis of col. 3. The ratio of col. 2 to col. 3 for 1929-33 is applied to col. 3 for 1934-42 to compute entries in col. 2.

1943: extrapolated from 1942 on the basis of changes in the flow of nondurable commodities (*Survey of Current Business*, April 1944, p. 13, Table 10) and changes between 1942 and 1943 in sales of retail stores (*ibid.*, Jan. 1944, p. 8, Table 10). Drug, eating and drinking, food stores, and filling stations were added as perishable; and apparel and general merchandise stores as semidurable. The totals for 1942 in col. 2 of Tables I 1 and I 2 were extrapolated to 1943 by the percentage change, 1942-43, in the sales of perishable and semidurable stores; the two totals for 1943 were then adjusted proportionally so that they would add to a total nondurable commodity flow in 1943 that would represent a percentage increase over nondurable commodity flow in 1942 equal to the one shown by that category of consumers' outlay in the April 1944 *Survey*.

3 Estimates by W. H. Shaw in the June 1944 *Survey*, particularly Table 2, pp. 9-11. The groups designated I; III 1; V 5; V 11; V 17; V 18; V 19; VI 1; VII 1; VIII 1f; IX 5b; IX 6 were classified as perishable in accordance with Shaw's advice.

4 *1919-33:* col. 2 divided by col. 5.

1934-38: estimated by linking in 1933 to indexes prepared by Henry Shavell (see *Survey*, May 1943, p. 17, Table 1).

1939-43: the price index implicit in nondurable commodities can be computed from the current price series given in the *Survey*, April 1944, p. 13, Table 10, and the 1939 price series provided by the Department of Commerce for 1939-43 and estimated by us for 1942 and 1943. The analysis in *National Product in Wartime*, Appendix II, indicates that the disparity between the Department of Commerce and our data for 1942 and 1943 on consumer commodities is confined to the nondurable, i.e., perishable and semidurable. With the help of *ibid.*, Appendix Table II 1, our estimates of nondurable commodities can be calculated.

The sum of perishable and semidurable commodities (Table I 1, col. 2, and I 2, col. 2) divided by the index described above yields the final total of nondurable commodities, 1939-43, in 1939 prices. Perishable and semidurable are converted to 1939 prices by means of the Shavell indexes (*Survey*, May 1943)

Table I 1 concluded:

extrapolated to 1943 by the percentage change in the index for the total nondurable group. The percentage breakdown of these preliminary estimates is applied to the final nondurable total in 1939 prices to yield final perishable and semidurable in 1939 prices. The price index implicit in each with 1939 as base is then derived. The indexes are reduced to 1929 levels by the ratios used for linking in 1933.

5 *1919-33:* the procedure parallels that followed in estimating the values in current prices. Output for domestic consumption is computed from the series in current prices by dividing by the price index of the minor commodity group to which the particular commodity belongs as shown in *Commodity Flow and Capital Formation,* Vol. One, Table II-6. Spread and net change in inventories are estimated from *ibid.,* Tables II-7 and V-7.

1934-43: col. 2 divided by col. 4.

Table I 2
Flow of Semidurable Commodities, at Cost to Consumers
Current and 1929 Prices, 1919-1943
(dollar figures in billions)

	Original Estimate in *Commodity Flow and Capital Formation* (1)	Adj. for Business Use of Passenger Cars (2)	Department of Commerce Estimate (Shaw) (3)	Price Index 1929 : 100 (4)	Total 1929 Prices (5)
1919	10.5	10.1		134.8	7.5
1920	12.2	11.7		180.2	6.5
1921	9.7	9.5		121.4	7.8
1922	10.0	9.8		110.9	8.9
1923	11.3	11.1		114.0	9.8
1924	10.7	10.5		116.2	9.0
1925	11.4	11.0		110.8	9.9
1926	11.9	11.5		115.2	10.0
1927	12.0	11.7		103.9	11.2
1928	12.2	11.8		105.6	11.2
1929	12.4	12.1	11.5	102.1*	11.8
1930	10.7	10.5	9.9	98.5	10.6
1931	9.0	8.8	8.5	84.1	10.5
1932	6.7	6.5	6.3	68.8	9.5
1933	6.5	6.3	5.8	73.4	8.7
1934		7.3	6.9	84.3	8.7
1935		7.9	7.5	82.8	9.5
1936		8.5	8.1	83.1	10.2
1937		8.6	8.2	86.6	9.9
1938		8.4	8.0	83.7	10.0
1939		9.2	8.7	82.5	11.2
1940		9.6	9.1	85.1	11.3
1941		11.3	10.7	90.5	12.5
1942		13.2	12.5	112.2	11.8
1943		15.6		126.1	12.4

* See note to Table I 1.

COLUMN

1 *Commodity Flow and Capital Formation*, Vol. One, p. 324, Table V-10, line A 2.

2 *1919-33:* col. 1 minus the flow of tires and tubes for business use of passenger cars. For the basis of estimating the proportion and the procedure of making the deduction from col. 1, see note to col. 2 of Table I 1.

1934-42: the average ratio of col. 2 to col. 3 for 1929-33 is applied to col. 3 for 1934-42.

1943: see note on the derivation of the 1943 entry for perishable commodities (Table I 1, col. 2).

3 Shaw's estimates in the *Survey of Current Business,* June 1944, Table 2, pp. 9-11. The following groups were included under semidurable: II 1; II 3; V 8 (65 percent of total); VIII 1c; VIII 1d; IX 5d. The 65 percent of V 8 (house furnishings and equipment, n.e.c.) classified as semidurable (the balance as durable) is Shaw's estimate.

4 See notes to col. 4 of Table I 1. 5 See notes to col. 5 of Table I 1.

Table I 3
Flow of Consumer Durable Commodities, at Cost to Consumers Current and 1929 Prices, 1919-1943
(dollar figures in billions)

	Original Estimate in *Commodity Flow and Capital Formation* (1)	Adj. for Business Use of Passenger Cars (2)	Department of Commerce Estimate (Shaw) (3)	Price Index 1929 : 100 (4)	TOTAL, 1929 PRICES RELATED TO Col. 1 (5)	Col. 2 (6)
1919	6.0	5.4		108.7	5.5	5.0
1920	6.9	6.2		126.8	5.4	4.9
1921	5.6	5.0		126.6	4.4	4.0
1922	6.2	5.5		108.4	5.7	5.1
1923	7.9	7.0		105.4	7.6	6.6
1924	7.9	7.0		101.5	7.8	6.9
1925	9.1	8.0		102.6	8.9	7.8
1926	9.4	8.3		96.3	9.9	8.6
1927	8.9	7.9		96.8	9.2	8.2
1928	9.2	8.1		97.0	9.5	8.4
1929	9.9	8.8	8.9	100.2*	9.9	8.8
1930	7.6	6.8	6.9	97.6	7.8	6.9
1931	5.7	5.2	5.4	90.2	6.4	5.7
1932	3.8	3.4	3.6	80.4	4.7	4.3
1933	3.9	3.5	3.4	83.2	4.6	4.2
1934		4.1	4.2	86.5		4.7
1935		5.0	5.1	85.0		5.9
1936		6.1	6.2	86.1		7.1
1937		6.6	6.7	89.9		7.3
1938		5.3	5.4	90.1		5.9
1939		6.2	6.3	89.1		7.0
1940		7.3	7.4	90.7		8.0
1941		9.0	9.2	97.2		9.3
1942		7.0	7.1	111.3		6.3
1943		7.1		120.1		5.9

* See note to Table I 1.

COLUMN

1 *Commodity Flow and Capital Formation*, Vol. One, p. 324, Table V-10, line A 3a.

2 *1919-33:* col. 1 minus the flow of passenger cars and motor vehicle bodies and parts for business use. For the basis of the estimate of the subtrahend see notes to col. 2 of Table I 1.

1934-42: the average ratio of col. 2 to col. 3 for 1929-33 is applied to col. 3 for 1934-42.

1943: extrapolated from 1942 on basis of change between 1942 and 1943 in Department of Commerce estimates of the durable category of consumers' outlay (see *Survey of Current Business*, April 1944, Table 10, p. 13).

3 Shaw's estimates in the *Survey,* June 1944, Table 2, pp. 9-11. Durables include II 11; V 1; V 2; V 3; V 4; V 5; V 7; V 8 (35 percent of total) ; V 9; V 10; V 16; VI 2; VI 18; VIII 1a; VIII 4; IX 5a; IX 5e; IX 5f; IX 5h; IX 5j; IX 5n.

ANNUAL ESTIMATES, 1919-1943

COLUMN

4 *1919-33:* from col. 2 and 6.

1934-41: linked at 1933 with Shavell's estimates (see *Survey,* May 1943, Table 1, p. 17).

1942-43: linked with Department of Commerce indexes obtained by dividing totals in 1939 prices into totals in current prices.

5 *1919-31:* the estimates in *Commodity Flow and Capital Formation,* Vol. One, Table V-7, line 14 under Consumers' Durable, had to be revised because of an error detected in the procedure. This error and the correction are as follows:

The flow to ultimate users of consumer (and producer) durable goods in 1929 prices was computed by: (a) estimating the value of output destined for domestic consumption at producers' prices for 1929 (*ibid.,* Table II-7); (b) allowing a mark-up representing transportation and distributive costs at their 1929 level, but modified by changes in the weights of the various minor commodity groups within the two major groups (Table V-7, line 2 under Consumers' [and Producers'] Durable); (c) applying this changing mark-up to the estimate under (a) to obtain a first estimate of the flow to ultimate users at final cost in 1929 prices, unadjusted for net changes in inventories (Table V-7, line 4 under Consumers' [and Producers'] Durable); (d) estimating the net changes in these inventories (Table V-7, line 13 under Consumers' [and Producers'] Durable); (e) subtracting these net changes from the estimate under (c) to obtain the final estimate of flow to ultimate users at final cost (Table V-7, line 14 under Consumers' [and Producers'] Durable).

The error in this procedure was to apply the index of shifting weights (Table V-7, line 2 under Consumers' [and Producers'] Durable) directly to the index of the value of commodities destined for domestic consumption, at 1929 producers' prices (line 1), without modifying the former by the weight of the mark-up compared with the weight of the value at producers' prices. The procedure would have been correct only if the 1929 mark-up for consumer (and for producer) durable goods were 100 percent of the value at producers' prices. Actually, the mark-up in these two commodity groups is lower—60.5 percent of consumer durable (and 16.2 percent of producer durable) at producers' prices. The revision to correct for this error is shown in the accompanying table.

1932-33: we retained the estimates in *Commodity Flow and Capital Formation,* Vol. One, Table V-7, line C 14, since the changes were extremely minor.

6 *1919-33:* from col. 5 by deduction of passenger cars, etc. purchased for business use. For a general description of the procedure see notes to col. 5 of Table I 1.

1934-43: col. 2 divided by col. 4.

Revision of the Estimates of Flow to Ultimate Users at Final Cost, Consumer Durable Commodities, 1919-1931

Published Estimates, Table V-7	1919	1920	1921	1922	1923	1924	1925	1926	1927	1928	1929	1930	1931
1 Index of value of commodities destined for domestic consumption, 1929 price (Table V-7, line 1)	53.3	53.6	40.9	60.3	81.8	78.2	91.7	101.4	88.9	95.8	100.0	70.7	57.3
2 Index of shifting weights, 1929:100, expressed as an index of mark-up (Table V-7, line 2)	110.8	107.8	107.6	102.7	98.3	100.8	98.6	97.6	102.4	101.4	100.0	102.6	105.8
3 Adj. index (Table V-7, line 3)	59.1	57.8	44.0	61.9	80.4	78.8	90.4	99.0	91.0	97.1	100.0	72.5	60.6
4 1st estimate of flow to ultimate users at final cost (Table V-7, line 4) ($ million)	5,929.8	5,799.4	4,414.7	6,210.7	8,066.9	7,906.4	9,070.3	9,933.2	9,130.5	9,742.5	10,033.5	7,274.3	6,080.3
5 Total net changes in inventories (Table V-7, line 13) ($ million)	+108.9	+92.7	−165.3	+391.9	+545.1	+33.5	+252.9	+181.7	−233.7	+187.9	+139.9	−600.6	−497.1
6 Final estimate of flow to ultimate users at final cost (Table V-7, line 14) ($ million)	5,820.9	5,706.7[a]	4,580.0	5,818.8	7,521.8	7,872.9	8,817.4	9,751.5	9,364.2	9,554.6	9,893.6	7,874.9	6,577.4

Revised Estimates

7 Line 2 adj. (line 2 x 1929 ratio of mark-up to value at producers' prices[b])	67.0	65.2	65.1	62.1	59.4	61.0	59.6	59.0	61.9	61.3	60.5	62.0	64.0
8 [Line 1 x (line 7 ÷ 100)] ÷ 100	89.0	88.5	67.5	97.7	130.4	125.9	146.4	161.2	143.9	154.5	160.5	114.5	94.0
9 Line 8 adj. to 1929:100	55.5	55.1	42.1	60.9	81.2	78.4	91.2	100.4	89.7	96.3	100.0	71.3	58.6
10 Revised 1st estimate of flow to ultimate users at final cost (1929 figure from Table III-5 x line 9) (Table V-7, line 4 revised) ($ million)	5,568.6	5,528.5	4,224.1	6,110.4	8,147.2	7,866.3	9,150.6	10,073.7	9,000.1	9,662.3	10,033.5	7,153.9	5,879.7
11 Revised final estimate of flow to ultimate users at final cost (line 10 –line 5) (Table V-7, line 14 revised) ($ million)	5,459.7	5,435.8	4,389.4	5,718.5	7,602.1	7,832.8	8,897.7	9,892.0	9,233.8	9,474.4	9,893.6	7,754.5	6,376.8

[a] Owing to a typographical error, this figure was published as 6,706.7.
[b] See *Commodity Flow and Capital Formation*, Vol. One, Table V-6, lines 5 and 6 under Consumers' Durable. The ratio is .6047.

Table I 4A

Flow of Services Not Embodied in New Commodities,
at Cost to Consumers, Current and 1929 Prices, 1919-1943
(dollar figures in billions)

	Total corr. to Commodity Flow and Capital Formation (1)	Adj. for Business Use of Passenger Cars (2)	Dept. of Commerce Estimate (Shaw) (3)	Estimate in National Product in Wartime, Part II (4)	Total 1929 Prices (rel. to col. 2) (5)	Dept. of Commerce Estimate 1939 Prices (6)	Direct Taxes incl. in Col. 2 (7)
1919	12.8	14.0			17.8		2.0
1920	16.5	18.1			19.8		2.3
1921	18.8	19.9			20.1		2.2
1922	18.6	19.8			20.0		1.9
1923	20.8	22.1			22.0		2.1
1924	23.8	25.2			24.8		2.0
1925	20.9	22.6			22.0		2.1
1926	23.9	25.7			25.1		2.4
1927	24.3	25.9			25.5		2.4
1928	25.6	27.1			26.9		2.6
1929	26.4	27.8	33.3		27.8		3.0
1930	28.4	30.3	31.2		30.6		2.8
1931	23.9	25.1	27.7		26.1		2.3
1932	18.5	19.5	23.6		21.6		1.9
1933	17.3	18.2	21.6		21.7		1.9
1934		20.7	22.1		25.2		2.1
1935		18.3	23.2		22.3		2.4
1936		19.3	25.3		23.3		2.9
1937		23.5	27.6		27.6		3.6
1938		25.5	27.4		29.6	24.8	3.5
1939		25.9	27.8	25.8	30.8	25.8	3.1
1940		27.1	29.0	27.0	32.1	26.9	3.1
1941		28.6	30.9	28.5	33.3	27.9	3.1
1942		30.8	33.0	30.7	34.0	28.5	3.1
1943		32.4		32.3	34.0	28.5	3.1

COLUMN

1 By subtraction from national income in current prices of net capital formation in current prices (see *National Income and Its Composition,* I, 269) and of the flow of perishable, semidurable, and consumer durable commodities as entered in col. 1 of Tables I 1, I 2, and I 3.

2 *1919-38:* by subtraction from national income in current prices of net capital formation (Table I 17) and of the flow of perishable, semidurable, and consumer durable commodities as entered in col. 2 of Tables I 1, I 2, and I 3.

1939: extrapolated from 1938 on the basis of col. 3.

1940-43: extrapolated from 1939 on the basis of col. 4.

3 Col. 7 plus Shaw's estimates in the *Survey of Current Business,* June 1944, Table 2, p. 11.

4 Estimates of services as part of the gross national product analysis, plus an allowance of $3.1 billion for the value of direct nonwar services by governments to individuals. For the Department of Commerce estimates see the *Survey,* April 1944, Table 10, p. 13. For the basis of the $3.1 billion allowance see *National Product in Wartime,* Part II.

ANNUAL ESTIMATES, 1919-1943

COLUMN

5 *1919-38:* col. 2 divided by the price index for services obtained by taking the weighted average of the components of the BLS cost of living index that represent services primarily (the weights are those of the BLS).

1939-43: by extrapolation from 1938 on the basis of col. 6.

6 *1939-43:* the service component of consumers' outlay, in 1939 prices, obtained directly from the Department of Commerce, plus the $3.1 billion allowance for the value of direct nonwar services by governments to individuals. The series was extrapolated from 1939 to 1938 on the basis of col. 3; the entry for 1938 was then reduced 0.8 percent to allow for a somewhat higher price level in 1938. According to Shavell's estimates (*Survey,* May 1943, p. 17) retail prices of consumer commodities were 1.7 percent higher in 1938 than in 1939. For services one-half of that differential was assumed.

7 *1919-38:* federal direct taxes include income, estate, and gift taxes, and were obtained from the Bureau of Internal Revenue for all years except 1919-25, when the tax liability for one year (*Statistics of Income, 1940,* Part I, p. 48) is used for the following year since taxes are paid after the close of the year. The tax liability figures are slight underestimates since they exclude back taxes, penalties, errors corrected in auditing returns, etc.

State and local direct personal taxes, given for 1939 in the *Survey,* March 1943, p. 21, Table 12, line 8, are extrapolated for the years back to 1914 by total state and local tax collections, given for fiscal years in the *Economic Almanac, 1943-44* (National Industrial Conference Board), p. 389. Calendar year estimates are averages of pairs of fiscal years.

1939-43: see notes to col. 4.

Table I 4B
Alternative Estimate of Services Not Embodied in New Commodities, at Cost to Consumers, Current and 1929 Prices, 1919-1943
(dollar figures in billions)

	TOTAL EXCL. DIRECT TAXES Current Prices (1)	DIRECT TAXES (2)	TOTAL INCL. DIRECT TAXES Current Prices (3)	PRICE INDEX 1929 : 100 (4)	TOTAL 1929 Prices (5)
1919	19.6	2.0	21.6	78.8	27.5
1920	21.4	2.3	23.7	91.5	25.9
1921	21.5	2.2	23.7	99.2	23.9
1922	22.4	1.9	24.3	99.0	24.6
1923	24.6	2.1	26.7	100.2	26.7
1924	26.0	2.0	28.0	101.8	27.5
1925	26.9	2.1	29.0	102.5	28.3
1926	27.8	2.4	30.2	102.4	29.5
1927	28.5	2.4	30.9	101.8	30.4
1928	29.1	2.6	31.7	100.8	31.5
1929	30.0	3.0	33.0	100.0	33.0
1930	28.3	2.8	31.1	99.0	31.5
1931	25.4	2.3	27.7	96.1	28.9
1932	21.8	1.9	23.7	90.5	26.2
1933	19.7	1.9	21.6	83.9	25.8
1934	20.2	2.1	22.3	81.9	27.2
1935	21.3	2.4	23.7	81.9	29.0
1936	23.1	2.9	26.0	82.8	31.4
1937	24.8	3.6	28.4	85.1	33.3
1938	24.6	3.5	28.1	86.2	32.6
1939	25.4	3.1	28.5	84.1	33.9
1940	26.6	3.1	29.7	84.4	35.2
1941	28.6	3.1	31.7	85.9	36.9
1942	30.8	3.1	33.9	90.6	37.4
1943		3.1	35.6	95.3	37.4

COLUMN

1 *1919-20:* extrapolated from 1921 with W. H. Lough's series on intangibles (*High-Level Consumption;* McGraw-Hill, 1935, p. 28) as index.

1921-28: extrapolated from 1929 with Harold Barger's series on services (*Outlay and Income in the United States, 1921-1938,* National Bureau of Economic Research, 1942, Table 22) as index.

1929-42: Shaw's series (*Survey of Current Business,* June 1944, p. 9, Table 2) except that for his rent and service series (groups IV 1, IV 2, IV 3, and V 26 in that table) we substituted those underlying the national income estimates (Barger, *op. cit.*).

2 Table I 4A, col. 7.

3 *1919-42:* col. 1 plus col. 2.
  1943: extrapolated from 1942 with Table I 4A, col. 4, as index.

4 Table I 4A, col. 2 divided by col. 5.

5 Col. 3 divided by col. 4.

TABLE I 5: Flow of Goods to Consumers, Current and 1929 Prices, 1919-1943 (billions of dollars)

	CURRENT PRICES					1929 PRICES				
	Perishable	Semidurable	Durable	Services	Flow of Goods to Consumers	Perishable	Semidurable	Durable	Services	Flow of Goods to Consumers
	(1)	(2)	(3)	(4)	(5)	(6)	(7)	(8)	(9)	(10)
1919	24.4	10.1	5.4	14.0	54.0	19.9	7.5	5.0	17.8	50.2
1920	26.9	11.7	6.2	18.1	63.0	21.0	6.5	4.9	19.8	52.2
1921	21.8	9.5	5.0	19.9	56.3	21.8	7.8	4.0	20.1	53.8
1922	21.1	9.8	5.5	19.8	56.2	22.6	8.9	5.1	20.0	56.5
1923	22.7	11.1	7.0	22.1	62.9	23.5	9.8	6.6	22.0	61.9
1924	23.4	10.5	7.0	25.2	66.2	25.3	9.0	6.9	24.8	66.0
1925	25.0	11.0	8.0	22.6	66.6	25.1	9.9	7.8	22.0	64.9
1926	26.6	11.5	8.3	25.7	72.1	26.3	10.0	8.6	25.1	70.0
1927	26.3	11.7	7.9	25.9	71.8	26.8	11.2	8.2	25.5	71.7
1928	26.9	11.8	8.1	27.1	73.9	26.7	11.2	8.4	26.9	73.2
1929	28.0	12.1	8.8	27.8	76.7	28.0	11.8	8.8	27.8	76.4
1930	25.9	10.5	6.8	30.3	73.5	27.5	10.6	6.9	30.6	75.7
1931	21.2	8.8	5.2	25.1	60.3	26.2	10.5	5.7	26.1	68.6
1932	17.8	6.5	3.4	19.5	47.3	25.9	9.5	4.3	21.6	61.2
1933	17.8	6.3	3.5	18.2	45.9	26.9	8.7	4.2	21.7	61.5
1934	20.7	7.3	4.1	20.7	52.8	28.6	8.7	4.7	25.2	67.2
1935	22.8	7.9	5.0	18.3	54.0	29.6	9.5	5.9	22.3	67.3
1936	25.3	8.5	6.1	19.3	59.2	32.9	10.2	7.1	23.3	73.5
1937	27.2	8.6	6.6	23.5	65.9	34.2	9.9	7.3	27.6	79.0
1938	25.7	8.4	5.3	25.5	64.9	34.2	10.0	5.9	29.6	79.7
1939	26.6	9.2	6.2	25.9	67.9	36.1	11.2	7.0	30.8	85.1
1940	28.2	9.6	7.3	27.1	72.2	37.7	11.3	8.0	32.1	89.1
1941	32.6	11.3	9.0	28.6	81.5	40.4	12.5	9.3	33.3	95.5
1942	38.9	13.2	7.0	30.8	89.9	40.0	11.8	6.3	34.0	92.1
1943	44.3	15.6	7.1	32.4	99.4	40.5	12.4	5.9	34.0	92.8

COLUMN

1 Table I 1, col. 2.
2 Table I 2, col. 2.
3 Table I 3, col. 2.
4 Table I 4A, col. 2.
5 Sum of col. 1-4.
6 Table I 1, col. 5.

COLUMN

7 Table I 2, col. 5.
8 Table I 3, col. 6.
9 Table I 4A, col. 5.
10 Sum of col. 6-9.

TABLE I 6
Flow of Producer Durable Commodities, at Cost to Purchasers
Current and 1929 Prices, 1919-1943
(dollar figures in billions)

	Original Estimate in Commodity Flow and Capital Formation (1)	Adj. for Business Use of Passenger Cars (2)	Dept. of Commerce Estimate (3)	Nonwar Producer Durable (4)	Price Index 1929 : 100 (rel. to col. 2) (5)	Total 1929 Prices (rel. to col. 2) (6)	Nonwar Producer Durable 1929 Prices (7)
1919	5.7	6.2		0.7	113.7	5.4	0.6
1920	5.7	6.3		5.4	118.6	5.3	4.5
1921	3.6	4.0		3.3	113.4	3.6	2.9
1922	3.5	4.1		3.9	99.1	4.2	3.9
1923	5.0	5.8		5.6	100.4	5.8	5.6
1924	4.7	5.4		5.2	100.0	5.4	5.2
1925	5.0	5.9		5.7	99.5	6.0	5.7
1926	5.4	6.4		6.2	97.8	6.5	6.3
1927	5.1	5.9		5.7	97.3	6.1	5.9
1928	5.5	6.3		6.1	97.7	6.5	6.2
1929	6.5	7.5	7.3	7.2	100.2*	7.5	7.2
1930	5.1	5.8	6.0	5.5	94.9	6.1	5.8
1931	3.3	3.7	4.2	3.3	90.5	4.1	3.7
1932	1.8	2.1	2.4	1.7	84.5	2.5	2.0
1933	1.9	2.2	2.1	1.9	81.1	2.7	2.4
1934		3.0	3.1	2.6	87.0	3.4	3.0
1935		3.9	4.0	3.5	86.4	4.5	4.1
1936		4.9	5.1	4.2	86.7	5.7	4.8
1937		6.1	6.3	5.5	92.6	6.6	5.9
1938		4.4	4.5	3.7	94.5	4.7	3.9
1939		6.2	6.4	5.3	101.6	6.1	5.7
1939		6.3		5.5	101.6	6.2	5.9
1940		8.0		6.9	102.6	7.8	7.3
1941		14.2		8.9	125.7	11.3	9.2
1942		35.1		5.1	181.9	19.3	4.9
1943		56.5		3.1	180.5	31.3	3.0

* See note to Table I 1.

In *Commodity Flow and Capital Formation,* Vol. One (and in *Bulletin 74*), the gross increase in the value of horses, mules, and milk cows on farms is included in the flow of producer durable commodities. This item, together with the corresponding estimate of the gross decrease, is now treated as a component of the net changes in inventories.

COLUMN

1 See *Commodity Flow and Capital Formation,* Vol. One, Table V-6, line D 11.

2 *1919-33:* col. 1 plus the flow of passenger cars for business use. For general basis of this adjustment see note to col. 2 of Table I 1.

1934-39: the average ratio for 1929-33 of col. 2 to col. 3 is applied to col. 3 for 1934-39.

1939-43: col. 4 plus col. 2 of Table I 9.

COLUMN

3 *1929-38:* Shaw's estimates (*Survey of Current Business,* April 1942, Table 1, p. 15).

1939: sum of producers' equipment estimated as part of private gross capital formation (*Survey,* April 1944, Table 10, p. 13) and munitions (Table I 9, col. 2, below).

4 *1919-39:* col. 2 minus col. 2 of Table I 9.

1939-43: *Survey,* April 1944, Table 10, p. 13.

5 *1919-33:* from col. 2 and 6.

1934-38: extrapolated from 1933 by movement in the index prepared by Henry Shavell and used by the Department of Commerce (*Survey,* May 1943, p. 19, Table 3).

1939-43: from col. 2 and 6.

6 *1919-33:* the basic estimate in 1929 prices is that comparable in scope with col. 1 and prepared in connection with the original work on capital formation. The estimates for 1919-31 in *Commodity Flow and Capital Formation,* Vol. One, Table V-7, line 14 under Producers' Durable, had to be revised because of the error described above (see the accompanying table and the note to col. 5 of Table I 3). For 1932-33 we retained the estimates in *Commodity Flow and Capital Formation,* Vol. One, Table V-7, line D 14.

The shift from the estimates revised as shown in the accompanying table to those including passenger cars for business use was by the procedure discussed in connection with this adjustment in notes to Tables I 1, I 2, and I 3.

1934-39: from col. 2 and 5.

1939-43: sum of (a) capital equipment as part of nonwar gross capital formation (col. 7) and (b) munitions (Table I 10, col. 2).

7 *1919-39:* col. 6 minus col. 2 of Table I 10.

1939-43: the Department of Commerce estimates in 1939 prices adjusted to the 1929 base by dividing by .93649, the ratio in 1933 of col. 5 to the Shavell index (*Survey,* May 1943, Table 3, p. 19).

REVISION OF THE ESTIMATES OF FLOW TO ULTIMATE USERS AT FINAL COST, PRODUCER DURABLE COMMODITIES, 1919-1931

Published Estimates, Table V-7	1919	1920	1921	1922	1923	1924	1925	1926	1927	1928	1929	1930	1931
1 Index of value of commodities destined for domestic consumption, 1929 prices (Table V-7, line 1)	81.4	75.5	47.3	55.3	76.5	70.6	76.5	83.6	77.4	84.1	100.0	81.2	52.8
2 Index of shifting weights, 1929:100, expressed as an index of mark-up (Table V-7, line 2)	80.8	86.0	87.2	93.6	93.0	94.2	98.8	97.7	108.1	102.3	100.0	99.4	98.8
3 Adj. index (Table V-7, line 3)	65.8	64.9	41.2	51.8	71.1	66.5	75.6	81.7	83.7	86.0	100.0	80.7	52.2
4 1st estimate of flow to ultimate users at final cost (Table V-7, line 4) ($ million)	4,346.4	4,287.0	2,721.5	3,421.6	4,696.5	4,392.7	4,993.8	5,396.7	5,528.8	5,680.7	6,605.5	5,330.6	3,448.1
5 Total net changes in inventories (Table V-7, line 13) ($ million)	+182.1	+14.2	−126.5	−0.4	+58.7	−34.5	+24.7	+30.5	−67.3	+5.6	+136.5	−30.6	−130.8
6 Final estimate of flow to ultimate users at final cost (Table V-7, line 14) ($ million)	4,164.3	4,272.8	2,848.0	3,422.0	4,637.8	4,427.2	4,969.1	5,366.2	5,596.1	5,675.1	6,469.0	5,361.2	3,578.9

Revised Estimates													
7 Line 2 adj. (line 2 x 1929 ratio of mark-up to value at producers' prices*)	13.1	13.9	14.1	15.2	15.1	15.3	16.0	15.8	17.5	16.6	16.2	16.1	16.0
8 [Line 1 x (line 7 ÷ 100)] ÷ 100	92.1	86.0	54.0	63.7	88.1	81.4	88.7	96.8	90.9	98.1	116.2	94.3	61.2
9 Line 8 adj. to 1929 : 100	79.3	74.0	46.5	54.8	75.8	70.1	76.3	83.3	78.2	84.4	100.0	81.2	52.7
10 Revised 1st estimate of flow to ultimate users at final cost (1929 figure from Table III-5 x line 9) (Table V-7, line 4 revised) ($ million)	5,238.2	4,888.1	3,071.6	3,619.8	5,007.0	4,630.5	5,040.0	5,502.4	5,165.5	5,575.1	6,605.5	5,363.7	3,481.1
11 Revised final estimate of flow to ultimate users at final cost (line 10 – line 5) (Table V-7, line 14 revised) ($ million)	5,056.1	4,873.9	3,198.1	3,620.2	4,948.3	4,665.0	5,015.3	5,471.9	5,232.8	5,569.5	6,469.0	5,394.3	3,611.9

* See *Commodity Flow and Capital Formation*, Vol. One, Table V-6, lines 5 and 6 under Producers' Durable. The ratio is .1620.

TABLE I 7
New Construction by Type, Current Prices, 1919-1943
(billions of dollars)

	RESI-DENTIAL (1)	OTHER PRIVATE (2)	PUBLIC UTILITY (3)	TOTAL BUSINESS (2+3) (4)	PUBLIC Incl. War Constr. (5)	PUBLIC Excl. War Constr. (6)	TOTAL Incl. War Constr. (1+4+5) (7)	TOTAL Excl. War Constr. (1+4+6) (8)
1919	1.9	1.4	0.7	2.0	2.0	0.8	5.9	4.7
1920	1.8	2.1	0.8	2.8	1.3	1.1	6.0	5.8
1921	1.9	1.6	0.6	2.2	1.6	1.5	5.6	5.5
1922	3.0	1.6	0.8	2.3	1.7	1.6	7.0	6.9
1923	3.9	1.8	1.2	3.0	1.6	1.5	8.5	8.4
1924	4.5	1.8	1.3	3.1	1.9	1.8	9.4	9.4
1925	4.8	2.2	1.3	3.5	2.1	2.0	10.4	10.3
1926	4.8	2.7	1.4	4.0	2.1	2.1	10.9	10.9
1927	4.5	2.7	1.4	4.1	2.4	2.3	10.9	10.9
1928	4.1	2.7	1.3	4.0	2.5	2.4	10.6	10.6
1929	3.7	2.6	1.6	4.2	2.4	2.3	10.3	10.3
1930	1.9	2.0	1.5	3.5	2.8	2.7	8.2	8.1
1931	1.6	1.2	0.9	2.1	2.6	2.4	6.2	6.1
1932	0.7	0.6	0.5	1.0	1.8	1.7	3.5	3.4
1933	0.5	0.5	0.2	0.7	1.2	1.1	2.4	2.3
1934	0.7	0.5	0.3	0.8	1.5	1.3	3.0	2.8
1935	1.0	0.5	0.3	0.9	1.4	1.2	3.4	3.1
1936	1.5	0.8	0.5	1.3	2.2	2.0	4.9	4.7
1937	1.8	1.1	0.6	1.7	2.0	1.8	5.5	5.3
1938	1.9	0.8	0.5	1.3	2.1	1.9	5.3	5.0
1939	2.5	0.8	0.5	1.4	2.4	2.1	6.3	6.0
1939	2.5	0.8	0.5	1.4	2.4	2.2	6.3	6.1
1940	2 8	1.1	0.7	1.7	2.7	1.9	7.3	6.4
1941	3.3	1.4	0.8	2.2	5.4	1.7	10.8	7.2
1942	1.6	0.6	0.7	1.3	10.7	1.5	13.6	4.4
1943	0.9	0.3	0.5	0.8	6.2	1.1	7.9	2.8

The estimates in *Commodity Flow and Capital Formation,* Vol. One, Table VI-6 (and in *Bulletin* 74) have been replaced by the series described below.

COLUMN

1 Sum of nonfarm and farm residential construction. For 1919-28 nonfarm residential construction, including major alterations and additions, is from *Residential Building* by L. J. Chawner (National Resources Committee, Housing Monograph Series, 1, Washington, D.C., 1939), Table V, and for 1929-43, from the *Survey of Current Business,* June 1943 and June 1944. Farm residential construction, for 1919-28, is estimated at 40 percent of total farm construction (*Construction Activity in the United States, 1915-37* by L. J. Chawner, Domestic Commerce Series, 99, Washington, D.C., 1938); for 1929-43, from the *Survey of Current Business,* June 1943 and June 1944. The apportionment of farm construction, 1919-28, is based on text discussion in *Construction Activity in the United States, 1915-37,* p. 13, and in *Commodity Flow and Capital Formation,* Vol. One, Note A to Table VI-7.

2 Private nonresidential construction plus farm nonresidential construction. Private nonresidential construction for 1919-28 is from *Construction Activity in the United States, 1915-37;* for 1929-43, from the *Survey,* June 1943 and June 1944. Farm nonresidential construction for 1919-28 is the difference between total farm construction and farm residential construction, both described in the note to col. 1; for 1929-43, from the *Survey,* June 1943 and June 1944.

3 & 5 From the sources indicated in the note to col. 2.

6 Col. 5 minus col. 3 of Table I 9.

TABLE I 8
New Construction by Type, 1929 Prices, 1919-1943
(billions of dollars)

	RESI-DENTIAL (1)	OTHER PRIVATE (2)	PUBLIC UTILITY (3)	TOTAL BUSINESS (2+3) (4)	PUBLIC Incl. War Constr. (5)	PUBLIC Excl. War Constr. (6)	TOTAL Incl. War Constr. (1+4+5) (7)	TOTAL Excl. War Constr. (1+4+6) (8)
1919	1.8	1.4	0.6	2.0	2.1	0.8	5.9	4.6
1920	1.4	1.6	0.6	2.3	1.0	0.8	4.7	4.5
1921	1.9	1.6	0.6	2.2	1.5	1.4	5.6	5.5
1922	3.2	1.7	0.8	2.5	1.7	1.6	7.4	7.4
1923	3.8	1.7	1.1	2.9	1.4	1.3	8.1	8.0
1924	4.4	1.7	1.3	3.0	1.7	1.6	9.1	9.0
1925	4.8	2.2	1.3	3.4	2.0	1.9	10.2	10.1
1926	4.8	2.6	1.4	4.0	2.0	1.9	10.7	10.7
1927	4.5	2.7	1.4	4.1	2.3	2.2	10.8	10.8
1928	4.1	2.7	1.4	4.1	2.4	2.4	10.6	10.6
1929	3.7	2.6	1.6	4.2	2.4	2.3	10.3	10.3
1930	2.1	2.1	1.6	3.7	2.9	2.8	8.7	8.5
1931	1.9	1.3	1.0	2.3	2.9	2.8	7.1	7.0
1932	1.0	0.7	0.5	1.3	2.2	2.1	4.5	4.3
1933	0.7	0.6	0.3	0.9	1.4	1.2	3.0	2.8
1934	0.9	0.6	0.3	0.9	1.6	1.4	3.5	3.2
1935	1.4	0.7	0.4	1.0	1.6	1.4	4.0	3.7
1936	1.9	0.9	0.5	1.4	2.3	2.1	5.6	5.3
1937	1.9	1.1	0.6	1.7	2.1	1.9	5.8	5.6
1938	2.1	0.8	0.5	1.3	2.3	2.0	5.6	5.4
1939	2.8	0.9	0.5	1.4	2.4	2.3	6.6	6.5
1939	2.8	0.9	0.5	1.4	2.5	2.4	6.6	6.5
1940	3.0	1.1	0.6	1.7	2.4	2.0	7.1	6.8
1941	3.3	1.4	0.7	2.1	3.1	1.7	8.4	7.1
1942	1.4	0.5	0.6	1.1	5.4	1.2	7.9	3.8
1943	0.8	0.2	0.4	0.6	3.4	0.9	4.8	2.3

COLUMN

1 Table I 7, col. 1, divided by the American Appraisal Company construction cost index published in the *Engineering News-Record,* Construction Costs Number.

2 Table I 7, col. 2, divided by the average of the American Appraisal Company index and that of the Aberthaw Company, also published in the *Engineering News-Record*.

3 Table I 7, col. 3, divided by the weighted average of the index for gas plant construction costs (weighted 1), electric light and power construction costs (weighted 5), and railroad construction costs (weighted 4). The first two, compiled by Whitman, Requardt, and Smith, Consulting Engineers, appear in the *Engineering News-Record;* the railroad index is from the Interstate Commerce Commission, Bureau of Valuation.

5 Col. 6 plus col. 3 of Table I 10.

6 Table I 7, col. 6, divided by the weighted average of the Aberthaw index (weighted 6) and the highway construction cost index (weighted 4) obtained from the Public Roads Administration.

Table I 9
War Output, Gross and Net, Current Prices, 1919-1943
(billions of dollars)

	NON-DURABLE (1)	MUNITIONS (2)	CONSTRUCTION (3)	GROSS WAR OUTPUT		CONSUMPTION OF		NET WAR OUTPUT	
				Wartime Concept (4)	Peacetime Concept (5)	Construction (6)	Munitions (7)	Wartime Concept (8)	Peacetime Concept (9)
1919	3.1	5.5	1.1	9.7	8.6	0.3		9.3	8.2
1920	0.9	0.9	0.2	2.0	1.3	0.5		1.6	0.8
1921	0.5	0.7	0.1	1.3	0.9	0.4		0.9	0.5
1922	0.2	0.3	0.1	0.6	0.5	0.4		0.2	0.1
1923	0.2	0.2	0.1	0.4	0.5	0.4		*	0.1
1924	0.2	0.2	0.1	0.5	0.5	0.4		*	*
1925	0.2	0.2	0.1	0.5	0.5	0.4		0.1	0.1
1926	0.2	0.2	0.1	0.5	0.5	0.4		0.1	0.1
1927	0.2	0.2	0.1	0.5	0.5	0.3		0.2	0.2
1928	0.2	0.3	0.1	0.6	0.6	0.1		0.5	0.5
1929	0.2	0.3	0.1	0.6	0.6	0.1		0.5	0.5
1930	0.2	0.3	0.1	0.6	0.7	0.1		0.5	0.5
1931	0.3	0.4	0.1	0.8	0.6	0.1		0.7	0.5
1932	0.3	0.4	0.1	0.8	0.6	0.1		0.7	0.5
1933	0.2	0.3	0.1	0.6	0.4	0.1		0.5	0.3
1934	0.3	0.4	0.2	0.9	0.6	0.1		0.7	0.5
1935	0.3	0.4	0.2	1.0	0.7	0.1		0.8	0.5
1936	0.3	0.7	0.2	1.2	0.9	0.2		1.0	0.7
1937	0.3	0.6	0.2	1.2	0.8	0.2		1.0	0.7
1938	0.4	0.7	0.2	1.3	1.0	0.2		1.1	0.8
1939	0.4	0.9	0.3	1.6	1.2	0.3		1.2	0.8
1939	0.4	0.8	0.2	1.4	1.0	0.3	0.1	1.1	0.6
1940	0.8	1.1	0.9	2.8	2.0	0.4	0.2	2.4	1.4
1941	3.8	5.3	3.6	12.8	9.0	0.8	0.7	12.0	7.5
1942	11.1	30.0	9.2	50.3	39.2	1.6	3.6	48.7	34.0
1943	22.8	53.4	5.1	81.3	58.5	1.9	8.6	79.4	48.0

* Less than $50 million.

COLUMN

1 Col. 4 multiplied by the percentage of nondurable in the total derived as follows:

1919-39: nondurable includes for those years in which they appear: (a) pay and subsistence of the armed forces (from data underlying the estimates in *National Income and Its Composition*), (b) foreign loans (largely for food exports), (c) the Food and Fuel Administration, (d) the Grain Corporation, and (e) the Sugar Equalization Board.

1939-43: the percentages are given in the President's Budget Message, 1945 (Washington, D.C., 1944), p. VI, for the period of preparedness (used for 1939-41); of defensive war (used for 1942); and of aggressive deployment (used for 1943).

2 Col. 4 minus col. 1 and 3.

3 *1919-39:* sum of (a) military and naval construction, (b) U. S. Army Engineers, and (c) Veterans' Administration construction. For (a) and (b) for 1919-28 see Chawner's *Construction Activity in the United States;* for 1929-39, the *Survey of Current Business,* June 1943 and June 1944. For (c) the estimates are Chawner's for 1919-36 and are assumed to be the same in 1937-39 as in 1936.

1939-43: sum of public residential, military and naval, and public nonresidential industrial construction (*Survey,* June 1944).

ANNUAL ESTIMATES, 1919-1943

COLUMN

4 *1919-39:* for fiscal years 1919 and 1920 only annual totals for war agencies are available; calendar year totals are based on the monthly data on total ordinary expenditures. For 1921 and later years, from the monthly expenditures by war agencies given in the *Annual Report of the Secretary of the Treasury,* calendar year totals are derived. The items included are the War and Navy Departments, Shipping Board, foreign loans, federal control of transportation, the War Finance Corporation, the Food and Fuel Administration in the report for 1919; minus the Food and Fuel Administration plus the Grain Corporation in the report for 1920; minus federal control of transportation in the report for 1921; plus the Sugar Equalization Board in 1922; minus the Grain Corporation and foreign loans in 1923; minus the Sugar Equalization Board in 1924; minus the War Finance Corporation in 1933. To the total is added Veterans' Administration construction and from it are subtracted major receipts on war account—interest on foreign obligations, principal payments on foreign obligations, sale of war supplies, and decrease in the capital stock of the Grain Corporation.

1939-43: see the *Survey,* April 1944, Table 10, p. 13.

5 Col. 2 plus col. 3 plus government war transactions entered under changes in claims against foreign countries (included here in col. 1). For sources of government foreign transactions see notes to Table I 13, col. 2.

6 Table I 10, col. 6, converted to current prices by the price index for war construction (see the notes to Table I 10, col. 3).

7 Table I 10, col. 7, converted to current prices by the price index for munitions (see the notes to Table I 10, col. 2).

8 Col. 4 minus col. 6.

9 Col. 5 minus col. 6 and 7.

TABLE I 10

War Output, Gross and Net, 1929 Prices, 1919-1943
(billions of dollars)

	NON-DURABLE (1)	MUNI-TIONS (2)	CONSTRUC-TION (3)	GROSS WAR OUTPUT		CONSUMPTION OF		NET WAR OUTPUT	
				War-time Concept (4)	Peace-time Concept (5)	Construc-tion (6)	Muni-tions (7)	War-time Concept (8)	Peace-time Concept (9)
1919	2.9	4.8	1.2	8.9	7.4	0.4		8.5	7.0
1920	0.8	0.8	0.2	1.7	1.1	0.4		1.3	0.7
1921	0.4	0.6	0.1	1.2	0.8	0.4		0.8	0.4
1922	0.2	0.3	0.1	0.6	0.5	0.4		0.2	0.1
1923	0.2	0.2	0.1	0.4	0.5	0.4		*	0.1
1924	0.2	0.2	0.1	0.5	0.4	0.4		0.1	*
1925	0.2	0.2	0.1	0.5	0.4	0.4		0.1	*
1926	0.2	0.2	0.1	0.5	0.5	0.4		0.1	0.1
1927	0.2	0.2	0.1	0.5	0.5	0.3		0.2	0.2
1928	0.2	0.3	0.1	0.6	0.6	0.1		0.5	0.5
1929	0.2	0.3	0.1	0.6	0.6	0.1		0.5	0.5
1930	0.2	0.3	0.1	0.7	0.7	0.1		0.5	0.6
1931	0.3	0.4	0.1	0.9	0.8	0.1		0.8	0.7
1932	0.4	0.4	0.1	0.9	0.7	0.1		0.8	0.6
1933	0.3	0.3	0.2	0.8	0.5	0.1		0.7	0.4
1934	0.3	0.5	0.2	1.0	0.7	0.1		0.9	0.5
1935	0.4	0.5	0.2	1.1	0.7	0.2		1.0	0.6
1936	0.4	0.8	0.2	1.4	1.0	0.2		1.2	0.8
1937	0.4	0.7	0.2	1.3	0.9	0.2		1.1	0.7
1938	0.4	0.8	0.2	1.5	1.0	0.2		1.3	0.8
1939	0.5	0.4	0.1	1.0	0.5	0.1		0.9	0.4
1939	0.5	0.3	0.1	0.9	0.4	0.1	*	0.8	0.2
1940	1.0	0.5	0.3	1.8	0.8	0.2	0.1	1.7	0.6
1941	4.4	2.1	1.4	7.9	3.5	0.3	0.3	7.7	2.9
1942	11.0	14.4	4.1	29.5	18.5	0.7	1.7	28.8	16.1
1943	19.6	28.3	2.5	50.4	30.8	1.0	4.6	49.4	25.3

* Less than $50 million.

COLUMN

1 *1919-39:* Table I 9, col. 1, divided by the price index implicit in the flow of goods to consumers (see Tables I 14 and I 15).

1939-43: the price index for 1939 is extrapolated through 1943 by the index for nondurable war output described in *National Product in Wartime,* Appendix II.

2 *1919-39:* Table I 9, col. 2, divided by col. 5 of Table I 6.

1939-43: the price index on a 1939 base (*National Product in Wartime*) is based on assumption *a*. It is the index implicit in munitions and war construction, and is converted to a 1929 base by multiplying by .93649, the ratio of our price index for producer durables to Shavell's (*Survey of Current Business,* May 1943).

3 *1919-39:* Table I 9, col. 3, divided by the Aberthaw construction cost index (see notes to Table I 8, col. 2, for source).

1939-43: the price index for munitions and war construction (see notes to col. 2 above). Since both 1929 and 1939 equal 100 in the Aberthaw index, no adjustment is necessary to convert to a 1929 base.

ANNUAL ESTIMATES, 1919-1943

COLUMN

4 Col. 1 plus col. 2 and 3 plus government war transactions (see notes to **Table I 13**, col. 2 and 4).

5 Col. 2 plus col. 3.

6 Consumption is based on col. 3 and the assumption of a 10-year life period for construction during the war periods, 1914-18 and 1939-43, and of a 20-year life period for 1919-38. The 1914-18 construction estimates are from the same sources as those from 1919 on.

7 Consumption is based on col. 2 and the assumption of a 10-year life for munitions during the war.

8 Col. 4 minus col. 6.

9 **Col. 5 minus col. 6 and 7.**

Table I 11

Net Changes in Inventories and in Claims against Foreign Countries Current and 1929 Prices, 1919-1939

(billions of dollars)

	Farm (1)	Mining[a] (2)	Mfg.[a] (3)	Construction (4)	Trade (5)	Monetary Metals (6)	All Other[b] (7)	Total (1-7) (8)	Net Changes in Claims against Foreign Countries (9)
Current Prices									
1919	+0.16	+0.5	+1.7	+0.03	+1.7	−0.10	−0.06	+4.0	+3.2
1920	+1.5	−0.08	+2.7	+0.38	+2.4	−0.09	+0.5	+7.3	+2.3
1921	−0.5	−0.03	+0.03	+0.16	+0.26	+0.09	+0.14	+0.15	+1.3
1922	−0.05	−0.28	+1.0	−0.18	+0.11	+0.07	−0.11	+0.6	+0.45
1923	−0.01	+0.17	+1.5	−0.01	+1.1	+0.06	+0.24	+3.1	+0.22
1924	−0.7	+0.08	−0.28	+0.10	−0.16	+0.05	+0.03	−0.9	+0.7
1925	+0.7	−0.10	+0.7	+0.14	+0.13	c	+0.22	+1.8	+0.33
1926	−0.37	−0.07	+0.5	+0.20	+0.8	+0.03	+0.42	+1.6	+0.12
1927	+0.01	+0.15	−0.06	+0.14	−0.12	+0.04	+0.28	+0.45	+0.45
1928	+0.08	−0.20	+0.05	−0.25	+0.40	+0.04	−0.46	−0.34	+0.7
1929	−0.08	+0.20	+0.9	+0.26	+0.7	+0.02	+0.39	+2.4	+0.43
1930	−0.13	−0.17	+0.44	−0.44	−0.36	+0.03	−0.46	−1.1	+0.6
1931	+0.30	+0.10	−0.9	−0.14	−0.5	+0.04	−0.21	−1.3	+0.15
1932	+0.14	−0.09	−1.3	+0.16	−1.1	+0.04	−0.24	−2.4	+0.05
1933	−0.24	−0.02	−0.21	+0.06	−0.7	−0.01	−0.05	−1.1	+0.12
1934	−0.7			+0.10	+0.03	−0.15	−1.0	−1.7	+0.35
1935	+0.6			+0.25	+0.14	+0.43	−0.17	+1.3	−0.15
1936	−0.6			+0.48	+0.9	+0.26	+1.6	+2.5	−0.30
1937	+0.9			−0.21	+0.37	+0.26	+1.2	+2.5	−0.10
1938	+0.22			+0.32	−0.18	+0.29	−0.9	−0.27	+0.8
1939	+0.19			−0.10	+0.40	+0.21	+0.8	+1.5	+0.7
1929 Prices									
1919	+0.03	+0.40	+1.2	+0.03	+1.3	−0.05	−0.05	+2.8	+2.1
1920	+0.8	−0.04	+1.6	+0.24	+1.4	−0.10	+0.34	+4.2	+1.4
1921	−0.6	−0.02	−0.04	+0.17	+0.28	+0.08	+0.13	−0.04	+1.3
1922	−0.14	−0.26	+0.8	−0.18	+0.10	+0.06	−0.11	+0.31	+0.45
1923	−0.03	+0.15	+1.4	−0.01	+1.1	+0.05	+0.22	+2.8	+0.22
1924	−0.8	+0.08	−0.24	+0.09	−0.18	+0.05	+0.03	−0.9	+0.6
1925	+0.5	−0.09	+0.7	+0.13	+0.14	d	+0.21	+1.6	+0.29
1926	−0.5	−0.06	+0.34	+0.19	+0.8	+0.02	+0.42	+1.2	+0.11
1927	−0.01	+0.14	−0.06	+0.14	−0.12	+0.04	+0.29	+0.42	+0.45
1928	+0.07	−0.20	+0.03	−0.26	+0.40	+0.04	−0.46	−0.38	+0.7
1929	−0.08	+0.20	+0.9	+0.26	+0.7	+0.02	+0.39	+2.4	+0.43
1930	−0.13	−0.18	+0.49	−0.46	−0.37	+0.03	−0.46	−1.1	+0.7
1931	+0.5	+0.12	−1.1	−0.17	−0.6	+0.04	−0.22	−1.4	+0.25
1932	+0.40	−0.12	−1.8	+0.22	−1.6	+0.04	−0.30	−3.2	+0.08
1933	−0.45	−0.03	−0.28	+0.08	−1.0	−0.01	−0.06	−1.7	+0.18
1934	−1.2			+0.11	+0.04	−0.02	−1.2	−2.3	+0.44
1935	+0.7			+0.27	+0.18	+0.37	−0.19	+1.3	−0.18
1936	−0.7			+0.51	+1.1	+0.24	+1.7	+2.9	−0.36
1937	+0.8			−0.21	+0.43	+0.23	+1.3	+2.6	−0.11
1938	+0.35			+0.32	−0.23	+0.29	−1.0	−0.30	+1.0
1939	+0.30			−0.10	+0.5	+0.24	+0.9	+1.8	+0.8

[a] For 1934-39, included with 'all other'.
[b] For 1934-39, including mining and manufacturing.
[c] Less than − $1 million.
[d] Less than + $1 million.

ANNUAL ESTIMATES, 1919-1943

The series on net changes in inventories and in claims against foreign countries in Table I 11 are somewhat different in scope from those in *Commodity Flow and Capital Formation,* Vol. One, Tables VII-9, VII-10, and VIII-2. To the former have been added net changes in the value of capital livestock and in stocks of monetary metals. Transfer to the latter of changes in the stock of gold resulting from international flow cancels the change in claims arising from that source.

CURRENT PRICES

COLUMN

1 Net changes in the inventories of crops, of capital livestock on farms (horses, mules, and milk cows) and of other livestock (cattle, calves, hogs, sheep and lambs, etc.). For 1919-33, net changes in the inventories of crops and in stocks of cattle, calves, hogs, sheep and lambs, etc., are from *ibid.,* Table VII-4. For 1934-39, they are estimated by the procedure outlined in Notes A-G to Table VII-4. Department of Agriculture revisions of the source material have been incorporated in the estimates for 1935-39 but not for the earlier years. The incomparability, however, is negligible.

Net changes in the value of capital livestock are estimated as the difference between the gross increase in value (formerly included in the flow of producer durable commodities) and the gross decrease in value (formerly included in the consumption of business capital) in horses, mules, and milk cows on farms. Gross increase for 1919-33 is from *ibid.,* Table V-9; for 1934-39, the procedure is that indicated in Notes A, B, and C to Table V-9. Gross decrease for 1919-35 is from *Capital Consumption and Adjustment,* Appendix B, Table VI; for 1936-39, the procedure is that outlined in that table.

2 & 3 From *Commodity Flow and Capital Formation,* Vol. One, Table VII-10.

4 *1919-33:* ibid., Table VI-4, line 6.

1934-39: net changes in 1929 prices (described below) are multiplied by the BLS wholesale price index for building materials adjusted by the procedure indicated in *ibid.,* Note C to Table VI-1, line 6.

5 *1919-33:* ibid., Table VII-10.

1934-39: net changes in 1929 prices (described below) are multiplied by the price index derived by dividing the net change in current prices for 1933 by the net change in 1929 prices and extrapolating by the BLS wholesale price index for all commodities other than farm.

6 Previously treated as a separate item, net changes in stocks of monetary metals are now included with net changes in business inventories. Net changes in gold stocks resulting from international flow, formerly included, have been transferred to net changes in claims against foreign countries, offsetting the change in these claims that arises from the international movement of gold.

1919-33: we deduct from net changes in stocks of monetary metals as shown in *ibid.,* Table VII-11, the net gold movement (reported annually in *Balance of International Payments of the United States;* Department of Commerce).

1934-39: net changes in stocks of gold, of silver bullion held in mints and assay offices, and of silver coin are estimated from the *Annual Report of the Director of the Mint* by the methods indicated in *Commodity Flow and Capital Formation,* Vol. One, Note A to Table VII-11. From these are subtracted net changes in gold stocks resulting from international flow (reported annually in the *Balance of International Payments of the United States*).

7 *1919-33:* the difference between net changes in 'all other' inventories, as shown in *Commodity Flow and Capital Formation,* Vol. One, Table VII-10, and net changes in construction inventories, col. 4.

Table I 11 continued:

CURRENT PRICES (*concl.*)

COLUMN

1934-39: 'all other' comprises mining, manufacturing, transportation and other public utilities, service, finance, and 'nature of business not given'. The net changes in 1929 prices (described below) are multiplied by the index computed by dividing the net change in current prices for 1933 by the net change in 1929 prices and extrapolating by the BLS wholesale price index for all commodities.

9 'Balance on commodity and service account' plus 'net currency movements' (reported annually in the *Balance of International Payments of the United States*).

1929 PRICES

1 In general, the adjustment for price changes follows the procedures adopted in *Commodity Flow and Capital Formation,* Vol. One. The cost or market, whichever is lower, basis of valuation is assumed for inventories reported in dollar values. For the price indexes used to convert the current price values to constant prices, the average of October and November is taken to represent cost, and the average of December and the following January, market.

2 & 3 *Ibid.,* Table VII-9.

4 *1919-33:* ibid., Table VI-4, line 5.

1934-39: inventories in current prices are estimated, converted to 1929 prices, and annual net changes in the latter determined.

For inventories in current prices, total new construction (Table I 7) is multiplied by the ratio of inventories to construction. This ratio is computed for 1933 by dividing inventories, as estimated from *ibid.,* Table VI-4 and Note A to Table VI-4, by new construction. It is extrapolated for 1934-37 by the ratio of inventories to sales for construction companies derived from *Statistics of Income.* Extrapolation of the ratio for 1938 and 1939 is by inventory sales ratios for wholesalers of lumber, millwork and other building materials, and plumbing and heating supplies (*Dun's Review,* May 1939 and 1940).

Inventories in current prices are converted to 1929 prices by the BLS wholesale price index for building materials adjusted by the procedure indicated in *Commodity Flow and Capital Formation,* Vol. One, Note C to Table VI-1, line 6.

5 *1919-33:* ibid., Table VII-9.

1934-39: inventories in current prices are estimated, converted to 1929 prices, and annual net changes in the result determined.

Inventories in current prices are estimated separately for wholesale and retail trade as follows:

Wholesale: the product of sales and the ratio of inventories to them. Sales for 1933-35 are from *Domestic Commerce,* February 20, 1937 and January 30, 1928. The figure for 1935 is extrapolated to 1936-39 by the sales of wholesalers proper (*ibid.,* Jan. 20, 1940).

The ratio of inventories to sales is computed for 1933 and extrapolated to 1935 by inventory-sales ratios derived from the *Census of Wholesale Distribution.* (Owing to minor changes in the structure of the Wholesale Census from census year to census year, the ratios for 1933 and 1935 derived from the 1933 and 1935 Censuses are not comparable with that derived from the 1929 Census which we use as a base. They are not used directly, therefore, but as an index of the change from 1933 to 1935.) The inventory-sales ratio

ANNUAL ESTIMATES, 1919-1943

COLUMN

for 1934 is extrapolated from 1935 by ratios derived from *Statistics of Income* for all corporations engaged in trade. The 1935 ratio is extrapolated for 1936 and 1937 by ratios derived from the *Census Survey of Wholesale Distribution*. The 1937 ratio is extrapolated for 1938 and 1939 by ratios derived from *Dun's Review*, May 1940.

Retail: the product of sales (*Domestic Commerce*, Jan. 20, 1940) and the ratio of inventories to them. The inventory-sales ratio is computed for 1933 and extrapolated to 1935 by inventory-sales ratios derived from the *Census of Retail Distribution*. The inventory-sales ratio for 1934 is extrapolated from 1935 by ratios derived from *Statistics of Income* for all corporations engaged in trade. The 1935 ratio is extrapolated to 1936-39 by ratios derived from *Dun's Review*, May 1940.

The sum of inventories in current prices for wholesale and retail trade is converted to 1929 prices by the index computed by dividing inventories in current prices for 1933 by those in 1929 prices and extrapolating for 1934-39 by the BLS wholesale price index for all commodities other than farm.

6 The procedure is that indicated in the note describing the estimates in current prices.

7 *1919-33:* the difference between net changes in 'all other' inventories, as shown in *Commodity Flow and Capital Formation*, Vol. One, Table VII-9, and net changes in construction inventories, col. 4.

1934-39: inventories in current prices are estimated, converted to 1929 prices, and annual net changes in the latter determined. 'All other' comprises mining, manufacturing, transportation and other public utilities, service, finance, and 'nature of business not given'. Inventories in current prices are estimated as follows:

Mining: for 1934-37, derived by the method outlined in *ibid.*, Note A to Table VII-1 and Note A to Table VII-2. 1937 is extrapolated to 1938 by manufacturing and transportation inventories combined (see below). For 1939, extrapolation is by manufacturing inventories alone.

Manufacturing: for 1934-37, derived by the method outlined in *ibid.* 1937 is extrapolated to 1938 and 1939 by data on inventories from *Dun's Review*, May 1940.

Transportation and other public utilities: for 1934-37, by the method outlined in *Commodity Flow and Capital Formation*, Vol. One, Note A to Table VII-1. 1937 is extrapolated to 1938 by materials and supplies held by Class I steam railroads, electric railways, pipe lines, carriers by water, telephone companies, and telegraph and cable companies (ICC reports). 1938 inventories are extrapolated to 1939 by manufacturing inventories.

Service, finance, and 'nature of business not given': estimated by the procedure indicated for mining.

The sum of inventories in current prices in these industries is converted to 1929 prices by the index derived by dividing inventories in current prices for 1933 by their values in 1929 prices (*Commodity Flow and Capital Formation*, Vol. One, Tables VII-6 and VII-8) and extrapolating by the BLS wholesale price index for all commodities.

9 The values in current prices are converted to 1929 prices by the BLS wholesale price index for all commodities adjusted to a 1929 base.

Table I 12

Net Changes in Inventories and in Claims against Foreign Countries
Current and 1929 Prices, 1939-1943
(billions of dollars)

	1939	1940	1941	1942	1943
Current Prices					
1 Net changes in business inventories	0.9	1.8	3.5	−0.5	−0.5
2 Net changes in claims against foreign countries	1.0	1.8	1.2	−0.1	−2.1
1929 Prices					
3 Net changes in business inventories	1.1	2.2	3.8	−0.5	−0.5
4 Net changes in claims against foreign countries	1.2	2.2	1.3	−0.1	−1.9

LINE

1 *Survey of Current Business,* April 1944, p. 13, Table 10, line 13.

2 *Ibid.,* lines 14 and 15.

3 & 4 The values in current prices are converted to 1929 prices by the BLS wholesale price index for all commodities adjusted to a 1929 base.

Table I 13

Gross Capital Formation, Total and Nonwar
Current and 1929 Prices, 1919-1943
(billions of dollars)

	Current Prices		1929 Prices	
	Total	Nonwar	Total	Nonwar
	(1)	(2)	(3)	(4)
1919	19.2	10.6	16.3	8.9
1920	21.9	20.6	15.6	14.6
1921	11.1	10.2	10.4	9.6
1922	12.2	11.7	12.4	11.9
1923	17.6	17.0	16.9	16.4
1924	14.7	14.2	14.2	13.8
1925	18.4	17.9	18.0	17.6
1926	19.0	18.5	18.6	18.1
1927	17.8	17.3	17.8	17.3
1928	17.3	16.8	17.4	16.8
1929	20.7	20.1	20.7	20.1
1930	13.5	12.9	14.3	13.7
1931	8.8	8.2	10.2	9.4
1932	3.3	2.7	3.8	3.1
1933	3.6	3.2	4.2	3.6
1934	4.6	4.0	5.0	4.4
1935	8.4	7.8	9.6	9.0
1936	12.0	11.1	13.8	12.6
1937	14.1	13.3	14.8	13.9
1938	10.2	9.3	11.0	10.0
1939	14.6	13.4	15.3	14.8
1939	14.5	13.5	15.1	14.7
1940	18.9	16.9	19.3	18.5
1941	29.7	20.8	24.8	21.4
1942	48.1	8.9	26.6	8.1
1943	61.8	3.3	33.7	2.9

COLUMN
1 Sum of Table I 6, col. 2; I 7, col. 7; I 11, col. 8 and 9; and I 12, lines 1 and 2.
2 Sum of Table I 6, col. 4; I 7, col. 8; I 11, col. 8 and 9; and I 12, lines 1 and 2; minus government foreign loans (*Annual Report of the Secretary of the Treasury*) and war debt receipts (*Balance of International Payments*).
3 Sum of Table I 6, col. 6; I 8, col. 7; I 11, col. 8 and 9; and I 12, lines 3 and 4.
4 Sum of Table I 6, col. 7; I 8, col. 8; I 11, col. 8; I 12, lines 3 and 4, and Table I 11, col. 9; minus government foreign loans and war debt receipts (see notes to col. 2 above) converted to 1929 prices by the index implicit in Table I 11, col. 9.

Total gross capital formation, 1941-43, is understated to the extent of Lend-Lease for nonwar products, statistics for which were not available when this report was being prepared.

Table I 14

Gross National Product, Peacetime and Wartime Concepts
Current Prices, 1919-1943
(billions of dollars)

	PEACETIME CONCEPT			WARTIME CONCEPT			
	Flow of Goods to Consumers	Gross Capital Formation	Gross National Product (1+2)	Flow of Goods to Consumers	Nonwar Gross Capital Formation	War Output	Gross National Product (4+5+6)
	(1)	(2)	(3)	(4)	(5)	(6)	(7)
1919	54.0	19.2	73.2	54.0	10.6	9.7	74.2
1920	63.0	21.9	84.9	63.0	20.6	2.0	85.6
1921	56.3	11.1	67.4	56.3	10.2	1.3	67.7
1922	56.2	12.2	68.4	56.2	11.7	0.6	68.4
1923	62.9	17.6	80.4	62.9	17.0	0.4	80.4
1924	66.2	14.7	80.8	66.2	14.2	0.5	80.9
1925	66.6	18.4	84.9	66.6	17.9	0.5	85.0
1926	72.1	19.0	91.1	72.1	18.5	0.5	91.1
1927	71.8	17.8	89.6	71.8	17.3	0.5	89.6
1928	73.9	17.3	91.3	73.9	16.8	0.6	91.3
1929	76.7	20.7	97.4	76.7	20.1	0.6	97.4
1930	73.5	13.5	87.1	73.5	12.9	0.6	87.0
1931	60.3	8.8	69.0	60.3	8.2	0.8	69.2
1932	47.3	3.3	50.5	47.3	2.7	0.8	50.7
1933	45.9	3.6	49.5	45.9	3.2	0.6	49.7
1934	52.8	4.6	57.4	52.8	4.0	0.9	57.6
1935	54.0	8.4	62.4	54.0	7.8	1.0	62.7
1936	59.2	12.0	71.2	59.2	11.1	1.2	71.5
1937	65.9	14.1	80.0	65.9	13.3	1.2	80.3
1938	64.9	10.2	75.1	64.9	9.3	1.3	75.5
1939	67.9	14.5	82.4	67.9	13.5	1.4	82.8
1940	72.2	18.9	91.1	72.2	16.9	2.8	91.9
1941	81.5	29.7	111.2	81.5	20.8	12.8	115.1
1942	89.9	48.1	138.0	89.9	8.9	50.3	149.1
1943	99.4	61.8	161.2	99.4	3.3	81.3	184.0

COLUMN
1 & 4 Table I 5, col. 5.
2 Table I 13, col. 1.

COLUMN
5 *Ibid.*, col. 2.
6 Table I 9, col. 4.

Table I 15
Gross National Product, Peacetime and Wartime Concepts
1929 Prices, 1919-1943
(billions of dollars)

	PEACETIME CONCEPT			WARTIME CONCEPT			
	Flow of Goods to Consumers (1)	Gross Capital Formation (2)	Gross National Product (1+2) (3)	Flow of Goods to Consumers (4)	Nonwar Gross Capital Formation (5)	War Output (6)	Gross National Product (4+5+6) (7)
1919	50.2	16.3	66.4	50.2	8.9	8.9	68.0
1920	52.2	15.6	67.8	52.2	14.6	1.7	68.5
1921	53.8	10.4	64.2	53.8	9.6	1.2	64.5
1922	56.5	12.4	68.9	56.5	11.9	0.6	69.0
1923	61.9	16.9	78.8	61.9	16.4	0.4	78.7
1924	66.0	14.2	80.3	66.0	13.8	0.5	80.3
1925	64.9	18.0	82.9	64.9	17.6	0.5	82.9
1926	70.0	18.6	88.5	70.0	18.1	0.5	88.5
1927	71.7	17.8	89.5	71.7	17.3	0.5	89.5
1928	73.2	17.4	90.6	73.2	16.8	0.6	90.6
1929	76.4	20.7	97.1	76.4	20.1	0.6	97.1
1930	75.7	14.3	90.0	75.7	13.7	0.7	90.0
1931	68.6	10.2	78.7	68.6	9.4	0.9	78.8
1932	61.2	3.8	65.1	61.2	3.1	0.9	65.3
1933	61.5	4.2	65.6	61.5	3.6	0.8	65.9
1934	67.2	5.0	72.3	67.2	4.4	1.0	72.7
1935	67.3	9.6	76.9	67.3	9.0	1.1	77.4
1936	73.5	13.8	87.3	73.5	12.6	1.4	87.5
1937	79.0	14.8	93.8	79.0	13.9	1.3	94.2
1938	79.7	11.0	90.7	79.7	10.0	1.5	91.1
1939	85.1	15.1	100.2	85.1	14.7	0.9	100.8
1940	89.1	19.3	108.4	89.1	18.5	1.8	109.4
1941	95.5	24.8	120.3	95.5	21.4	7.9	124.8
1942	92.1	26.6	118.7	92.1	8.1	29.5	129.7
1943	92.8	33.7	126.5	92.8	2.9	50.4	146.0

COLUMN
1 & 4 Table I 5, col. 10.
    2 Table I 13, col. 3.

COLUMN
5 *Ibid.,* col. 4.
6 Table I 10, col. 4.

TABLE I 16
Capital Consumption, Current and 1929 Prices, 1919-1943
(billions of dollars)

	CURRENT PRICES					1929 PRICES				
		PUBLIC		TOTAL			PUBLIC		TOTAL	
		Incl.	Excl.	Incl.	Excl.		Incl.	Excl.	Incl.	Excl.
	PRIVATE	War	War	War (1+2)	War (1+3)	PRIVATE	War	War	War (6+7)	War (6+8)
	(1)	(2)	(3)	(4)	(5)	(6)	(7)	(8)	(9)	(10)
1919	8.2	0.8	0.4	8.9	8.6	7.5	0.8	0.4	8.3	7.9
1920	9.7	1.0	0.5	10.7	10.2	7.4	0.8	0.4	8.2	7.8
1921	7.2	0.8	0.4	8.0	7.6	7.1	0.8	0.4	7.8	7.4
1922	6.9	0.7	0.4	7.7	7.3	7.4	0.8	0.4	8.3	7.9
1923	7.9	0.9	0.4	8.8	8.4	7.7	0.8	0.4	8.5	8.1
1924	7.9	0.9	0.5	8.8	8.3	7.7	0.8	0.4	8.6	8.2
1925	8.0	0.9	0.5	8.9	8.5	8.1	0.9	0.5	8.9	8.5
1926	8.6	0.9	0.5	9.5	9.1	8.7	0.9	0.5	9.6	9.2
1927	8.7	0.9	0.6	9.5	9.2	8.7	0.8	0.6	9.6	9.3
1928	8.9	0.7	0.6	9.6	9.5	9.1	0.7	0.6	9.7	9.6
1929	9.5	0.7	0.6	10.2	10.1	9.5	0.7	0.6	10.2	10.1
1930	9.0	0.7	0.6	9.7	9.6	9.4	0.7	0.6	10.1	10.0
1931	8.0	0.7	0.6	8.7	8.6	9.2	0.8	0.7	10.0	9.9
1932	7.0	0.7	0.5	7.6	7.5	8.7	0.8	0.7	9.5	9.4
1933	6.6	0.7	0.6	7.3	7.2	8.5	0.9	0.7	9.3	9.2
1934	7.0	0.8	0.6	7.8	7.7	8.4	0.9	0.8	9.3	9.1
1935	7.1	0.8	0.7	7.9	7.8	8.4	0.9	0.8	9.3	9.1
1936	7.4	0.9	0.8	8.4	8.2	8.5	1.0	0.9	9.5	9.3
1937	8.4	1.1	0.9	9.5	9.3	8.7	1.1	1.0	9.8	9.6
1938	8.4	1.2	1.0	9.6	9.4	8.8	1.2	1.0	10.0	9.8
1939	8.6	1.4	1.0	10.0	9.6	8.9	1.2	1.1	10.1	10.0
1940	8.8	1.6	1.0	10.4	9.8	9.1	1.3	1.0	10.4	10.1
1941	9.7	2.5	1.0	12.2	10.7	9.7	1.6	1.0	11.3	10.7
1942	10.6	6.2	1.0	16.8	11.6	10.3	3.4	1.0	13.7	11.3
1943	11.3	11.5	1.0	22.8	12.3	10.8	6.5	1.0	17.3	11.8

COLUMN

1 *1919-35: Capital Consumption and Adjustment* by Solomon Fabricant (National Bureau of Economic Research, 1938), Table 31, p. 170. The estimates include business capital depreciation and depletion, provision for fire and marine losses, and depreciation on residences.

1936-39: estimates prepared by Mr. Fabricant by methods similar to those for 1919-35.

1940-43: extrapolated from 1939 with the Department of Commerce series (*Survey of Current Business*, April 1944, p. 14, Table 13) as index.

2 Table I 9, col. 6 and 7, plus col. 3, below.

3 *1919-38:* see notes to col. 1.
1939-43: assumed to be $1 billion annually.

6 & 8 *1919-39:* see notes to col. 1.

1939-43: col. 1 divided by the price index obtained by extrapolating the 1939 index by that derived from *National Product in Wartime*, Appendix Table II 3.

7 Col. 8 plus Table I 10, col. 6 and 7.

TABLE I 17

Net Capital Formation, Total and Nonwar
Current and 1929 Prices, 1919-1943
(billions of dollars)

| | CURRENT PRICES | | 1929 PRICES | |
	Total (1)	Nonwar (2)	Total (3)	Nonwar (4)
1919	10.2	2.0	8.0	1.0
1920	11.2	10.4	7.5	6.8
1921	3.1	2.6	2.6	2.1
1922	4.5	4.4	4.1	4.0
1923	8.7	8.6	8.4	8.3
1924	5.9	5.9	5.6	5.6
1925	9.5	9.4	9.1	9.0
1926	9.4	9.4	9.0	8.9
1927	8.2	8.1	8.2	8.0
1928	7.7	7.3	7.7	7.2
1929	10.5	10.0	10.5	10.0
1930	3.8	3.3	4.2	3.6
1931	a	−0.5	0.2	−0.5
1932	−4.4	−4.8	−5.7	−6.3
1933	−3.7	−4.0	−5.2	−5.6
1934	−3.2	−3.7	−4.2	−4.7
1935	0.4	b	0.3	−0.1
1936	3.7	2.9	4.3	3.3
1937	4.6	4.0	5.0	4.3
1938	0.6	−0.2	1.0	0.2
1939	4.7	3.8	5.2	4.8
1939	4.5	3.9	5.0	4.8
1940	8.5	7.1	8.9	8.4
1941	17.5	10.1	13.5	10.7
1942	31.3	−2.7	12.9	−3.2
1943	39.0	−9.0	16.4	−8.9

ᵃ Less than $50 million. ᵇ Less than −$50 million.

COLUMN
1 Table I 13, col. 1, minus Table I 16, col. 4.
2 Table I 13, col. 2, minus Table I 16, col. 5.
3 Table I 13, col. 3, minus Table I 16, col. 9.
4 Table I 13, col. 4, minus Table I 16, col. 10.

TABLE I 18
Net National Product, Peacetime and Wartime Concepts
Current Prices, 1919-1943
(billions of dollars)

	PEACETIME CONCEPT			WARTIME CONCEPT			
	Flow of Goods to Consumers	Net Capital Formation	Net National Product (1+2)	Flow of Goods to Consumers	Nonwar Net Capital Formation	Net War Output	Net National Product (4+5+6)
	(1)	(2)	(3)	(4)	(5)	(6)	(7)
1919	54.0	10.2	64.2	54.0	2.0	9.3	65.3
1920	63.0	11.2	74.2	63.0	10.4	1.6	75.0
1921	56.3	3.1	59.4	56.3	2.6	0.9	59.8
1922	56.2	4.5	60.7	56.2	4.4	0.2	60.8
1923	62.9	8.7	71.6	62.9	8.6	a	71.6
1924	66.2	5.9	72.1	66.2	5.9	a	72.1
1925	66.6	9.5	76.0	66.6	9.4	0.1	76.1
1926	72.1	9.4	81.6	72.1	9.4	0.1	81.6
1927	71.8	8.2	80.1	71.8	8.1	0.2	80.1
1928	73.9	7.7	81.7	73.9	7.3	0.5	81.7
1929	76.7	10.5	87.2	76.7	10.0	0.5	87.3
1930	73.5	3.8	77.3	73.5	3.3	0.5	77.3
1931	60.3	a	60.3	60.3	−0.5	0.7	60.4
1932	47.3	−4.4	42.9	47.3	−4.8	0.7	43.1
1933	45.9	−3.7	42.2	45.9	−4.0	0.5	42.4
1934	52.8	−3.2	49.5	52.8	−3.7	0.7	49.8
1935	54.0	0.4	54.4	54.0	b	0.8	54.7
1936	59.2	3.7	62.9	59.2	2.9	1.0	63.1
1937	65.9	4.6	70.5	65.9	4.0	1.0	70.9
1938	64.9	0.6	65.5	64.9	−0.2	1.1	65.9
1939	67.9	4.5	72.4	67.9	3.9	1.1	72.9
1940	72.2	8.5	80.7	72.2	7.1	2.4	81.7
1941	81.5	17.5	99.0	81.5	10.1	12.0	103.6
1942	89.9	31.3	121.2	89.9	−2.7	48.7	135.9
1943	99.4	39.0	138.4	99.4	−9.0	79.4	169.7

a Less than $50 million.   b Less than −$50 million.

COLUMN
1&4 Table I 5, col. 5.
2 Table I 17, col. 1.

COLUMN
5 Ibid., col. 2.
6 Table I 9, col. 8.

TABLE I 19
Net National Product, Peacetime and Wartime Concepts
1929 Prices, 1919-1943
(billions of dollars)

	PEACETIME CONCEPT			WARTIME CONCEPT			
	Flow of Goods to Consumers	Net Capital Formation	Net National Product (1+2)	Flow of Goods to Consumers	Nonwar Net Capital Formation	Net War Output	Net National Product (4+5+6)
	(1)	(2)	(3)	(4)	(5)	(6)	(7)
1919	50.2	8.0	58.2	50.2	1.0	8.5	59.7
1920	52.2	7.5	59.6	52.2	6.8	1.3	60.3
1921	53.8	2.6	56.3	53.8	2.1	0.8	56.7
1922	56.5	4.1	60.7	56.5	4.0	0.2	60.7
1923	61.9	8.4	70.3	61.9	8.3	a	70.3
1924	66.0	5.6	71.7	66.0	5.6	0.1	71.7
1925	64.9	9.1	74.0	64.9	9.0	0.1	74.0
1926	70.0	9.0	79.0	70.0	8.9	0.1	79.0
1927	71.7	8.2	79.9	71.7	8.0	0.2	79.9
1928	73.2	7.7	80.8	73.2	7.2	0.5	80.9
1929	76.4	10.5	86.9	76.4	10.0	0.5	86.9
1930	75.7	4.2	79.9	75.7	3.6	0.5	79.8
1931	68.6	0.2	68.7	68.6	−0.5	0.8	68.8
1932	61.2	−5.7	55.5	61.2	−6.3	0.8	55.7
1933	61.5	−5.2	56.3	61.5	−5.6	0.7	56.6
1934	67.2	−4.2	63.0	67.2	−4.7	0.9	63.4
1935	67.3	0.3	67.6	67.3	−0.1	1.0	68.1
1936	73.5	4.3	77.8	73.5	3.3	1.2	78.0
1937	79.0	5.0	84.0	79.0	4.3	1.1	84.4
1938	79.7	1.0	80.7	79.7	0.2	1.3	81.1
1939	85.1	5.0	90.1	85.1	4.8	0.8	90.7
1940	89.1	8.9	98.0	89.1	8.4	1.7	99.2
1941	95.5	13.5	109.0	95.5	10.7	7.7	113.8
1942	92.1	12.9	105.0	92.1	−3.2	28.8	117.7
1943	92.8	16.4	109.2	92.8	−8.9	49.4	133.3

a Less than $50 million.

COLUMN
1 & 4 Table I 5, col. 10.
 2 Table I 17, col. 3.

COLUMN
5 *Ibid.*, col. 4.
6 Table I 10, col. 8.

PART II

Decade Estimates, 1869-1939

A CHARACTER OF THE ESTIMATES

Since, for lack of data, annual estimates could not be made, the estimates of national product and its major categories by type of use, 1869-1938, are averages calculated for decades overlapping at five-year intervals. For the full span covered, each series comprises therefore thirteen decade averages.

In general, the series are derived by combining annual estimates, 1919-38, with Shaw's data on the flow of finished commodities and construction materials, at producers' prices, back to 1879 and extrapolated to 1869. The annual estimates for recent years are given in Part I; and the important steps in their derivation are set forth in detail in *Commodity Flow and Capital Formation,* Volume One. Shaw's series on the flow of commodities at producers' prices are summarized in *Occasional Paper 3* (National Bureau of Economic Research, Aug. 1941) and will be set forth in detail in his *Value of Commodity Output since 1869.* The various devices used to combine the two bodies of data to get the decade estimates of national product and its components are described in the tables in this Part and their notes. The purpose of the brief discussion here is merely to indicate the basic steps and attempt to appraise some assumptions that had to be made in calculating the decade estimates.

1 *Commodity Flow*

a COVERAGE OF BASIC SERIES

Before we consider how Shaw's series, derived mainly from successive Censuses of Manufactures, were treated to arrive at the flow of finished commodities to consumers and the value of new construction, the coverage and comparability of the Shaw series proper must be noted. These are in turn determined largely by the adequacy of the underlying data in the *Census of Manufactures.*[1]

In Shaw's estimates no adjustments were made for (a) exclusion from Census data of establishments with an annual value of product of less than $500; (b) exclusion from Census data of government manufacturing establishments; (c) possible understatement in the 1869 Census. In addition, (d) products of hand trades and custom establishments were excluded by applying to

[1] For a more detailed discussion of the latter see W. H. Shaw, *Value of Commodity Output since 1869* (in press), particularly Part II, Sec. A.

the Census years before 1899 the ratio estimated for 1899 (somewhat less than 3 percent).

The shortages in coverage represented by the omissions under (a) and (b) are definitely negligible. For 1899 the value product of establishments below the reporting minimum was less than 0.5 percent of the total covered; and it is doubtful that the omission was as much as 1 percent even in the earlier years. Manufacturing plants owned and operated by the government are of slight importance in peacetime; and their output could have been large only in 1918, although even then most war production was flowing through privately owned or operated enterprises. The effect on the decade averages, could it have been measured, would have been negligible, even for 1909-18 and 1914-23.

Concerning the 1869 Census there seems to be unanimity on the fact of understatement, but considerable difficulty in measuring it. The official estimate of understatement in the *Census of Population* is 1.5 million (most of it in the South), or 5 percent of the reported total; others place it at 0.9 million, or less than 3 percent of the reported total.[2] In his book Shaw states that the possible undercoverage in the *Census of Manufactures* is perhaps "as much as 5 percent"; and in a recent discussion "between 5 and 10 percent". Such undercoverage would presumably be due to incomplete coverage of several smaller industries and failure to use special schedules and employ 'expert special agents' (as was done in the later censuses).

If we accept the upper figure, 10 percent, which seems high in comparison even with the upper limit of the adjustment of the population census, two factors materially reduce the effect on our decade averages. First, since this particular understatement applies to the census data for 1869 alone, the averaging involved in deriving the estimate for the 1869-78 decade means cutting the relative understatement in the *decade average* in half; in the decade average for 1874-83 to one-quarter. The adjustment called for would then be to raise the averages for the two decades by at most 5 and 2.5 percent respectively. Second, manufactured products are not the only items entering the flow of consumers' commodities and of capital formation. In the former, nonmanu-

[2] See reference to F. A. Walker's estimate in W. F. Willcox, *International Migrations* (National Bureau of Economic Research, 1931) II, 98.

factured foods (i.e., foods sold to ultimate consumers without any fabrication, or retained by farmers for their own consumption) are important; in the latter, nonmanufactured construction materials, changes in inventories and in net claims against foreign countries affect the total, and of these inventory change alone is partly affected by the estimates of manufactured output. Consequently, the maximum upward adjustment in either the flow of goods to consumers or national product would have to be cut further to some 4 percent for 1869-78 and to 2 percent for 1874-83.

The omission of hand trades and custom establishments may be compensated by the inclusion of part of their value product under services not embodied in new commodities, or under value added to construction materials in estimating new construction. So far as the activities of these trades and establishments are not so covered, their omission from the Shaw series restricts unwarrantedly coverage for the present purposes. Fortunately, their exclusion is admittedly incomplete for the earlier Census dates. By the same token, any upward adjustment on this account would be quite small. The somewhat less than 3 percent allowance Shaw used to exclude this item for years before 1899, must, if used as an upward adjustment, be reduced by (a) possible coverage under services and construction; (b) absence of distributive margins on the products in question, which renders their weight in the flow of finished goods, at cost to ultimate users, less than their weight in the flow at manufacturers' values. All told, an allowance of 1 percent, in terms of the larger aggregates of flow of commodities to consumers and national product, seems ample, even for the earliest decade in the series.

The foregoing discussion suggests that the *maximum* upward adjustment called for by undercoverage of the basic series would, for national product and its major components, be about 5 percent for 1869-78; 4 percent for the subsequent decades through 1889-98; and gradually dwindle to insignificant levels by 1919-28. For some of the smaller components the adjustment might be somewhat larger, but in none apparently much more than 5 percent even in the earliest decades. Were there adequate evidence upon which to estimate these adjustments carefully, and especially to set them separately for each component of the flow of goods to consumers and of capital formation, it might have been advisable to introduce them into the detailed series in the basic tables, and eventually into the over-all totals. But because of lack of such evidence, and in view of the slightness of the adjustment even when assigned maximum values, it did not seem worth while to introduce the correction. The approximation to it given above may be used, in full cognizance that it is the maximum adjustment on account of the undercoverage discussed and is, in the nature of the case, exceedingly crude.

b PASSING FROM OUTPUT AT MANUFACTURERS' PRICES TO FLOW AT FINAL COST

Shaw's series are for the value of commodities destined for domestic consumption, i.e., output adjusted for exports and imports, at producers' current and 1913 prices. To link this series with the more recent estimates, 1929 rather than 1913 was used as the constant price base. More important were the steps taken to pass from the flow to domestic consumption at producers' prices to the flow to ultimate consumers at cost to them.

Shaw's series on output destined for domestic consumption of finished commodities are grouped into four major categories: perishables, semidurables, consumer durables, and producer durables. Output of construction materials, adjusted for imports and exports, was also estimated by Shaw. To estimate the flow of finished commodities to consumers, at cost to them, the totals of output destined for domestic consumption had to be raised to include transportation and distribution costs, and adjusted for changes in finished inventories. To estimate the final value of new construction, i.e., to pass from the value of raw materials consumed to the full value of new construction, additional steps were taken. All the steps just indicated were applied to the series on output destined for domestic consumption, in both current and 1929 prices after the latter had been calculated from Shaw's series, using his minor rather than major commodity groups, and thus allowing for differences in minor group weights between the 1913 and 1929 bases.[3]

[3] This refinement in shifting the price adjustment base from 1913 to 1929 was found indispensable when the results of a shift, using major commodity groups alone, were compared with the price series beginning with 1919 in the detailed analysis in

In general the allowance for transportation and distribution costs and the adjustment for inventory changes were calculated by assuming that their proportional weights—for each major commodity group valued at *constant* prices—during the earlier decades were the same as those during 1919-33 or 1919-28. For transportation and distribution costs the relative share for 1919-33 was used,[4] because it is the longest period for which we have both detailed data and analysis of these two constituents of commodity costs to ultimate consumers and because it includes enough years of both cyclical expansion and contraction to yield levels from which long term, secular levels could be extrapolated. To estimate changes in finished inventories we used the ratio of additions to inventories to additions to flow for 1919-28, thereby omitting the severe cyclical contraction that followed 1928. Since the estimates to which the adjustments were to be applied showed a continuous secular increase in the real volume of goods, any ratios that were to be applied to them to get a rough estimate of inventory changes had to be based upon a period of marked increase in real volume. Finally, in estimating total new construction from the output of construction materials, the basic ratios were for periods similar to those used for finished commodities: 1919-28 for changes in inventories, and 1919-33 for the proportional weight of other items. The procedure called for approximating not only distribution and transportation charges and changes in inventories but also the proportional weight of costs other than that of raw materials and the relative importance of repairs.

How large were the adjustments entailed by these crude assumptions? Table II a shows the allowance for transportation and distribution charges, as well as the adjustment for changes in finished inventories, expressed in percentages of the final value

---

Commodity Flow and Capital Formation. The differences between the price indexes obtained by shifting Shaw's base from 1913 to 1929 by *major* commodity groups and those based on the detailed work for recent years were clearly due to the fact that the former set of price indexes retained within each major group the 1913 weights of the minor groups. When the shift in bases was made by the minor groups, the indexes obtained from Shaw's data and those in *Commodity Flow and Capital Formation* were closely similar for the years compared.

[4] Except for the semidurable commodity group and for construction materials, where the ratio was for 1929 alone.

TABLE II a
Steps in Estimating Gross Commodity Flow and Construction Average Value per Year, 1869-1918

	PERISH-ABLE (1)	SEMI-DURABLE (2)	CONSUMER DURABLE (3)	PRODUCER DURABLE (4)	CONSTRUCTION MATERIALS & CONSTRUCTION (5)
	\multicolumn{5}{c}{MILLIONS OF DOLLARS}				
1 Output destined for domestic consumption, current prices	4,380	1,607	785	937	1,214
2 Output destined for domestic consumption, 1929 prices	6,958	2,662	1,394	1,577	2,173
3 Retail value of (2), 1929 prices	10,438	4,223	2,268	1,826	3,168
4 Net change in finished inventories, 1929 prices	+54	+64	+32	+6	+18
5 Flow to industrial consumers, 1929 prices					3,150
6 Net change in inventories of industrial consumers, 1929 prices					+14
7 Flow into consumption, 1929 prices					3,136
8 Final value, 1929 prices	10,383	4,159	2,236	1,820	4,402
9 Final value, current prices	6,538	2,513	1,260	1,076	2,123
	\multicolumn{5}{c}{PERCENTAGE DISTRIBUTION}				
10 Output destined for domestic consumption, 1929 prices	67.0	64.0	62.3	86.6	49.4
11 Retail value of (2), 1929 prices	100.5	101.5	101.4	100.3	72.0
12 Net change in finished inventories, 1929 prices	0.5	1.5	1.4	0.3	0.4
13 Flow to industrial consumers, 1929 prices					71.6
14 Net change in inventories of industrial consumers, 1929 prices					0.3
15 Flow into consumption, 1929 prices					71.2
16 Final value, 1929 prices	100.0	100.0	100.0	100.0	100.0

Averages of estimates for successive decades in Tables II 1, II 2, II 3, II 4, and II 5, lines 1, 3, 5, 7, and 9.

LINE
1 Col. 1 of the respective tables.
2 Col. 2 of the respective tables.
3 Col. 3 of the respective tables.
4 Col. 4 of the respective tables except for col. 5 which is based on data underlying col. 4 of Table II 5.

LINE
5 Line 3 minus line 4.
6 Based on data underlying col. 4 of Table II 5.
7 Line 5 minus line 6.
8 Col. 5 of the respective tables.
9 Col. 7 of the respective tables.
10-16 Percentage distribution of line 8.

of each of the four major finished commodity groups, and also the proportional weight of various additions to the value of construction materials (destined for domestic consumption) made in obtaining the final cost of new construction. The percentage share of the added cost items ranges from 13 for producer durables to 38 for consumer durables; while the largest addition, about one-half of the final total, is made to the value of construction materials flowing into domestic consumption.

Even sizable errors in estimating the transportation and distributive margins would be much smaller when measured as percentages of the final totals, i.e., in terms of costs to ultimate consumers or recipients of the commodities. For example, a 20 percent error in the combined allowance for transportation and distribution charges would mean an error of less than 7 percent in the final estimate of the flow of perishable commodities; of about 7 percent, for semidurable commodities; of 7-8 percent, for consumer durables; and of less than 3 percent for producer durables. In construction alone would the reduction in the error in the various adjustments be smaller; although even here a 20 percent error in the combined adjustment would mean an error of only 10 percent in the final estimate of the value of new construction.

The validity of one set of assumptions can be checked, roughly, by estimates of the distribution of national income by industrial origin. Of the charges by railroads and other transportation agencies for carrying freight, the preponderant proportion must be accounted for by payments to labor and on invested capital. Of retailers' and wholesalers' margins, an overwhelming proportion must be accounted for by the compensation of employees in wholesale and retail establishments, the net income of entrepreneurs, and the property income payments on invested capital. The share of national income originating in transportation and trade, compared with that originating in all commodity producing industries combined (agriculture, mining, manufacturing, and construction), if studied for a long period, can at least suggest whether there have been noteworthy secular shifts in the proportional weight of transportation and distribution margins in the value of commodities, at producers' prices, and, by implication, in the final value of finished commodities (Table II b).

TABLE II b
Ratios of Income Originating in Transportation and Trade to National Income and to Income Originating in Commodity Production
1869-1928
(dollar figures in millions, current prices)

AVERAGES PER YEAR	NATIONAL INCOME (1)	INCOME ORIGINATING IN Commodity Production (2)	Transportation & Trade (3)	%(3) IS OF (1) (4)	%(3) IS OF (2) (5)
\multicolumn{6}{c}{NATIONAL INDUSTRIAL CONFERENCE BOARD ESTIMATES}
1 1869 & 1879	7,027	2,925	1,910	27.2	65.3
2 1879 & 1889	8,964	3,623	2,510	28.0	69.3
3 1889 & 1899	13,032	5,560	3,532	27.1	63.5
4 1899 & 1909	20,910	9,432	5,532	26.5	58.7
5 1899-1908	19,928	8,863	5,413	27.2	61.1
6 1904-13	25,614	11,656	6,862	26.8	58.9
7 1909-18	34,942	16,367	8,990	25.7	54.9
\multicolumn{6}{c}{NATIONAL BUREAU OF ECONOMIC RESEARCH ESTIMATES}
8 1909-18	39,815	16,779	7,652	19.2	45.6
9 1914-23	55,602	23,147	11,252	20.2	48.6
10 1919-28	70,541	27,859	14,165	20.1	50.8

COLUMN 1

LINE

1-7 Robert F. Martin, *National Income in the United States, 1799-1938* (National Industrial Conference Board, 1939), pp. 6-7.

8 & 9 Data comparable with *National Product in Wartime*, App. Table III 9, plus imputed rent.

10 Estimated by multiplying the 1919-28 data in *National Income and Its Composition*, I, 310, Table 44 (excl. government savings), by the ratio of the 1919-23 data in line 9 to the 1919-23 data in *ibid*.

COLUMN 2

1-7 Martin, *op. cit.*, pp. 58-9. Includes agriculture, mining, manufacturing, and construction.

8 & 9 See note to col. 1, lines 8 and 9. Includes agriculture, mining, manufacturing, and construction.

10 Extrapolated by the procedure used for col. 1, line 10, with estimates in *National Income and Its Composition*, I, 310, Table 44, as index.

COLUMN 3

1-7 Martin, *op. cit.*, pp. 58-9. Includes transportation and communication and trade.

8 & 9 See note to col. 1, lines 8 and 9. Includes steam railroads, Pullman, and express; water transportation; and trade.

10 Extrapolated by the procedure used for col. 1, line 10, with estimates in *National Income and Its Composition*, I, 310, Table 44, for trade; II, 660, Table P 2, for steam railroads; and II, 661, Table P 3, for water transportation, as index.

Unfortunately, net income originating in the transportation and distribution activities that concern finished commodities alone cannot be segregated. Furthermore, the estimates in Table II b are in current prices, whereas our assumption that the relative weight of transportation and distribution charges is constant is for values in constant prices. Nevertheless, the comparison is of some interest. It shows (col. 5) that the ratio of the net income originating in transportation and trade to that originating in the commodity producing industries declines, from a percentage ratio of about 65 during the first three decades to about 55 in 1909-18.

These figures suggest that instead of assuming a constant proportional weight of transportation and distribution charges we should have allowed for a mild down trend, thereby raising slightly the allowance in the early decades of the long period covered by our estimates. But for several reasons it did not seem advisable to apply the trend suggested by Table II b. The main reason was doubt concerning the extent to which the numerator and denominator used in deriving the ratio in column 5 truly described transportation and distribution costs, and the value of commodities destined for domestic consumption, with which we are concerned. The producers' value already includes some transportation and distribution charges, as well as contributions of other industries (service, government) not included under *net* income originating in the commodity producing industries. In this sense the denominator (col. 2) is incomplete. On the other hand, the numerator (col. 3) is too large in that it includes charges for services on unfinished commodities or to individuals. It is perhaps significant that while column 5 shows a distinct down trend, column 4, in which the numerator remains the same but the denominator is extended to cover the full product of the economy, shows a secular decline so small as to be negligible.

Also, the estimates in Table II b are in current prices; and differences among secular movements in compensation of resources in production and in trade may be important. Of the total gainfully occupied, the percentage attached to manufacturing and hand trades grew from 16.7 in 1870 to an average of 24.1 in 1920 and 1930; that attached to trade from 6.3 to 11.2 (recent revisions by Daniel Carson of his estimates in *Labor Supply and Employment, Preliminary Statement of Estimates Prepared and Methods Used,* WPA, mimeo., Nov. 1939). The ratio of gainfully occupied attached to trade to those attached to manufacturing rose, therefore, from 0.38 to 0.46. This suggests a rise in the ratio of distribution margins to the value of manufactured products at producers' prices, rather than the decline indicated in Table II b. But the trend may well be more than offset by a greater increase in productivity per worker in manufacturing industries than in trade.

The considerations adduced made it inadvisable to use the evidence in column 5 of Table II b to alter our basic assumption. But even were we to accept the evidence in Table II b at full face value, the modification in our final estimates would be minor. A drop in column 5 from 65 percent in 1869-79 to 55 percent in 1909-18 and a subsequent rise to roughly 60 percent in 1919-28 [5] would mean both raising the adjustments for the early decades and lowering the adjustment for the 1909-18 decade less than one-tenth. This, in terms of final values, would imply changes of 1.5 to 3 percent in the four major categories of finished commodities and in construction (for the latter taking account only of transportation and distribution costs). Therefore, the assumption of the long term stability of relative transportation and distribution costs probably does not make for a large error.

The construction estimates are based on assumptions, in addition to those relating to distribution and transportation margins, concerning the ratio of the total value of construction, including repairs and maintenance, to the cost of construction materials consumed; and the ratio of total construction to new, i.e., excluding current repairs and maintenance (see Table II 5). The validity of assuming that these two ratios remained constant (for values in 1929 prices) during the decades preceding 1919 can be checked but crudely, but crude checks are better than none.

Of the total difference between the value of construction and the cost of construction materials consumed, a substantial proportion is constituted by net income originating in the industry,

[5] Allowing for the disparity in levels between the two series in col. 5, as indicated by the two entries for 1909-18.

TABLE II c

Comparison of Allowance for Construction Costs other than Materials with Income Originating in Contract Construction, 1869-1928
(dollar figures in millions, current prices)

	AVERAGES PER YEAR (1)	INCOME ORIGINATING IN CONTRACT CONSTRUCTION (2)	AVERAGES PER YEAR (3)	DIFFERENCE BETWEEN TOTAL CONSTRUCTION & FLOW OF CONSTR. MATERIALS (4)	RATIO OF (4) TO (2) (5)
1	1869 & 1879	373.5	1869-78	263.5	0.71
2	1879 & 1889	495.5	1879-88	460.1	0.93
3	1889 & 1899	643.0	1889-98	831.9	1.29
4	1899 & 1909	904.0	1899-1908	1,215.4	1.34
5	1899-1908	886.9	1899-1908	1,215.4	1.37
6	1904-13	1,107.1	1904-13	1,612.1	1.46
7	1909-18	1,115.7	1909-18	1,902.3	1.71
8	1914-23	1,571.7	1914-23	2,495.2	1.59
9	1919-28	2,588.7	1919-28	4,096.1	1.58
	PERCENTAGE CHANGE				
10	1869-89 to 1889-1908	+76.1		+182.9	
11	1889-1908 to 1909-28	+142.1		+193.0	

COLUMN

2 R. F. Martin, *National Income in the United States, 1799-1938*, pp. 58-9. The average, 1919-28, for income originating in construction, as estimated in *National Income and Its Composition*, I, 310-1, Table 44, is $3,223 million.

4 Difference between col. 5 and 6 of Table II 5, multiplied by the index of wages in construction (see notes to Table IV 4, line 1).

i.e., payments to employees, net income of entrepreneurs, and payments on the invested capital. We may, therefore, compare the level and particularly the movement of the spread between the cost of materials and the final value of construction implicit in our estimates with independent estimates of net income originating in the construction industry (Table II c).

The comparison is subject to three qualifications. First, income originating is merely part of the spread between the cost of materials and the final value of construction, the other part being payments to other industries (fees to various professional groups, rent, payments for equipment, taxes, etc.). Second, the estimates in column 2 are for income originating in contract construction alone, i.e., exclude all construction on force account; our estimates of the spread, and indeed of all aspects of construction, include force account work. Third, Martin's estimates of net income originating in construction are some 20 percent lower than those in *National Income and Its Composition,* chiefly because all undistributed savings and construction work in connection with oil wells (drilling, etc.) are excluded.

The third qualification may not have any definite bearing upon the comparison of *trends* in Table II c. But the effect of the first two can be surmised. The portion of the total difference between the value of construction and the cost of materials not represented by net income originating could be expected to constitute a growing proportion of the spread because of an increasing use of services of other industries and a growing burden of taxes. Likewise, at least during part of the period, the increasing importance of construction by public utilities, by government, and by large enterprises in other industrial areas may have raised the proportion of force account work. On both scores, we would expect the trend in the spread between the value of construction and the cost of materials consumed to be algebraically greater than the trend in net income originating in the construction industry.

And it is. In current prices net income originating, as measured by Martin's series, rises from about $435 million in the first two decades to $2,589 million in 1919-28, or fivefold (col. 2). The spread increases from $360 million to $4,096, or over tenfold (col. 4). We do not know whether this difference is too great to be accounted for by the considerations adduced; but in view of the crudity of the comparison, one is inclined to accept the indicated trend in the difference between the two series without assigning too much significance to its magnitude.

A more perplexing circumstance is that, for the first two decades, the spread is smaller than net income originating. Perhaps our assumptions tend to underestimate the spread; or, what is more probable, our index of construction wages, used to convert the spread from 1929 prices into current, indicates a lower wage level relative to that in recent years than is implied in the Martin estimates. It is not clear that the fault lies with our estimates. Martin's estimates are perforce based upon scanty evidence for this early period and are for single years rather than decade averages—an important factor in estimating a process so subject to well defined and long cycles as construction. At any rate, the evidence did not seem sufficient to warrant revising our estimates for the earlier decades.[6]

Even were the revision to be made, the effect on the final estimates of new construction would be small. If the ratio of the entries in columns 4 and 2 (lines 1 and 2) should be 1.1 rather than 0.7 and 0.9 respectively, the final estimates of construction in current prices (Table II 5) would be raised, for 1869-78, from $702 to $884 million; and for 1879-88 from $1,162 to $1,262 million—26 and 9 percent, respectively. But to repeat, the evidence for such revision is inconclusive.

TABLE II d

Ratio of Allowance for Repairs and Maintenance Construction to Total Value of Real Estate Improvements, 1880-1922
(dollar figures in millions, 1929 prices)

YEAR (1)	VALUE OF REAL ESTATE IMPROVEMENTS 1ST VARIANT (2)	AVERAGES PER YEAR (3)	ALLOWANCE FOR REPAIRS & MAINTENANCE (4)	% (4) IS OF (2) (5)
1880	27,480	1874-83	642	2.3
1890	48,462	1884-93	1,312	2.7
1900	68,510	1894-1903	1,671	2.4
1912	116,329	1909-18	2,441	2.1
1922	117,405	1919-28	2,670	2.3

COLUMN
2 Table IV 5, line 19.
4 Difference between col. 6 and 7 of Table II 5.

Is it valid to allow for repairs and maintenance as a constant percentage of total construction, with the percentage at the level of the 1920's? Perhaps the most revealing check feasible is to compare the resulting estimate of repairs and maintenance, in 1929 prices, with the value of all existing construction in 1929 prices (Table II d). If the level looks reasonable, and there is no puzzling trend that runs counter to a reasonable expectation that the ratio of repairs and maintenance to existing structures should remain fairly constant, our assumption can be said to be confirmed.

The ratio in Table II d may at first seem too large, since ordi-

[6] The possible undercoverage of the *1869 Census of Manufactures* is relevant here (see discussion in Sec. 1a above). Even a generous allowance for such understatement would account for only a small part of the discrepancy in line 1 and for none of that in line 2.

narily annual expenses on repairs and maintenance do not run so high—more than 2 percent of the value of a real estate unit. But the ratio customarily used is to the value of a unit, including land; and the latter is important, even if we exclude agriculture and mining. Omitting the latter and using current values as reported, improvements proper constitute roughly 60 percent of the total value including land (see Tables IV 1 and IV 2). The application of this percentage would reduce the entries in Table II d, column 5, to 1-1.5 percent; and to less, if agriculture and mining are included. So stated, the ratios do not seem unduly high.

Nor do they show any significant long term movement. Perhaps the crudities of the estimates, especially of the denominator, conceal some trends due to the shifting composition of total improvements, of which repairs and maintenance are a part. But if so, the trends are too weak to emerge. And apparently Table II d suggests no basis upon which to disqualify the assumption used in passing from total to new construction in Table II 5.

A final check upon our estimates of new construction lies in comparing, for the four overlapping decades 1914-38, the independent estimates of new construction with those calculated from the flow of construction materials (Table II e, lines 5a-c). The check is of limited significance because the estimates of the value of new construction derived from the flow of construction materials use ratios for distribution and transportation margins, spreads, etc. that are based upon data for new construction in *part* of the period under comparison. Yet the distribution and transportation margins are based upon data for one year alone, 1929; and those for the spread between the value of total construction and the cost of materials, and for the proportion of repairs and maintenance, upon 1919-33, i.e., fifteen of the twenty-five years compared. There are thus elements of independence between the two series.

The average values (means of the four overlapping decades) differ little: in current and in 1929 prices they run about 3 percent higher in the crude estimates derived from the flow of construction materials than in those derived from independent data on new construction. Of more interest is the greater prominence of the long cycle in the latter. In 1929 prices the latter rise almost 40 percent from 1914-23 to 1924-33, and decline more than 30 percent from 1924-33 to 1929-38; the former rise almost 20 percent and decline about 20 percent. We can therefore assume that the proportion of distribution and transportation charges, or of the spread between the cost of materials and the value of total construction, increases during the rising phase of the long cycle and declines during the declining phase; and that perhaps the proportion of repairs and maintenance to total construction declines during the rising phase and increases during the declining phase. Whether all or only some of these movements occur, one may surmise that for the past decades also our crude estimates understate the amplitude of the long cycle in construction more than could be attributed to the use of decade averages rather than of data for single years or months.

The crude tests discussed above are far from conclusive, and indeed cannot help being: in all except one the estimates against which our approximations were checked have perhaps even a wider margin of error and a less secure foundation in statistical detail. But they indicate no substantial ground for inferring that the assumptions made in our estimates of the flow of finished commodities and of total new construction lead to appreciable errors, a conclusion that is of particular relevance not to the single decade totals but to such grouping of them as is involved in attempts to establish the broader trends for the long period covered.

C ADJUSTMENT FOR BUSINESS USE OF PASSENGER CARS AND RELATED PRODUCTS

We finally compare the estimates of the flow of finished commodities based upon the assumptions indicated above with those based upon the more detailed analysis for recent years (Table II e). The comparison does not fully test the reliability of the estimates for past years, because it can be made for only three overlapping decades—1919-28, 1924-33, and 1929-38; and the basic ratios upon which the cruder estimates are grounded are taken from the more detailed information for 1919-28 or 1919-33. Consequently, the two sets of estimates overlap sufficiently to make the comparison spurious for most commodity categories, at least for one of the three decades, viz., 1919-28. The comparison in Table II e (lines 1-4) is intended, therefore, not to test the

Table II e
Gross Commodity Flow and Construction
Decade Estimates and Averages of Annual Estimates, 1919-1938
(dollar figures in millions)

	Current Prices				1929 Prices			
	1919-28 (1)	1924-33 (2)	1929-38 (3)	Av. of 1919-28 & 1929-38 (4)	1919-28 (5)	1924-33 (6)	1929-38 (7)	Av. of 1919-28 & 1929-38 (8)
1 Perishable Commodities								
a Av. of annual estimates	24,505	23,893	23,243	23,874	23,895	26,456	29,391	26,643
b Decade estimates	24,679	23,293	21,994	23,336	23,549	25,824	27,254	25,402
c Diff. as % of (a)	+0.7	−2.5	−5.4	−2.3	−1.4	−2.4	−7.3	−4.7
2 Semidurable Commodities								
a Av. of annual estimates	10,889	10,080	8,495	9,692	9,190	10,252	9,940	9,565
b Decade estimates	10,806	9,766	8,094	9,450	9,058	9,915	9,261	9,160
c Diff. as % of (a)	−0.8	−3.1	−4.7	−2.5	−1.4	−3.3	−6.8	−4.2
3 Consumer Durable Commodities								
a Av. of annual estimates	6,860	6,705	5,475	6,168	6,554	6,982	6,080	6,317
b Decade estimates	7,991	7,633	6,628	7,310	7,596	7,869	7,212	7,404
c Diff. as % of (a)	+16.5	+13.8	+21.1	+18.5	+15.9	+12.7	+18.6	+17.2
d Decade estimates, adj.	6,928	6,705	5,475	6,202	6,585	6,982	6,080	6,332
4 Producer Durable Commodities								
a Av. of annual estimates	5,650	5,129	4,356	5,003	5,479	5,335	4,774	5,126
b Decade estimates	4,965	4,329	3,903	4,434	4,738	4,486	4,202	4,470
c Diff. as % of (a)	−12.1	−15.6	−10.4	−11.4	−13.5	−15.9	−12.0	−12.8
d Decade estimates, adj.	5,735	5,129	4,356	5,046	5,472	5,335	4,774	5,123
5 Construction								
a Av. of annual estimates	8,528	8,303	5,274	6,901	8,310	8,504	5,797	7,054
b Decade estimates	8,188	8,038	6,008	7,098	7,981	8,235	6,602	7,292
c Diff. as % of (a)	−4.0	−3.2	+13.9	+2.9	−4.0	−3.2	+13.9	+3.4

DECADE ESTIMATES, 1869-1939

Notes to Table II e:

Line 1 a

COLUMN	COLUMN
1-3 Table II 1, col. 7, lines 15-17.	5-7 *Ibid.*, col. 5, lines 15-17.

Line 1 b

1-3 *Ibid.*, col. 7, lines 11-13.	5-7 *Ibid.*, col. 5, lines 11-13.

Line 2 a

1-3 Table II 2, col. 7, lines 15-17.	5-7 *Ibid.*, col. 5, lines 15-17.

Line 2 b

1-3 *Ibid.*, col. 7, lines 11-13.	5-7 *Ibid.*, col. 5, lines 11-13.

Line 3 a

1-3 Table II 3, col. 7, lines 14-16.	5-7 *Ibid.*, col. 5, lines 14-16.

Line 3 b

1-3 Table II 3, col. 7, lines 11-13.	5-7 *Ibid.*, col. 5, lines 11-13.

Line 3 d

1 & 5 Table II 6, lines 5 and 7.	2, 3, 6, 7 Identical with line 3 a.

Line 4 a

1-3 Table II 4, col. 7, lines 14-16.	5-7 *Ibid.*, col. 5, lines 14-16.

Line 4 b

1-3 *Ibid.*, col. 7, lines 11-13.	5-7 *Ibid.*, col. 5, lines 11-13.

Line 4 d

1 & 5 Table II 6, lines 9-11.	2, 3, 6, 7 Identical with line 4 a.

Line 5 a

1-3 Table II 5, col. 9, lines 16-18.	5-7 *Ibid.*, col. 7, lines 16-18.

Line 5 b

1-3 *Ibid.*, col. 9, lines 11-13.	5-7 *Ibid.*, col. 7, lines 11-13.

validity of the assumptions, already discussed in connection with Tables II a and II b, but rather to bring out an additional adjustment—the allowance for the business use of passenger cars and related products (gasoline and oil in the perishable group; tires, etc. in the semidurable).

The estimates of the final flow of finished commodities in Tables II a and II 1-II 4, are based upon extrapolation of the totals for recent years and Shaw's data, which do not allow for the business use of passenger cars and related products. Such an allowance has recently been made for the annual estimates beginning in 1919 (see Part I). Should a similar adjustment be made for the decade estimates for the years before 1919?

The difference between the unadjusted (lines b) and the adjusted totals (lines a) for the perishable and semidurable commodity groups is minor. Indeed, the unadjusted totals based upon the cruder assumptions are somewhat smaller rather than larger than the totals from which automobile products used by business units have been deducted. But the differences are so minor that we can treat as fairly comparable the cruder estimates for the period before 1919 and the more detailed estimates for the years since 1919, the latter adjusted for the business use of products related to passenger cars; and construct a continuous series of decade estimates without additional adjustments for the decades preceding 1919-28.

It is for the consumer durable and producer durable commodity groups that the allowance for the business use of passenger cars is relatively large. The reduction in the total for consumer durables and the increase in that for producer durables are too great to warrant considering the decade estimates for years before 1919 and those after 1919 comparable without further adjustment of the former. For this reason we introduce (in Table II 6) into the cruder decade estimates this further adjustment for the business use of passenger cars back to 1899-1908 (by which decade the correction is negligible). This adjustment makes the cruder decade estimates for consumer and producer durable commodity groups closely comparable with decade averages of the more detailed annual estimates for the years beginning with 1919.

2 Flow of Goods to Consumers

The data and procedures discussed so far yield estimates for three groups of finished commodities—perishable, semidurable, and consumer durable—which constitute major components of the total flow of goods to consumers, at cost to them. But these three series are for commodities alone, and to complete the measurement of the total flow of goods to consumers we have to estimate also services not embodied in new commodities. The latter group is large, including services of various descriptions flowing to ultimate consumers: those yielded by commodities (e.g., residential housing); those provided by individuals and applied to commodities already in the possession of ultimate consumers (e.g., passenger car repair); those rendered by individuals or enterprises directly to ultimate consumers (e.g., professional services of physicians or services of governments to individuals).

In Part I we gave our reasons for estimating such services flowing to ultimate consumers in recent years as a residual, that is, by subtracting from national product independently estimated final product categories except services (i.e., commodity flow to ultimate consumers and capital formation).

The results of the residual procedure are also used here—in deriving decade estimates for the years before 1919. Data needed for extrapolation back to the earlier decades are samples on the composition of budgets, primarily of low income urban consumers, in combination with the only detailed study of such budgets available for all consumers in this country for a recent period, 1935/36. Though it suffers from many gaps and deficiencies, this is the sole body of data with which a reasonably acceptable approximation can be constructed. From it we estimate the long term movement in the proportion of services to the total flow of goods to consumers back to 1869. The data and the procedures used in deriving the secular movement of this basic proportion are discussed in detail in Part III, which indeed, is in the nature of a long note to Table II 7.

As the sample data are for the composition of consumers' budgets in current prices, they provide a basis for estimating the value of services in current prices. An index of the changes in the ratio of services to the total flow of goods to consumers, in current prices, is constructed; it is then used to extrapolate back the proportions established for recent years and presented in detail in Part I. The remaining task, to adjust the value of services in current prices to 1929 prices, offers particular difficulties. For the years before 1919 no price data for services are available, with the single though important exception of rents. And comparison for recent years of the movement of the prices of finished commodities with that of the prices of services other than rent does not yield a relation that can be applied, for the decades before 1919, to the commodity price indexes to give an acceptable picture of the long term movements in the prices of services.

The qualitative changes in services during the long period give rise to greater difficulties in estimating price movements properly than would seem to be the case for commodity prices. For many commodities a fair degree of standardization had been attained early in the period under study; e.g., a loaf of bread or a suit of clothes or a bed in the 1870's and in the 1920's were similar enough for their prices to be compared. Only in some of the newer consumer durable goods was quality improvement so great as to render price comparisons over a long period subject to an exceedingly wide margin of error (ordinarily in the direction of underestimating the decline). In most services the quality change seems to have been much greater: certainly the improvement in the quality of at least professional services, and those rendered either by or in connection with durable commodities, was enormous. Even if the customary price indexes were available for the long period, the legitimacy of their use without substantial adjustments, the basis for which would have been exceedingly difficult to establish, would be subject to serious doubt.

The procedure finally adopted to adjust the value of services, *other than rent*,[7] for price changes was, for reasons just indicated, merely a crude expedient. We used the index of prices of all finished consumer commodities (perishable, semidurable, and durable), holding that the broad secular sweeps in such finished commodity prices could not but affect the prices of services; that any practicable index of the prices of services must be subject to the same biases as these commodity price indexes because of failure to take account of improvement in quality; and that while the magnitude of the long term movements in the prices of services, if not their direction, may have been different from those in commodity prices, we had no evidence upon which to estimate such possible differences.

The relative importance of the category under discussion is revealed in Table II f, which shows both the large share services constitute of the total flow of goods to consumers—from over one-quarter to over one-third—and the secular rise in that share revealed by the sample data underlying the estimate. This secular rise is the result of the shift in consumers' expenditures, and indeed in the final product structure of national income, to a larger proportion for services as per capita levels of product and of consumption rise.[8]

[7] For rent, an important subcomponent of the service category, the price adjustment was made by a specific index of rents.
[8] The service share as estimated here includes implicitly direct taxes paid by individuals as a measure of government services to individuals. In including this item (and imputed rent) the flow of goods to consumers differs from 'consumers' outlay' as estimated by the Department of Commerce for recent years.

Table II f
Share of Services in the Flow of Goods to Consumers, 1869-1938

		$ MILLION, AVERAGES PER YEAR			% OF FLOW OF GOODS TO CONSUMERS	
		Commodities (1)	Services (2)	Total (3)	Commodities (4)	Services (5)
		CURRENT PRICES				
1	1869-1888	5,237	1,932	7,169	73.1	26.9
2	1889-1908	9,484	4,152	13,636	69.6	30.4
3	1909-1928	32,042	16,006	48,048	66.7	33.3
4	1919-1938	39,733	22,433	62,166	63.9	36.1
		1929 PRICES				
5	1869-1888	8,356	3,302	11,658	71.7	28.3
6	1889-1908	18,556	7,701	26,257	70.7	29.3
7	1909-1928	34,644	18,356	53,000	65.4	34.6
8	1919-1938	42,524	23,992	66,516	63.9	36.1

COLUMN 1
LINE
1-4 Table II 8, col. 1-3.
LINE
5-8 Ibid., col. 6-8.

COLUMN 2
1-4 Ibid., col. 4.
5-8 Ibid., col. 9.

Since the total flow of goods to consumers accounts, in turn, for a large proportion of net national product, ranging above 80 percent during the period under study, the value of services flowing to ultimate consumers also accounts for a sizable share of total product—from one-fifth to over one-quarter.

3 Capital Formation

The data and procedures used to derive commodity flow, discussed in Section 1, yield estimates of two major components of gross capital formation: gross flow of producer durable commodities and gross value of new construction. For the former, the crude decade estimates for the years before 1919, after adjustment for the business use of passenger cars, can be combined with the decade averages of annual estimates for years beginning with 1919 to form a continuous series, 1869-1938; and for the latter, the crude pre-1914 decade estimates can be combined, without adjustment, with decade averages of annual estimates for years beginning with 1914.

To compute both gross and net capital formation, two other groups of estimates are needed. (a) To pass from gross to net capital formation, the current consumption of construction and of producer durable equipment has to be estimated. (b) To form totals of capital formation we must add to the value of construction and the flow of producer durable commodities net changes in inventories and in claims against foreign countries.

a) Annual estimates of current consumption, for construction and producer durable equipment combined, are available beginning with 1919 (see Table I 16 and the discussion in Part I); and are calculated, with various adjustments and extensions, largely from accounts of business enterprises. To divide these totals between construction and producer durables, and to extend them back through the decades preceding 1919, we used one and the same device: consumption was calculated on the basis of a constant life period for each of the two major categories and apportioned on a straight line principle. For producer durable equipment the life period assumed was 13 years, equivalent to an annual depreciation rate of almost 8 percent; for construction it was fifty years (six decades, with the terminal decades at half weight), equivalent to an annual depreciation rate of 2 percent. These periods were selected on the basis of information in *Capital Consumption and Adjustment*, pp. 176-83, for recent years.

By assuming these periods and adopting the principle of apportioning consumption over life, we could, with the help of annual data on the current flow of producer durable equipment and decade data on the value of new construction, calculate consumption for all the decades up to 1919; and use the extensions beyond 1919 to apportion the already calculated consumption total (in Part I) between that of construction and of producer durables.

Table II g shows the large proportion that current consumption of construction and producer durable equipment constitutes of the gross value of production during any substantial period. For the more durable construction, the proportion ranges from one- to two-thirds; for producer durable equipment, from one-half to eight-tenths. Notable also is the upward trend in the proportion of consumption to gross value.

It would be idle to speculate whether the basic assumption of

TABLE II g
Consumption of Construction and of Producer Durable Commodities Compared with Gross Flow, 1869-1938
(dollar figures in millions, averages per year)

		CURRENT PRICES			1929 PRICES		
		Gross Flow (1)	Consumption (2)	% (2) is of (1) (3)	Gross Flow (4)	Consumption (5)	% (5) is of (4) (6)
		CONSTRUCTION					
1	1869-1888	932	387	41.5	2,087	864	41.4
2	1889-1908	2,285	846	37.0	5,269	1,940	36.8
3	1909-1928	6,156	3,482	56.6	7,459	4,154	55.7
4	1919-1938	6,901	4,809	69.7	7,053	5,046	71.5
		PRODUCER DURABLE					
5	1869-1888	456	258	56.6	753	426	56.6
6	1889-1908	951	606	63.7	2,001	1,285	64.2
7	1909-1928	4,208	2,927	69.6	4,680	3,201	68.4
8	1919-1938	5,003	4,049	80.9	5,126	4,175	81.4
		CONSTRUCTION AND PRODUCER DURABLE					
9	1869-1888	1,388	645	46.5	2,840	1,290	45.4
10	1889-1908	3,236	1,452	44.9	7,270	3,225	44.4
11	1909-1928	10,364	6,409	61.8	12,139	7,355	60.6
12	1919-1938	11,904	8,858	74.4	12,179	9,221	75.7

COLUMN 1
LINE
1-4 Derived from Table II 5, col. 9, lines 1, 3, 5, 7, 14, 16, 18.

5-8 Derived from Table II 4, col. 7, lines 1, 3, 5, 14, and 16, and Table II 6, line 9.

9-12 Sum of lines 1 and 5, 2 and 6, 3 and 7, 4 and 8, respectively.

COLUMN 2
1-4 From data underlying Table II 14, col. 6, lines 1, 3, 5, 7, 9, 11, 13.

5-8 From data underlying Table II 14, col. 3, lines 1, 3, 5, 7, 9, 11, 13.

9-12 Sum of lines 1 and 5, 2 and 6, 3 and 7, 4 and 8, respectively.

COLUMN 4
1-4 From Table II 5, col. 7, lines 1, 3, 5, 7, 14, 16, 18.

5-8 From Table II 4, col. 5, lines 1, 3, 5, 14, and 16, and Table II 6, line 11.

9-12 Sum of lines 1 and 5, 2 and 6, 3 and 7, 4 and 8, respectively.

COLUMN 5
1-4 From Table II 14, col. 4, lines 1, 3, 5, 7, 9, 11, 13.

5-8 From *ibid.*, col. 1, lines 1, 3, 5, 7, 9, 11, 13.

9-12 Sum of lines 1 and 5, 2 and 6, 3 and 7, 4 and 8, respectively.

the procedure, a constant life period for construction and equipment, is historically valid. Perhaps we should assume a shorter life for these capital goods in the early years of the period than in the later because of the greater rapidity of technological improvement and hence of obsolescence; or, a shorter life in recent decades than in the earlier because of greater competitive pressures and of the attraction the depreciation charge as a deduction in calculating corporate income taxes had for business enterprises. Suffice it to say that there is no evidence at hand to invalidate an assumption of constant life; and that whatever rough checks on the application of these assumptions can be made do not reveal bias. In Part IV the cumulated additions of net values of construction and producer durable equipment are compared with the net changes in corresponding categories of reproducible wealth, the latter adjusted to a constant valuation base. Because the underlying data are crude, this comparison cannot be a definitive check on our estimates of the consumption of construction and durable equipment; but it does not indicate that this particular step in our procedure should be revised.

b) Net changes in *all* inventories, for decades preceding 1919, were estimated by a procedure somewhat analogous to that used in estimating changes in inventories of finished commodities and construction materials (Sec. 1). From data for 1919-28, a ratio of inventories (end and beginning of period) to an index of the volume of activity is established; the index is extrapolated to earlier decades for as many sectors of activity as are covered by available data; the ratio is applied to compute terminal inventories; and the net change in inventories is calculated. Then the sum of these inventory changes in the several sectors of activity, supplemented in some sectors by estimates based upon inventory holdings, is raised to a more comprehensive coverage by the ratio, calculated for 1919-28, of the 'separately estimated sectors' to the total comprised in the more detailed annual estimates for years beginning with 1919.

The chief difference between this procedure and that used in estimating changes in finished inventories in Section 1 lies in the use of a ratio of terminal inventories to the average level of activity (measured in index form) instead of a ratio of the additions to inventories to the additions to the flow. Absence of data on the flow of *all* commodities, for both recent and earlier years, necessitated this approach. So far as it neglects the possible downward trend in the ratio of inventories to total activity, it may underestimate additions to inventories in the early decades. However, the bias cannot be appreciable; certainly not in its effect on the estimates of national product or even on gross or net capital formation.

Net changes in claims against foreign countries rest upon the flow of goods and services into and out of the country. The longest series, constituting the backbone of the estimates, is for the balance of merchandise exports and imports. It is either combined with other items in the international balance of payments or raised to complete coverage on the basis of crude ratios. The whole calculation is an adaptation of the work for years before 1919 by Messrs. Bullock, Williams, and Tucker.

The proportion of either of these two categories of capital formation, or even of the two combined, in gross capital formation, is fairly small (Table II h). Net changes in inventories range from about one-quarter to less than one-tenth of gross capital formation; net changes in claims against foreign countries from -8 to $+8$ percent. In net capital formation the categories loom larger, but do not exceed a third. A notable trend is the rise of the net claims against foreign countries from a consistently negative share in the 19th century to a sizable positive share in the 20th—reflecting the transition of this country from an international debtor to an international creditor status.

Since these two categories constitute only moderate shares of capital formation, they are quite small when measured as shares of national product, gross or net. Gross capital formation ranges consistently below one-quarter of gross national product; and net capital formation consistently below one-fifth of net national product. Consequently, neither net changes in inventories nor net changes in claims against foreign countries, nor their combined total, when expressed as decade averages, can run much above 5 percent of national product. The items, being small and based on scanty data, are subject to wide relative error, and should not be used as independent measures of change in inventories or in the net balance of foreign claims. But

TABLE II h

Net Changes in Inventories and in Claims Against Foreign Countries Compared with Total Capital Formation, 1869-1938
(dollar figures in millions, averages per year)

		CURRENT PRICES			1929 PRICES	
			PERCENTAGE OF			PERCENTAGE OF
	DOLLAR TOTAL	Gross Capital Formation	Net Capital Formation	DOLLAR TOTAL	Gross Capital Formation	Net Capital Formation
	(1)	(2)	(3)	(4)	(5)	(6)
	NET CHANGES IN INVENTORIES					
1 1869-1888	383	22.6	36.6	503	15.5	25.8
2 1889-1908	315	8.9	15.2	494	6.4	11.0
3 1909-1928	1,272	10.1	20.5	1,057	7.5	15.5
4 1919-1938	920	6.9	20.2	566	4.3	14.0
	NET CHANGES IN CLAIMS AGAINST FOREIGN COUNTRIES					
5 1869-1888	−80	−4.7	−7.6	−104	−3.2	−5.3
6 1889-1908	−30	−8.5	−1.4	−48	−0.6	−1.1
7 1909-1928	976	7.7	15.7	962	6.8	14.1
8 1919-1938	585	4.4	12.9	506	3.8	12.6
NET CHANGES	IN INVENTORIES AND IN CLAIMS AGAINST FOREIGN COUNTRIES					
9 1869-1888	303	17.9	29.0	399	12.3	20.5
10 1889-1908	285	8.1	13.8	446	5.8	9.9
11 1909-1928	2,248	17.8	36.2	2,019	14.3	29.7
12 1919-1938	1,505	11.2	33.1	1,072	8.1	26.6

COLUMN 1

LINE
1-4 Derived from Table II 13, col. 3, lines 1, 3, 5, 7, 9, 11, 13.

5-8 Derived from *ibid.*, col. 4, lines 1, 3, 5, 7, 9, 11, 13.

9-12 Sum of lines 1 and 5, 2 and 6, 3 and 7, 4 and 8, respectively.

COLUMN 2
Based on col. 1 and gross capital formation derived from Table II 13, col. 5, lines 1, 3, 5, 7, 9, 11, 13.

COLUMN 3
Based on col. 1 and net capital formation derived from Table II 15, col. 5, lines 1, 3, 5, 7, 9, 11, 13.

COLUMN 4
1-4 Derived from Table II 13, col. 8, lines 1, 3, 5, 7, 9, 11, 13.

5-8 Derived from *ibid.*, col. 9, lines 1, 3, 5, 7, 9, 11, 13.

9-12 Sum of lines 1 and 5, 2 and 6, 3 and 7, 4 and 8, respectively.

COLUMN 5
Based on col. 4 and gross capital formation derived from Table II 13, col. 10, lines 1, 3, 5, 7, 9, 11, 13.

COLUMN 6
Based on col. 4 and net capital formation derived from Table II 15, col. 10, lines 1, 3, 5, 7, 9, 11, 13.

an error in the estimates of these categories cannot affect the estimates of national product or capital formation greatly.

4 *National Product*

Capital formation is a component of national product, peacetime concept, as defined in *National Product in Wartime* and as measured in Part I. Including all construction, public and private, war and nonwar, it is assumed to include the full flow of producer durable equipment and net changes in all inventories. Statistical difficulties preclude estimating changes in government-held inventories and may result in incomplete coverage of the output of munitions. But except for a few years (such as 1917 and 1918) the omissions are negligible; and even those for the World War I years are not likely to form large proportions of the *decade* averages. The present series can thus be taken as tolerable approximations to the capital formation component of national product, peacetime concept.

With decade estimates covering both the flow of goods to consumers and capital formation, we can obtain by simple addition estimates of total national product, gross and net. Since only the peacetime concept is used in this Part and is relevant to longer term studies, it is not designated as such in the text and tables that follow.

What is the margin of error in the decade estimates of national product and its major components? In the nature of the case, any appraisal must be tentative; but one may be helpful to possible users of the series as an opinion of their reliability based upon familiarity with the underlying data and the procedures.

For the comprehensive totals of national product and their major components, such as flow of goods to consumers, gross value of producer durables, gross construction, the maximum error in the estimates for the decades before 1919 can be said to be 15 percent; for the later three decades, less than 10 percent. The maximum errors may be somewhat larger for the various categories of the flow of goods to consumers; and, on a percentage basis, much larger for the net totals—net producer durables, net construction, changes in inventories, changes in claims against foreign countries, particularly the last two.

Owing to possible shortages in the underlying data or errors inherent in some of the assumptions, the comprehensive totals for the 1869-78 decade may be understated by as much as 10 percent; for the 1874-83 decade by as much as 5 percent; for the subsequent decades through 1899-1908 by as much as 2 to 3 percent. As suggested, particularly by the discussion in Section 1, these percentages for the earliest two decades in the series are a maximum rather than a medium allowance.

Naturally, the possible errors would be lessened by combining the single decades. In any study of secular trends, a combination of the series into periods covering two or more decades would yield results subject to much narrower margins of maximum error than those just suggested.

These judgments, and they cannot be more, can be strengthened, but not confirmed, by two comparisons. The first is of the present series for net national product or national income with Martin's recent estimates of national income, covering a comparable period and based throughout upon the flow of income payments approach (Table II i).

Certain differences in concept must be noted. The Martin series does not include undistributed net profits of enterprises

TABLE II i

Net National Product Derived from Commodity Flow Data Compared with Martin's Estimates of Realized National Income, 1869-1938
(dollar figures in millions, averages per year, current prices)

		PRESENT ESTIMATES (1)	MARTIN'S ESTIMATES (2)	DIFFERENCE AS % OF (1) (3)
1	1869-78	6,489	7,027	+8.3
2	1879-88	9,941	8,964	−9.8
3	1889-98	11,671	13,032	+11.7
4	1899-1908	19,740	19,928	+1.0
5	1904-13	26,273	25,614	−2.5
6	1909-18	36,341	34,942	−3.8
7	1914-23	55,324	51,672	−6.6
8	1919-28	72,160	67,135	−7.0
9	1924-33	70,139	66,397	−5.3
10	1929-38	61,274	60,829	−0.7
	PERCENTAGE CHANGE			
11	1869-98 to 1889-1918	+141.1	+134.0	
12	1889-1918 to 1909-38	+150.6	+139.9	

COLUMN
1 Table II 16, col. 5.

2 R. F. Martin, *National Income in the United States, 1799-1938* (National Industrial Conference Board, 1939), p. 6, Table 1.

and makes no allowance for net savings of governments. The inclusion of these items for recent years in the present series explains the shortage of the Martin estimates. But it is to be doubted that in the earlier decades the excluded items constitute as much as 5 percent of the total; and their relative importance must diminish as we go back in time.

The present series is too complex to be described simply as being based upon commodity flow. For years beginning with 1919, the controlling totals, though allocated by final product categories with the help of additional data on commodity flow, are, as indicated in Part I, based upon the flow of income payments. For the years before 1919, the decade estimates are based largely upon commodity flow data, supplemented by a study of samples relating to services; and these decade estimates are combined with the decade averages of annual estimates for recent years either without adjustment or adjusted only for the business use of passenger cars. But, at least for one important category, viz., services not embodied in new commodities, the cruder pre-1919 decade estimates are spliced to the more detailed estimates for subsequent years by extrapolating the ratios based for recent years on income payments. To that extent, the entire series for national product back to 1869 is an extension of the annual series that begins in 1919, i.e., of the series controlled by the flow of income payments approach.

The present series may, therefore, be described as an extension into the past, primarily on the basis of commodity flow data, of recent estimates derived by the flow of income payments approach; and the Martin series, as an extension, primarily on the basis of flow of income payments data, of recent estimates. So far as these different bases of extension mean that the two series are independent, they are a check on each other.

The greatest difference between them is for the 1889-98 decade, about 15 percent, if we take into account the narrower scope of the Martin estimates. The smallest is for the decades 1904-13 and 1909-18. Nor are the differences distributed in such a fashion as to suggest that the longer trends indicated by the two series would diverge widely (see lines 11 and 12).

Another interesting comparison is of percentage changes from decade to decade in the present estimates of gross national

TABLE II j
Rates of Growth, Successive Overlapping Decades
Gross National Product in 1929 Prices and
Two Indexes of 'Total' Production, 1869-1928

		% INCREASE SHOWN BY		
		Gross National Product 1929 Prices	Day-Persons Index	Warren-Pearson Index
		(1)	(2)	(3)
1	1869-78 to 1874-83	43.6	30.6	32.8
2	1874-83 to 1879-88	31.1	27.5	28.6
3	1879-88 to 1884-93	18.9	21.1	21.4
4	1884-93 to 1889-98	15.6	18.0	20.2
5	1889-98 to 1894-1903	23.1	20.1	24.3
6	1894-1903 to 1899-1908	25.1	23.2	26.6
7	1899-1908 to 1904-13	21.0	17.8	19.8
8	1904-13 to 1909-18	13.4	17.1	15.3
9	1909-18 to 1914-23	14.2	12.9	7.5
10	1914-23 to 1919-28	20.5	13.0	10.8

COLUMN
1 Based on Table II 16, col. 9.

2 W. M. Persons, *Forecasting Business Cycles* (Wiley & Sons, 1931), p. 170. The index was converted to arithmetic means per decade, and their percentage increases calculated.

3 G. F. Warren and F. A. Pearson, *Physical Volume of Production in the United States* (Cornell Agricultural Experiment Station Memoir 144, Nov. 1932), Table 1, pp. 5-7. The variable weight index, weighted by value plus value of manufacture, was used.

product, in 1929 prices, with those in the most comprehensive indexes of the physical volume of production now available (Table II j). Since these indexes do not cover total national output, the point of the comparison is not in the levels of the rates of increase, or even in the degree of their retardation, but primarily in the fluctuations in the three measures.

The fluctuations in the rate of increase of gross national product, as estimated here, are similar to those in the production indexes based upon a quite different set of data. The peaks appear in all three columns in lines 1, 6, and 10; the troughs in lines 4 and 8 or 9. The only difference in timing is the occurrence of the trough in column 1 in line 8; in columns 2 and 3 a quinquennium later (line 9). But there is a marked difference in amplitude: the fluctuations in the rate of increase in gross national product, as estimated here, are much more pronounced than in either the Day-Persons or the Warren-Pearson index—possibly a reflection of the greater sensitivity of our estimates and of the more comprehensive inclusion of activities in which long trend cycles are especially prominent (notably construction).

In the light of the discussion in Section 1a of the possible bias resulting from the inadequacy of the 1869 Census, the comparison of lines 1 and 2 with the other lines of Table II j is specially instructive. The high rate of increase in our estimates of gross national product in lines 1 and 2 may be due to too low a base. But the relative difference between the entries in columns 1 and 2 for line 1 is not any greater than for line 10, another high period in the 'trend-cycle'; and that between entries in columns 1 and 3 for line 1 is appreciably smaller than for line 10. So perhaps our estimate for 1869-78 does not exaggerate the rate of increase for periods in which it is used as a base any more than does our estimate for 1914-23.

The smaller relative difference in the rate of increase between gross national product and the two 'total' production indexes in line 6 (the third high period in the trend-cycle covered by Table II j) than in lines 1 and 10 suggests a possible explanation. Both periods covered in lines 1 and 10 follow major military conflicts (the Civil War and World War I). During such wars the reduction in the rate of growth of the basic commodities that dominate production indexes is not noticeable, since these basic commodities are wanted for war purposes as much as for peacetime, or more; and by the same token, the rise in their volume after the war is not as great as in other sectors of the economy. In contrast, consumer goods of more finished character and all types of service, whose output tends to be curtailed during a major conflict, enjoy an accelerated rate of growth after it. Gross national product, being a more comprehensive measure of output than the indexes of production, gives full weight to these consumer goods and services. This hypothesis may explain why our estimates, whose changes are measured in column 1, show such a relatively greater excess in lines 1 and 10 over the changes in the Day-Persons and Warren-Pearson indexes than in line 6; and also suggest why the second trough is reached in column 1 in line 8, i.e., in the first decade covering World War I rather than in line 9, i.e., in the decade in which the postwar expansion is already felt.

The rough agreement in Table II i between the *levels* of the present estimates of national income and Martin's, and the plausible concurrence of the *fluctuations* in the rate of change between the present estimates of gross national product in 1929 prices and the indexes of production should not be attributed decisive significance. Perhaps they should be interpreted as a confirmation of the other series rather than of the comprehensive estimates assembled here. But since there is considerable independence of data underlying our estimates and the others in Tables II i and II j, the rough agreement in the levels and in the fluctuations of the rate of change from decade to decade encourages the belief that, within the margin of error suggested, the decade estimates are useful in studying long term trends in the level and composition of national product.

B BASIC TABLES

TABLE II 1

Perishable Commodities, Averages per Year by Decades, 1869-1938
(all columns except 6 in millions of dollars)

	OUTPUT DESTINED FOR DOMESTIC CONSUMPTION		RETAIL VALUE OF COL. 2	NET CHANGE IN FINISHED INVEN- TORIES	FLOW TO ULTIMATE USERS AT FINAL COST	PRICE INDEX	FLOW TO ULTIMATE USERS AT FINAL COST
	Current Prices	1929 Prices	1929 Prices	1929 Prices	1929 Prices	1929: 100	Current Prices
	(1)	(2)	(3)	(4)	(5)	(6)	(7)
DECADE ESTIMATES							
1 1869-78	1,737	2,341	3,512	+44	3,467	74.2	2,573
2 1874-83	2,265	3,534	5,302	+58	5,244	64.1	3,360
3 1879-88	2,658	4,612	6,918	+36	6,882	57.6	3,964
4 1884-93	2,822	5,914	7,792	+23	7,769	54.3	4,219
5 1889-98	3,043	6,030	9,046	+66	8,980	50.5	4,535
6 1894-1903	3,795	7,612	11,419	+83	11,336	49.9	5,657
7 1899-1908	5,124	9,451	14,178	+77	14,100	54.2	7,642
8 1904-13	6,706	11,132	16,698	+80	16,619	60.2	10,005
9 1909-18	9,338	12,356	18,536	+49	18,487	75.6	13,976
10 1914-23	13,514	13,608	20,414	+87	20,327	99.3	20,185
11 1919-28	16,529	15,775	23,664	+116	23,549	104.8	24,679
12 1924-33	15,544	17,236	25,856	+32	25,824	90.2	23,293
13 1929-38	14,716	18,232	27,350	+96	27,254	80.7	21,994
14 1914-23					20,514	98.1	20,123
AVERAGES OF ANNUAL ESTIMATES							
15 1919-28					23,895	102.6	24,505
16 1924-33					26,456	90.3	23,893
17 1929-38					29,391	79.1	23,243

COLUMN 1

LINES 1-3: sums of estimates for (1) food and kindred products; (2) cigars, cigarettes, and tobacco; (3) fuel and lighting products; (4) all other perishable commodities. For each group annual estimates are derived and averaged for the decade. Values for 1869, 1879, and 1889 are in the series prepared by W. H. Shaw on the basis of Censuses of Manufactures. Annual estimates for 1870-78 and 1880-88 are interpolated between or extrapolated from these dates by sample data weighted by the value of output for 1869, 1879, and 1889 (*Census of Manufactures*). The years for which estimates are interpolated or extrapolated and the sample series used are indicated below.

1) Food and kindred products
   a) Manufactured
      1870-78 interpolated between 1869 and 1879 by value of coffee imports (*Production Trends in the United States since 1870* by A. F. Burns; National Bureau of Economic Research, 1934); gross income from peanuts, sugar, rice, condensed milk, and slaughter of animals (*Gross Farm Income and Indices of Farm Production and Prices in the United States, 1869-1937* by Frederick Strauss and L. H. Bean, Department of Agriculture Technical Bulletin 703); total value of butter and cheese produced (quantity production, from *Production and Consumption of Manufactured Dairy Products* by E. E. Vial, Department of Agriculture Technical Bulletin 722, multiplied by BLS price indexes); value of flour shipments received at New York (*Internal Commerce of the United States*).

      1880-88 interpolated between 1879 and 1889 by the same series as for 1870-78, with the following changes: value of natural mineral waters (*Mineral Resources of the United States*) is added; total value of butter and cheese produced is replaced by value of factory production (source cited for total value); value of flour shipments received at New York is replaced by value of wheat flour produced (*Stanford Wheat Studies*, Vol. IV, No. 2).
   b) Nonmanufactured
      1870-78 and 1880-88 interpolated between 1869 and 1879 and between 1879 and 1889 by gross income from all farm crops (*Gross Farm Income and Indices of Farm Production and Prices in the United States, 1869-1937*).

2) Cigars, cigarettes, and tobacco
   1870-78 estimated with 'all other' perishable commodities.

   1880-88 extrapolated from 1889 by quantity production of cigars, cigarettes, tobacco and snuff (*Annual Report of the Commissioner of Internal Revenue*) multiplied by appropriate price indexes.

3) Fuel and lighting products
   a) Manufactured
      1870-78 and 1880-88 interpolated between 1869 and 1879 and between 1879 and 1889 by value of crude petroleum produced (*Mineral Resources*).
   b) Nonmanufactured (anthracite and bituminous coal)
      1870-78 and 1880-88 estimated by the method outlined in *Commodity Flow and Capital Formation* (National Bureau of Economic Research, 1938), Vol. One, Table II-1, d and e.

4) All other perishable commodities
   1870-78, including cigars, cigarettes, and tobacco, interpolated between 1869 and 1879 by the sum of the estimates under food and kindred products and fuel and lighting products.

   1880-88 interpolated between 1879 and 1889 by the sum of the estimates under food and kindred products, cigars, cigarettes, and tobacco, and fuel and lighting products.

Table II 1 concluded:

LINES 4-13: averages of annual estimates. For 1884-88, see note to lines 1-3; for 1889-1938, see Shaw's 'Finished Commodities since 1879', *Occasional Paper 3* (National Bureau of Economic Research, Aug. 1941).

COLUMN 2

LINES 1-13: the annual estimates from which col. 1 is derived, converted to 1929 prices and averaged. Conversion is carried through separately for each minor group for which indexes are available. The indexes used for 1869, 1879, 1889, and subsequent years are those underlying Shaw's estimates in 1913 prices (see *Occasional Paper 3,* pp. 47-9), the index for each minor group being recomputed to a 1929 base. Annual price data for the major group for 1870-78 and 1880-88 are interpolated between 1869 and 1879 and between 1879 and 1889 by a weighted index of prices for food, fuel and lighting, drugs and chemicals, and tobacco. These price series (*Wholesale Prices, Wages and Transportation,* Part I, Senate Report 1394, Finance Committee, 52d Cong., 2d Sess., pp. 91, 107) are weighted by rough approximations to output totals for 1869, 1879, and 1889 (*Census of Manufactures*).

COLUMN 3

LINES 1-13: col. 2 multiplied by a raising ratio, 1.5001, representing the relation in 1919-33 of the retail value of output destined for domestic consumption (the value of output destined for domestic consumption at producers' prices plus transportation and distribution costs) plus the farm value of products retained by farmers for their own consumption, to the value of output destined for domestic consumption at producers' prices plus the farm value of products retained by farmers for their own consumption. Data for this ratio are from *Commodity Flow and Capital Formation,* Vol. One, Tables II-7, V-7, and V-8.

COLUMN 4

LINES 1-13: total net change in finished inventories for each period is estimated by multiplying the net change in the retail value of output destined for domestic consumption (the difference between output in the first year of the period and that in the year following the close of the period) by a constant ratio, .1587 (total net change in finished inventories for 1919-28, +$1,273.6, divided by the net change between 1919 and 1929 [$27,106.0 − $19,082.6] in the retail value of output destined for domestic consumption). Data for this ratio are from *ibid.,* Table V-7, lines A11 and A2, respectively. Finally, total net change for each period is reduced to an average per year basis.

COLUMN 5

LINES 1-13: col. 3 minus col. 4.

LINE 14: average of 1914-18, derived by the method used for lines 1-13, and of 1919-23, by the method used for lines 15-17.

LINES 15-17: averages of annual estimates in Table I 1, col. 5.

COLUMN 6

LINES 1-13: col. 1 divided by col. 2.

LINES 14-17: col. 7 divided by col. 5.

COLUMN 7

LINES 1-13: col. 5 multiplied by col. 6.

LINE 14: average of 1914-18, derived by the method used for lines 1-13, and of 1919-23, by the method used for lines 15-17.

LINES 15-17: averages of annual estimates in Table I 1, col. 2.

TABLE II 2
Semidurable Commodities, Averages per Year by Decades, 1869-1938
(all columns except 6 in millions of dollars)

	OUTPUT DESTINED FOR DOMESTIC CONSUMPTION		RETAIL VALUE OF COL. 2	NET CHANGE IN FINISHED INVEN- TORIES	FLOW TO ULTIMATE USERS AT FINAL COST	PRICE INDEX	FLOW TO ULTIMATE USERS AT FINAL COST
	Current Prices	1929 Prices	1929 Prices	1929 Prices	1929 Prices	1929: 100	Current Prices
	(1)	(2)	(3)	(4)	(5)	(6)	(7)
DECADE ESTIMATES							
1 1869-78	760	1,007	1,598	+53	1,546	75.5	1,167
2 1874-83	894	1,378	2,187	+59	2,128	64.9	1,381
3 1879-88	1,038	1,771	2,810	+53	2,757	58.6	1,616
4 1884-93	1,114	2,066	3,278	+35	3,244	53.9	1,748
5 1889-98	1,139	2,356	3,738	+69	3,669	48.3	1,772
6 1894-1903	1,320	2,853	4,527	+114	4,413	46.3	2,043
7 1899-1908	1,810	3,536	5,609	+105	5,503	51.2	2,818
8 1904-13	2,347	4,202	6,666	+93	6,573	55.9	3,675
9 1909-18	3,288	4,640	7,361	+40	7,320	70.9	5,190
10 1914-23	5,385	4,977	7,895	+62	7,833	108.2	8,475
11 1919-28	6,967	5,842	9,267	+210	9,058	119.3	10,806
12 1924-33	6,136	6,228	9,880	−35	9,915	98.5	9,766
13 1929-38	5,058	5,789	9,184	−76	9,261	87.4	8,094
14 1914-23					7,914	107.7	8,525
AVERAGES OF ANNUAL ESTIMATES							
15 1919-28					9,190	118.5	10,889
16 1924-33					10,252	98.3	10,080
17 1929-38					9,940	85.5	8,495

COLUMN 1

LINES 1-3: averages of annual estimates. Values for 1869, 1879, and 1889 in current and 1913 prices are in the series prepared by Mr. Shaw on the basis of *Census of Manufactures* reports and other data. We adjust the 1913 price series to the 1929 level, adjustment being carried through separately for each minor group (see note to Table II 1, col. 2, lines 1-3). Annual estimates for the major group for 1870-78 and 1880-88 are interpolated by an index of physical output derived from sample data appropriately weighted. The sample series—boot and shoe shipments from Boston (*Shoe and Leather Reporter*), cotton consumption, wool consumption, and raw silk imports (*Production Trends in the United States since 1870*) —are weighted by output values for 1869, 1879, and 1889 (*Census of Manufactures*). Shaw's price index for 1869, 1879, and 1889 is adjusted to a 1929 base, adjustment being carried through separately for each minor group. Annual data for the major group for 1870-78 and 1880-88 are interpolated by the index for cloths and clothing (*Wholesale Prices, Wages and Transportation*, Part I, p. 91). Multiplication of the values in 1929 prices by this index yields the current price series.

LINES 4-13: averages of annual estimates. For 1884-88, see note to lines 1-3; for 1889-1938, see *Occasional Paper 3*.

COLUMN 2

LINES 1-3: see note to col. 1.

LINES 4-13: the annual estimates underlying col. 1, converted to 1929 prices and averaged. Conversion is carried through separately for each minor group for which indexes are available. For 1884-88 conversion is by the index described in

Table II 2 concluded:

the note to col. 1, lines 1-3; for 1889-1938, by those described in *Occasional Paper 3* (pp. 47-9), the index for each minor group being recomputed to a 1929 base.

COLUMN 3

LINES 1-13: col. 2 multiplied by a raising ratio, 1.5864, representing the relation in 1929 of the retail value of output destined for domestic consumption, $12,248,232 (the value of output destined for domestic consumption at producers' prices plus transportation and distribution costs), to the value of output destined for domestic consumption at producers' prices, $7,720,777. Data for this ratio are from *Commodity Flow and Capital Formation,* Vol. One, p. 212, col. 5 and 4, respectively.

COLUMN 4

LINES 1-13: total net change in finished inventories for each period is estimated by multiplying the net change in the retail value of output destined for domestic consumption (the difference between output in the first year of the period and that in the year following the close of the period) by a constant ratio, .4977 (total net change in finished inventories for 1919-28, +$2,066.7, divided by the net change between 1919 and 1929 [$12,248.2 − $8,096.1] in the retail value of output destined for domestic consumption). Data for this ratio are from *ibid.,* Table V-7, lines B11 and B2, respectively. Finally, total net change for each period is reduced to an average per year basis.

COLUMN 5

LINES 1-13: col. 3 minus col. 4.

LINE 14: average of 1914-18, derived by the method used for lines 1-13, and of 1919-23, by the method used for lines 15-17.

LINES 15-17: averages of annual estimates in Table I 2, col. 5.

COLUMN 6

LINES 1-13: col. 1 divided by col. 2.

LINES 14-17: col. 7 divided by col. 5.

COLUMN 7

LINES 1-13: col. 5 multiplied by col. 6.

LINE 14: average of 1914-18, derived by the method used for lines 1-13, and of 1919-23, by the method used for lines 15-17.

LINES 15-17: averages of annual estimates in Table I 2, col. 2.

DECADE ESTIMATES, 1869-1939

TABLE II 3

Consumer Durable Commodities, Averages per Year by Decades,
1869-1938
(all columns except 6 in millions of dollars)

	OUTPUT DESTINED FOR DOMESTIC CONSUMPTION Current Prices (1)	1929 Prices (2)	RETAIL VALUE OF COL. 2 1929 Prices (3)	NET CHANGE IN FINISHED INVEN- TORIES 1929 Prices (4)	FLOW TO ULTIMATE USERS AT FINAL COST 1929 Prices (5)	PRICE INDEX 1929: 100 (6)	FLOW TO ULTIMATE USERS AT FINAL COST Current Prices (7)
DECADE ESTIMATES							
1 1869-78	295	431	701	+15	686	68.6	470
2 1874-83	345	610	993	+20	972	56.5	549
3 1879-88	428	859	1,397	+23	1,375	49.8	685
4 1884-93	497	1,081	1,759	+12	1,747	46.0	804
5 1889-98	511	1,233	2,007	+27	1,980	41.4	820
6 1894-1903	606	1,474	2,398	+35	2,363	41.1	971
7 1899-1908	872	1,816	2,956	+34	2,922	48.0	1,403
8 1904-13	1,220	2,194	3,571	+34	3,537	55.6	1,966
9 1909-18	1,821	2,629	4,279	+60	4,219	69.3	2,924
10 1914-23	3,278	3,318	5,400	+126	5,274	98.8	5,211
11 1919-28	4,997	4,751	7,733	+137	7,596	105.2	7,991
12 1924-33	4,651	4,796	7,806	−63	7,869	97.0	7,633
13 1929-38	4,046	4,401	7,162	−50	7,212	91.9	6,628
AVERAGES OF ANNUAL ESTIMATES							
14 1919-28					6,554	104.7	6,860
15 1924-33					6,982	96.0	6,705
16 1929-38					6,080	90.1	5,475

COLUMN 1

LINES 1-3: averages of annual estimates. Values for 1869, 1879, and 1889 are in the series prepared by Mr. Shaw on the basis of *Census of Manufactures* reports. Annual estimates for 1870-78 and 1880-88 are interpolated between 1869 and 1879 and between 1879 and 1889 by an index of output computed by weighting output of semidurable commodities 2 (see note to Table II 2, col. 1) and output of construction materials 1 (see note to Table II 5, col. 1).

LINES 4-13: averages of annual estimates. For 1884-88, see note to lines 1-3; for 1889-1938, see *Occasional Paper 3*.

COLUMN 2

LINES 1-13: the annual estimates underlying col. 1, converted to 1929 prices and averaged. Conversion is carried through separately for each minor group for which indexes are available. The indexes used for 1869, 1879, 1889, and subsequent years are those underlying Shaw's estimates in 1913 prices (see *Occasional Paper 3*, pp. 47-9), the index for each minor group being recomputed on a 1929 base. Annual price data for the major group for 1870-78 and 1880-88 are interpolated between 1869 and 1879 and between 1879 and 1889 by the index for house furnishing goods (*Wholesale Prices, Wages and Transportation,* Part I, p. 91).

COLUMN 3

LINES 1-13: col. 2 multiplied by a raising ratio, 1.6275, representing the relation in 1919-33 of the retail value of output destined for domestic consumption (the value of output destined for domestic consumption at producers' prices plus trans-

Table II 3 concluded:

portation and distribution costs), to the value of output destined for domestic consumption at producers' prices. Data for this ratio are from *Commodity Flow and Capital Formation,* Vol. One, Table II-7, and a revision of Table V-7 (for which see notes to Table I 3, col. 5, above).

COLUMN 4

LINES 1-13: total net change in finished inventories for each period is estimated by multiplying the net change in the retail value of output destined for domestic consumption (the difference between output in the first year of the period and that in the year following the close of the period) by a constant ratio, .3126 (total net change in finished inventories for 1919-28, + $1,395.6, divided by the net change between 1919 and 1929 [$10,033.5 − $5,568.6] in the retail value of output destined for domestic consumption). Data for this ratio are from *ibid.,* Table V-7, line C13, and a revision of line C4 (for which see notes to Table I 3, col. 5). Finally, total net change for each period is reduced to an average per year basis.

COLUMN 5

LINES 1-13: col. 3 minus col. 4.

LINES 14-16: averages of annual estimates in Table I 3, col. 6.

COLUMN 6

LINES 1-13: col. 1 divided by col. 2.

LINES 14-16: col. 7 divided by col. 5.

COLUMN 7

LINES 1-13: col. 5 multiplied by col. 6.

LINES 14-16: averages of annual estimates in Table I 3, col. 2.

TABLE II 4
Producer Durable Commodities, Averages per Year by Decades, 1869-1938
(all columns except 6 in millions of dollars)

	OUTPUT DESTINED FOR DOMESTIC CONSUMPTION Current Prices (1)	1929 Prices (2)	RETAIL VALUE OF COL. 2 1929 Prices (3)	NET CHANGE IN FINISHED INVEN- TORIES 1929 Prices (4)	FLOW TO ULTIMATE USERS AT FINAL COST 1929 Prices (5)	PRICE INDEX 1929: 100 (6)	FLOW TO ULTIMATE USERS AT FINAL COST Current Prices (7)
DECADE ESTIMATES							
1 1869-78	314	415	481	+2	479	75.6	362
2 1874-83	398	651	754	+2	751	61.1	459
3 1879-88	477	891	1,031	+4	1,027	53.6	551
4 1884-93	506	1,070	1,238	+2	1,236	47.3	585
5 1889-98	534	1,231	1,425	+3	1,422	43.4	617
6 1894-1903	727	1,581	1,831	+7	1,823	46.0	839
7 1899-1908	1,100	2,208	2,556	+6	2,550	49.8	1,270
8 1904-13	1,382	2,618	3,030	+4	3,026	52.8	1,598
9 1909-18	2,238	3,140	3,635	+15	3,620	71.3	2,581
10 1914-23	3,593	3,665	4,243	+11	4,233	98.0	4,148
11 1919-28	4,298	4,100	4,746	+8	4,738	104.8	4,965
12 1924-33	3,733	3,867	4,477	−10	4,486	96.5	4,329
13 1929-38	3,365	3,622	4,193	−9	4,202	92.9	3,903
AVERAGES OF ANNUAL ESTIMATES							
14 1919-28					5,479	103.1	5,650
15 1924-33					5,335	96.1	5,129
16 1929-38					4,774	91.2	4,356

COLUMN 1

LINES 1-3: averages of annual estimates. Values for 1869, 1879, and 1889 in current and 1913 prices are in the series prepared by Mr. Shaw on the basis of *Census of Manufactures* reports and other data. We adjust the 1913 price series to 1929 levels, adjustment being carried through separately for each minor group (see note to Table II 1, col. 2, lines 1-13). Annual estimates for 1856-68, 1870-78, and 1880-88 are interpolated and extrapolated by an index of physical output derived from sample data appropriately weighted. The sample series used are output of pig iron and of steel ingots and castings (American Iron and Steel Association reports), gross tonnage of vessels built (*Merchant Marine Statistics, 1936*, pp. 43-5), and locomotives constructed (for 1856-80, production at the Baldwin Locomotive Works from the *History of the Baldwin Locomotive Works, 1832-1923*, Philadelphia, 1924; for 1880-89, total United States production from *Railroad Gazette*, Jan. issues). The weights are approximated from the value of output for 1869, 1879, and 1889 (*Census of Manufactures*). Shaw's price index for 1869, 1879, and 1889 is adjusted to a 1929 base, adjustment being carried through separately for each minor group. The major group index is interpolated between 1869 and 1879 and 1879 and 1889 and extrapolated to 1856 by the index for metals and implements excluding pocket knives (*Wholesale Prices, Wages and Transportation*, Part I, p. 92). Multiplication of the values in 1929 prices by this price index yields the series in current prices. The values for 1856-68 are needed for our estimates of the consumption of producer durable goods (see notes to Table II 14, col. 1).

LINES 4-13: averages of annual estimates. For 1884-88, see note to lines 1-3; for 1889-1938, see *Occasional Paper 3*.

Table II 4 concluded:

COLUMN 2

LINES 1-3: see note to col. 1.

LINES 4-13: the annual estimates underlying col. 1, converted to 1929 prices and averaged. Conversion is carried through separately for each minor group for which indexes are available. For 1884-88 conversion is by the index described in the note to col. 1, lines 1-3; for 1889-1938, by those described in *Occasional Paper 3* (pp. 47-9), the index for each minor group being recomputed to a 1929 base.

COLUMN 3

LINES 1-13: col. 2 multiplied by a raising ratio, 1.1576, representing the relation in 1919-33 of the retail value of output destined for domestic consumption (the value of output destined for domestic consumption at producers' prices plus transportation and distribution costs) to the value of output destined for domestic consumption at producers' prices. Data for this ratio are from *Commodity Flow and Capital Formation*, Vol. One, Table II-7, and a revision of Table V-7 (for which see notes to Table I 6, col. 6, above).

COLUMN 4

LINES 1-13: total net change in finished inventories for each period is estimated by multiplying the net change in the retail value of output destined for domestic consumption (the difference between output in the first year of the period and that in the year following the close of the period) by a constant ratio, .0637 (total net change in finished inventories for 1919-28, + $87.1, divided by the net change between 1919 and 1929 [$6,605.5 − $5,238.2] in the retail value of output destined for domestic consumption). Data for this ratio are from *ibid.*, Table V-7, line D13, and a revision of line D4 (for which see notes to Table I 6, col. 6, above). Finally, total net change for each period is reduced to an average per year basis.

COLUMN 5

LINES 1-13: col. 3 minus col. 4.

LINES 14-16: averages of annual estimates in Table I 6, col. 6.

COLUMN 6

LINES 1-13: col. 1 divided by col. 2.

LINES 14-16: col. 7 divided by col. 5.

COLUMN 7

LINES 1-13: col. 5 multiplied by col. 6.

LINES 14-16: averages of annual estimates in Table I 6, col. 2.

TABLE II 5

Construction, Averages per Year by Decades, 1869-1938
(all columns except 8 in millions of dollars)

	OUTPUT OF CONSTRUCTION MATERIALS DESTINED FOR DOMESTIC CONSUMPTION Current Prices (1)	OUTPUT INCL. TRANSPORTATION & DISTRIBUTION COSTS 1929 Prices (2)	NET CHANGES IN ALL INVENTORIES 1929 Prices (3)	1929 Prices (4)	FLOW INTO CONSUMPTION 1929 Prices (5)	TOTAL CONSTRUCTION 1929 Prices (6)	NEW CONSTRUCTION 1929 Prices (7)	PRICE INDEX 1929: 100 (8)	NEW CONSTRUCTION Current Prices (9)
DECADE ESTIMATES									
1 1869-78	441	743	1,083	+17	1,066	1,997	1,496	46.9	702
2 1874-83	529	961	1,401	+33	1,368	2,562	1,920	43.8	841
3 1879-88	717	1,344	1,960	+51	1,908	3,575	2,679	43.4	1,162
4 1884-93	969	1,959	2,856	+62	2,793	5,233	3,921	42.4	1,662
5 1889-98	1,036	2,320	3,381	+40	3,341	6,260	4,690	39.7	1,862
6 1894-1903	1,130	2,464	3,591	+35	3,556	6,662	4,991	40.8	2,036
7 1899-1908	1,529	2,912	4,245	+78	4,166	7,805	5,848	46.3	2,708
8 1904-13	1,934	3,411	4,972	+76	4,897	9,173	6,873	51.1	3,512
9 1909-18	2,348	3,547	5,170	−29	5,198	9,738	7,297	57.3	4,181
10 1914-23	3,242	3,381	4,928	+27	4,901	9,181	6,879	84.1	5,785
11 1919-28	4,362	3,990	5,816	+130	5,686	10,651	7,981	102.6	8,188
12 1924-33	3,840	3,922	5,716	−151	5,867	10,991	8,235	97.6	8,038
13 1929-38	2,896	3,151	4,592	−111	4,703	8,811	6,602	91.0	6,008
14 1909-18							6,609	57.3	3,784
AVERAGES OF ANNUAL ESTIMATES									
15 1914-23							6,114	84.1	5,141
16 1919-28	4,467	4,076					8,310	102.6	8,528
17 1924-33	3,910	3,996					8,504	97.6	8,303
18 1929-38							5,797	91.0	5,274

COLUMN 1

LINES 1-3: averages of annual estimates. Values for 1869, 1879, and 1889 in current and 1913 prices are in the series prepared by Mr. Shaw on the basis of *Census of Manufactures* reports and other data. We adjust the latter to 1929 levels and interpolate annual estimates for 1870-78 and 1880-88 by an index of physical output derived from sample data appropriately weighted. The sample series used for interpolation between 1869 and 1879 are production of nails and of rails (American Iron and Steel Association reports), and of lumber (*American Lumberman*). For interpolation between 1879 and 1889, production of cement and of roofing slate (*Mineral Resources of the United States*) are also used. The weights by which these series are combined are approximations to the value of output for 1869, 1879, and 1889 (*Census of Manufactures*). Shaw's price index for 1869, 1879, and 1889 is adjusted to a 1929 base, and annual price data for 1870-78 and 1880-88 interpolated by the index for lumber and building materials (*Wholesale Prices, Wages and Transportation*, Part I, p. 91). Multiplication of the values in 1929 prices by the price index yields the series in current prices.

LINES 4-13: averages of annual estimates. For 1884-88, see note to lines 1-3; for 1889-1938, the series prepared by Mr. Shaw is used.

LINES 16 & 17: the annual estimates underlying col. 2, multiplied by the price index for building materials in *Commodity Flow and Capital Formation*, Vol. One, Table VI-1, line 2, and averaged.

Table II 5 continued:

COLUMN 2

LINES 1-3: see note to col. 1, lines 1-3.

LINES 4-13: averages of annual estimates. For 1884-88, see note to col. 1, lines 1-3; for 1889-1938, Shaw's series in 1913 prices is used, after adjustment to 1929 price levels.

LINES 16 & 17: averages of annual estimates of the output of construction materials minus the excess of exports (reduced by wholesalers' margins) over imports. *Commodity Flow and Capital Formation,* Vol. One, gives annual series on output in 1929 prices (Table VI-1, line 3), on exports and imports in current prices (Table VI-2, lines 12 and 2), and on the ratio of wholesalers' margins to exports (Table VI-2, line 8). Exports and imports in current prices are converted to 1929 prices by the price index of building materials (Table VI-1, line 2).

COLUMN 3

Col. 2 multiplied by a raising ratio, 1.4576, representing the relation in 1929 of output of construction materials destined for domestic consumption including transportation and distribution costs, $7,404.7, to the value of output destined for domestic consumption at producers' prices, $5,080.1. Transportation charges in 1929 are from *ibid.,* Table VI-1; distributive costs, from *ibid.,* Tables VI-2 and VI-3.

COLUMN 4

Total net change in all inventories for each period is estimated by applying to the net change in output (the difference between output in the terminal years of the period) a constant ratio, .4554 (total net change in inventories for 1919-28 divided by the net change in output, after mark-up, from 1919 to 1928). Total net change in inventories for 1919-28 is the sum of annual net changes in stocks held by producers, wholesalers, retailers, and consumers (derived from *ibid.,* Tables VI-1, VI-2, VI-3, and VI-4, respectively). Output, after mark-up, is estimated by multiplying output destined for domestic consumption by the mark-up ratio described in the note to col. 3. Finally, total net change for each period is reduced to an average per year basis.

COLUMN 5

Col. 3 minus col. 4.

COLUMN 6

Col. 5 multiplied by 1.8733, the ratio of total construction in 1919-33 to the cost of materials consumed, both in 1929 prices. Total construction is the sum of (a) new construction, (b) maintenance, and (c) work relief. These series are shown annually in current prices in the following sources: (a) Table I 7, col. 7, above; (b) *Construction Activity in the United States, 1915-37,* by L. J. Chawner (Domestic Commerce Series, 99, Washington, D. C., 1938) for 1919-28, and the *Survey of Current Business,* June 1943 and June 1944, for 1929-33; (c) which begins in 1933, *Survey,* June 1943. Total construction in current prices is converted to 1929 prices by the index of construction costs implicit in new construction (col. 7 of Table I 7 ÷ col. 7 of Table I 8), a revision of the index in *Commodity Flow and Capital Formation,* Vol. One, Table VI-5, line 22. This table (line 19) shows also the cost of materials consumed.

COLUMN 7

LINES 1-13: col. 5 multiplied by 1.4036, the ratio of new construction in 1919-33 (Table I 8, col. 7) to the cost of materials consumed (see note to col. 6), both in 1929 prices.

LINE 14: average of 1909-13, derived by the method used for lines 1-13, and of 1914-18, by the method used for lines 15-18.

LINES 15-18: averages of annual estimates: for 1919-38, from Table I 8, col. 7; for 1914-18, computed by converting the values in current prices (see note to col. 9, lines 15-18) by the procedure indicated in the notes to Table I 8 with the public utility index extrapolated from 1919 by the Richey index given in Solomon Fabricant, *Capital Consumption and Adjustment*, p. 178.

Column 8

LINES 1-8: extrapolation of line 10 by cost of construction index described in Part IV.

LINES 9-13: same as lines 14-18.

LINES 14-18: col. 9 divided by col. 7.

Column 9

LINES 1-13: col. 7 multiplied by col. 8.

LINE 14: average of 1909-13, derived by the method used for lines 1-13, and of 1914-18, by the method used for lines 15-18.

LINES 15-18: averages of annual estimates: for 1919-38, from Table I 7, col. 7. The procedure indicated in the notes to that table yields estimates for 1915-18 also. That for 1915 is extrapolated to 1914 by nonfarm residential construction.

TABLE II 6

Calculation of Flow of Consumer and Producer Durable Commodities Adjusted for Business Use of Passenger Cars, 1899-1923
(dollar figures in millions, averages per year)

	1899-1908	1904-13	1909-18	1914-18	1914-23	1919-28
1 Av. value, passenger cars & accessories used for business, domestic consumption	12.7	53.9	162.1	239.5		666.6
2 % (1) is of domestic consumption of consumer durables	1.5	4.4	8.9	10.8		13.3
3 % (1) is of domestic consumption of producer durables	1.2	3.9	7.2	8.1		15.5
4 Flow of consumer durables, unadj. for business use of passenger cars, current prices	1,403	1,966	2,924	3,660		7,991
5 Flow of consumer durables, adj., current prices	1,382	1,880	2,663	3,265	4,553	6,928
6 Flow of consumer durables, unadj. for business use of passenger cars, 1929 prices	2,922	3,537	4,219	4,670		7,596
7 Flow of consumer durables, adj., 1929 prices	2,878	3,381	3,843	4,166	4,644	6,585
8 Flow of producer durables, unadj. for business use of passenger cars, current prices	1,270	1,598	2,581	3,554		4,965
9 Flow of producer durables, adj., current prices	1,285	1,660	2,767	3,842	4,567	5,735
10 Flow of producer durables, unadj. for business use of passenger cars, 1929 prices	2,550	3,026	3,620	4,151		4,738
11 Flow of producer durables, adj., 1929 prices	2,580	3,144	3,881	4,487	4,670	5,472

LINE

1 It is assumed that 30 percent of the total value of the output of passenger cars and accessories for domestic use is used for business. Annual estimates of total value are from Shaw's data underlying the estimates in *Occasional Paper 3*.

2 & 3 The denominator is from *Occasional Paper 3*, Table 1.

4 Table II 3, col. 7. The 1914-18 average is estimated similarly.

5 Line 4 multiplied by (100% − line 2). The 1914-23 estimate is an average of that for 1914-18 and the average for 1919-23 derived from Table I 3, col. 2.

6 Table II 3, col. 5. The 1914-18 average is estimated similarly.

7 Line 6 multiplied by (100% − line 2). The 1914-23 estimate is an average of that for 1914-18 and the average for 1919-23 derived from Table I 3, col. 6.

… DECADE ESTIMATES, 1869-1939

LINE

8 Table II 4, col. 7. The 1914-18 average is estimated similarly.

9 Line 8 multiplied by (100% + line 3). The 1914-23 estimate is an average of that for 1914-18 and the average for 1919-23 derived from Table I 6, col. 2.

10 Table II 4, col. 5. The 1914-18 average is estimated similarly.

11 Line 10 multiplied by (100% + line 3). The 1914-23 estimate is an average of that for 1914-18 and the average for 1919-23 derived from Table I 6, col. 6.

Table II 7
Services Not Embodied in New Commodities
Averages per Year by Decades, 1869-1938
(all columns except 2 and 4 in millions of dollars)

	FLOW OF COMMODITIES TO ULTIMATE USERS AT FINAL COST Current Prices (1)	RATIO OF SERVICE TO COMMODITY EXPENDITURES BASED ON VALUES IN CURRENT PRICES (2)	SERVICES NOT EMBODIED IN NEW COMMODITIES Current Prices (3)	PRICE INDEX FOR SERVICES 1929:100 (4)	SERVICES NOT EMBODIED IN NEW COMMODITIES 1929 Prices (5)
DECADE ESTIMATES					
1 1869-78	4,210	.3552	1,496	63.4	2,358
2 1874-83	5,291	.3665	1,939	58.7	3,305
3 1879-88	6,264	.3780	2,368	55.8	4,246
4 1884-93	6,770	.3899	2,640	53.9	4,900
5 1889-98	7,127	.4061	2,894	51.5	5,618
6 1894-1903	8,671	.4298	3,727	51.4	7,244
7 1899-1908	11,642	.4569	5,410	55.3	9,784
8 1904-13	15,559	.4846	7,540	60.1	12,540
9 1909-18	21,830	.4567	9,970	69.6	14,319
10 1914-23	33,200	.4602	15,277	86.6	17,647
AVERAGES OF ANNUAL ESTIMATES					
11 1919-28	42,254	.5217	22,043	98.4	22,393
12 1924-33	40,678	.6084	24,750	98.2	25,210
13 1929-38	37,212	.6133	22,823	89.2	25,591

Column 1
Flow of perishable, semidurable, and consumer durable commodities.

LINES 1-6: Tables II 1-II 3, col. 7, lines 1-6.

LINES 7-9: Tables II 1 and II 2, col. 7, lines 7-9, plus Table II 6, line 5.

LINE 10: Tables II 1 and II 2, col. 7, line 14, plus Table II 6, line 5.

LINES 11-13: Tables II 1 and II 2, col. 7, lines 15-17, plus Table II 3, lines 14-16.

Column 2
LINES 1-9: Extrapolation of line 11 by ratios derived for 1909-18 from over-all estimates of consumers' outlay by W. H. Lough (*High-Level Consumption;* McGraw-Hill, 1935), and for 1869-1908 from sample expenditure data on low-income urban workers (selected from various state reports) supplemented by data for all consumer groups (*Family Expenditures in the United States;* National Resources Planning Board; Washington, D. C., 1941; and *Family Spending and Saving in Wartime;* preliminary releases by the Department of Agriculture, Bureau of Home Economics; and 'Income and Spending and Saving of City Families in Wartime', *Monthly Labor Review,* Sept. 1942). See Part III for a detailed description of the basic material and the procedures followed.

LINES 10-13: col. 3 divided by col. 1.

Column 3
LINES 1-9: col. 1 multiplied by col. 2.

LINE 10: average of 1914-18, derived by the method indicated for lines 1-9, and of 1919-23, by the method indicated for lines 11-13.

LINES 11-13: averages of annual estimates in Table I 4A, col. 2.

COLUMN 4
Col. 3 divided by col. 5.

COLUMN 5
LINES 1-9: sums of separate estimates of rent and 'other' services derived by converting the current price values of each to 1929 levels. Values in current prices are derived from col. 3 by ratios extrapolated from 1919-28 (for which decade they are ascertainable from data underlying the national income estimates) on the basis of the sample data described in the notes to col. 2. See Part III for a detailed description of the basic material and the procedures followed.

Conversion of rents to 1929 prices is by the BLS cost index extrapolated from 1913 by an index based upon an unpublished study by the Russell Sage Foundation (see *Business Cycles and Business Measurements* by Carl Snyder; Macmillan, 1927; pp. 137 and 291).

Conversion of 'other' services to 1929 prices is by the price index implicit in consumer commodities (derived from Tables II 1, II 2, II 3, and II 6 by dividing the total in current prices by the total in 1929 prices).

LINE 10: average of estimates for 1914-18, derived by the method indicated for lines 1-9, and for 1919-23, by the method indicated for lines 11-13.

LINES 11-13: averages of annual estimates in Table I 4A, col. 5.

TABLE II 8: Flow of Goods to Consumers, Averages per Year by Decades, 1869-1938 (millions of dollars)

	CURRENT PRICES					1929 PRICES				
	Perishable (1)	Semi-durable (2)	Durable (3)	Services (4)	Flow of Goods to Consumers (5)	Perishable (6)	Semi-durable (7)	Durable (8)	Services (9)	Flow of Goods to Consumers (10)
DECADE ESTIMATES										
1 1869-78	2,573	1,167	470	1,496	5,706	3,467	1,546	686	2,358	8,056
2 1874-83	3,360	1,381	549	1,939	7,230	5,244	2,128	972	3,305	11,649
3 1879-88	3,964	1,616	685	2,368	8,632	6,882	2,757	1,375	4,246	15,260
4 1884-93	4,219	1,748	804	2,640	9,410	7,769	3,244	1,747	4,900	17,660
5 1889-98	4,535	1,772	820	2,894	10,021	8,980	3,669	1,980	5,618	20,248
6 1894-1903	5,657	2,043	971	3,727	12,398	11,336	4,413	2,363	7,244	25,356
7 1899-1908	7,642	2,818	1,382	5,410	17,252	14,100	5,503	2,878	9,784	32,265
8 1904-13	10,005	3,675	1,880	7,540	23,099	16,619	6,573	3,381	12,540	39,114
9 1909-18	13,976	5,190	2,663	9,970	31,799	18,487	7,320	3,843	14,319	43,970
10 1914-23	20,123	8,525	4,553	15,277	48,478	20,514	7,914	4,644	17,647	50,719
AVERAGES OF ANNUAL ESTIMATES										
11 1919-28	24,505	10,889	6,860	22,043	64,298	23,895	9,190	6,554	22,393	62,031
12 1924-33	23,893	10,080	6,705	24,750	65,428	26,456	10,252	6,982	25,210	68,900
13 1929-38	23,243	8,495	5,475	22,823	60,036	29,391	9,940	6,080	25,591	71,002

COLUMN 1
LINES 1-9: Table II 1, col. 7, lines 1-9.
LINES 10-13: *ibid.*, lines 14-17.

COLUMN 2
LINES 1-9: Table II 2, col. 7, lines 1-9.
LINES 10-13: *ibid.*, lines 14-17.

COLUMN 3
LINES 1-6: Table II 3, col. 7, lines 1-6.
LINES 7-10: Table II 6, line 5.
LINES 11-13: Table II 3, col. 7, lines 14-16.

COLUMN 4
Table II 7, col. 3.

COLUMN 5
Sum of col. 1-4.

COLUMN 6
LINES 1-9: Table II 1, col. 5, lines 1-9.
LINES 10-13: *ibid.*, lines 14-17.

COLUMN 7
LINES 1-9: Table II 2, col. 5, lines 1-9.
LINES 10-13: *ibid.*, lines 14-17.

COLUMN 8
LINES 1-6: Table II 3, col. 5, lines 1-6.
LINES 7-10: Table II 6, line 7.
LINES 11-13: Table II 3, col. 5, lines 14-16.

COLUMN 9
Table II 7, col. 5.

COLUMN 10
Sum of col. 6-9.

TABLE II 9

Flow of Goods to Consumers, Per Capita and Per Consuming Unit
Averages per Year by Decades, 1929 Prices, 1869-1938

	POPULATION	CONSUMING UNITS	FLOW OF GOODS TO CONSUMERS	
			Per Capita	Per Consuming Unit
	(thousands)		(dollars)	
	(1)	(2)	(3)	(4)
DECADE ESTIMATES				
1 1869-78	43,541	28,981	185	278
2 1874-83	48,847	32,923	238	354
3 1879-88	54,762	37,370	279	408
4 1884-93	61,152	42,250	289	418
5 1889-98	67,625	47,067	299	430
6 1894-1903	74,269	51,973	341	488
7 1899-1908	81,540	57,363	396	562
8 1904-13	89,646	63,407	436	617
9 1909-18	97,743	69,417	450	633
10 1914-23	104,963	74,807	483	678
AVERAGES OF ANNUAL ESTIMATES				
11 1919-28	112,841	80,715	550	769
12 1924-33	120,619	86,580	571	796
13 1929-38	125,963	90,517	564	784

COLUMN

1 *Statistical Abstract, 1942*, p. 11, decade averages.

2 Thompson & Whelpton, *Population Trends in the United States* (McGraw-Hill, 1933), p. 169, for 1870, 1890, 1910, and 1930; interpolated on the basis of total population.

3 Col. 10 of Table II 8 divided by col. 1.

4 Col. 10 of Table II 8 divided by col. 2.

TABLE II 10

Net Changes in Inventories
Averages per Year by Decades, 1929 Prices, 1869-1938
(millions of dollars)

	FARM								TOTAL EXCL.
	Crops	Live-stock	MIN-ING	MFG.	CON-STRUC-TION	TRADE	TOTAL COL. 1-6	ALL OTHER	MONE-TARY METALS
	(1)	(2)	(3)	(4)	(5)	(6)	(7)	(8)	(9)

DECADE ESTIMATES

		(1)	(2)	(3)	(4)	(5)	(6)	(7)	(8)	(9)
1	1869-78	+17	+128	+2	+113	+8	+95	+363	+34	+397
2	1874-83	+16	+160	+2	+194	+14	+139	+525	+49	+574
3	1879-88	+29	+170	+4	+149	+22	+104	+479	+45	+524
4	1884-93	+28	+52	+6	+126	+27	+85	+324	+30	+354
5	1889-98	+28	+9	+8	+139	+17	+120	+322	+30	+352
6	1894-1903	+27	+127	+10	+370	+15	+180	+729	+68	+797
7	1899-1908	+22	+64	+13	+187	+34	+163	+483	+45	+528
8	1904-13	+15	−22	+14	+374	+33	+252	+665	+62	+728
9	1909-18	+10	+112	+14	+306	−12	+358	+787	+74	+861
10	1914-23	+3	+42	+11	+498	+12	+513	+1,080	+101	+1,180
11	1919-28	−7	−148	+7	+510	+56	+525	+944	+88	+1,032
12	1924-33	+8	+20	+10	−248	−66	−230	−506	−47	−553
13	1929-38	−4	+18	+6	−253	−48	−98	−380	−36	−415

AVERAGES OF ANNUAL ESTIMATES

		(1)	(2)	(3)	(4)	(5)	(6)	(7)	(8)	(9)
14	1919-28	+14	−81	+10	+567	+56	+515	+1,080	+101	+1,181
15	1924-33	−35	−7	−14	−95	+23	−183	−311	−17	−328
16	1929-38	+28	−6	a	a	+93	−138	−22[b]	−172[c]	−194

a Included with 'all other'.   b Excluding mining and manufacturing.
c Including mining and manufacturing.

COLUMN 1

LINES 1-13: the total net change for each period is the difference between inventories in the terminal years estimated on the basis of their relation to output during the period. For each decade an index of physical output is derived, the data for 1869-1937 being those for 12 important crops recorded annually in *Gross Farm Income and Indices of Farm Production and Prices in the United States, 1869-1937*, p. 130. For 1938, these are extrapolated by data for 22 field crops (*Statistical Abstract, 1941*). The ratio of inventories as of December 31, 1918 and 1928, in 1929 prices (*Commodity Flow and Capital Formation,* Vol. One, Table VII-4) to the average index of output for 1919-28 is multiplied by the average index of output for the other periods to yield beginning and end of period inventories for each. This procedure yields two figures for each date (one by applying the beginning of the period ratio for the following period, the other by applying the end of the period ratio for the current period), which are averaged. (For the beginning of the first two decades, and for the end of the last two, only a single estimate is derived; this affects but slightly the comparability of the estimates for these decades and the others.) Finally, the total net change for each period is reduced to an average per year basis.

LINES 14-16: averages of the annual estimates of crop changes described in the note to Table I 11, col. 1.

COLUMN 2

LINES 1-13: sums of net changes in the inventories of horses and mules on farms, cattle (including calves and milk cows), hogs, sheep and lambs. The total net change for each period in the number of horses and mules on farms (the difference between the number on January 1 of the first year of the period and January 1 of the year following the close of the period), derived from *Agricultural Statistics, 1940,* is multiplied by 1929 prices. For cattle, hogs, sheep and lambs, the total net change in liveweight during each period (recorded annually for 1869-1937 in *Gross Farm Income and Indices of Farm Production and Prices in the United States, 1869-1937,* and derived for 1938 from the series on number in *Agricultural Statistics, 1940*) is multiplied by 1929 prices. The price data (average of farm prices on January 1, 1929 and 1930) are from the same sources as those on number and liveweight. Finally, the total net change for each period is reduced to an average per year basis.

LINES 14-16: averages of the annual estimates of livestock changes described in the note to Table I 11, col. 1.

Column 3

LINES 1-13: the total net change for each period is the difference between inventories in the terminal years as estimated on the basis of their relation to output during the period. For each decade, an index of physical output is computed from annual data recorded for 1869-1930 in *Forecasting Business Cycles* by W. M. Persons (Wiley, 1931), pp. 170-1, and extrapolated through 1938 by the Federal Reserve Board index of production (*Statistical Abstract, 1941*). Stocks as of December 31, 1918 and 1928, in current prices (*Commodity Flow and Capital Formation,* Vol. One, Table VII-6, lines A2a, A2b, C1a, and C1b) are converted to 1929 prices by the appropriate indexes in *ibid.,* Table VII-7. The ratio of these beginning and end of period inventories to the average index of output for 1919-28 is multiplied by the average index of output for the other periods to yield beginning and end of period inventories for each. This procedure yields two figures for each date (see note to col. 1, lines 1-13), which are averaged. Finally, the total net change for each period is reduced to an average per year basis.

LINES 14-16: averages of annual estimates in Table I 11, col. 2.

Column 4

LINES 1-13: net changes in inventories of manufactured perishable, semidurable, consumer durable, and producer durable commodities estimated on the basis of their relation to changes in output. The total net change in output for each period, estimated as the difference between the output in the terminal years in 1929 prices (see notes to col. 2 of Tables II 1-II 4), is multiplied by the ratio of the total net change in inventories, 1919-28, to the total net change in output from 1919 to 1928. Data for annual net changes in inventories, 1919-28, are from *Commodity Flow and Capital Formation,* Vol. One, Table VII-9, line 1 under Manufacturers'; those for output, from *ibid.,* Table II-7. Finally, the total net change for each period is reduced to an average per year basis.

LINES 14-16: averages of annual estimates in Table I 11, col. 3.

Column 5

LINES 1-13: net changes in stocks held by consumers, estimated by multiplying net changes in all construction inventories by the ratio for 1919-28 of net changes in stocks held by consumers to net changes in all construction inventories (see Table II 5, col. 4, and the notes).

LINES 14-16: averages of annual estimates in Table I 11, col. 4.

Column 6

LINES 1-13: the total net change in sales for each period in 1929 prices (the difference between sales in the terminal years) multiplied by the ratio of the total net change in inventories, 1919-28, to the total net change in sales from 1919 to 1928. Annual

Table II 10 concluded:

COLUMN 6 (*concl.*)

net changes in inventories, 1919-28, are given in *Commodity Flow and Capital Formation*, Vol. One, Table VII-9. Sales in 1919 and 1928 in current prices, by type of commodity (*ibid.*, Tables VII-5 and V-5, final approximation), are converted to 1929 prices by the appropriate indexes in *ibid.*, Table VII-7 and in Note A to Table V-7, and added. Total sales in 1929 prices for terminal years of periods back to 1899-1908 and forward to 1929-38 are extrapolated from 1919-28 by N. H. Engle's index of the physical volume of goods marketed at wholesale (given in the *Survey of Current Business*, May 1936, p. 18, through 1935, and extended through 1938 by the volume of wholesale trade and by sales by service and limited function wholesalers, both presented in the *Statistical Abstract, 1941*). Extrapolation of total sales from 1899-1908 for the terminal years of the periods back to 1869-78 is by a weighted index of crops (weight 2), slaughter of cattle, etc. (weight 1), mining (weight 1), and manufacturing (weight 6). The index of cattle slaughter is from *Gross Farm Income and Indices of Farm Production and Prices in the United States, 1869-1937*. The other series are described in the notes to col. 1, 3, and 4. The total net change in sales, 1894-1903, is the sum of total net changes for 1894-98 (estimated by the procedure indicated for the decades before 1899-1908) and for 1899-1903 (estimated by the procedure indicated for the decade 1899-1908). Finally, the total net change in inventories for each period is reduced to an average per year basis.

LINES 14-16: averages of annual estimates in Table I 11, col. 5.

COLUMN 8

LINES 1-13: col. 7 multiplied by .0935, representing the relation in 1919-28 of 'all other' to the total excluding 'all other' (see line 14, col. 7 and 8).

LINES 14-16: averages of annual estimates in Table I 11, col. 7.

COLUMN 9

LINES 1-16: col. 7 plus col. 8.

TABLE II 11

Net Changes in Inventories, Averages per Year by Decades, 1869-1938
(all columns except 2 in millions of dollars)

	TOTAL EXCL. MONETARY METALS 1929 Prices (1)	PRICE INDEX 1929: 100 (2)	TOTAL EXCL. MONETARY METALS Current Prices (3)	NET CHANGES IN STOCKS OF MONETARY METALS Current Prices (4)	TOTAL INCL. MONETARY METALS Current Prices (5)	NET CHANGES IN STOCKS OF MONETARY METALS 1929 Prices (6)	TOTAL INCL. MONETARY METALS 1929 Prices (7)
DECADE ESTIMATES							
1 1869-78	+397	83.0	+329	+51	+380	+46	+443
2 1874-83	+574	71.2	+409	+53	+462	+41	+616
3 1879-88	+524	63.6	+333	+52	+386	+40	+563
4 1884-93	+354	59.0	+209	+57	+265	+42	+395
5 1889-98	+352	53.8	+189	+42	+231	+36	+388
6 1894-1903	+797	54.6	+435	+47	+482	+48	+844
7 1899-1908	+528	62.1	+328	+71	+399	+71	+599
8 1904-13	+728	68.4	+498	+72	+570	+72	+799
9 1909-18	+861	85.4	+735	+52	+787	+53	+914
10 1914-23	+1,180	111.2	+1,313	+24	+1,337*	+27	+1,208*
11 1919-28	+1,032	113.5	+1,171	+18	+1,189	+20	+1,052
12 1924-33	−553	92.2	−510	+29	−481	+29	−524
13 1929-38	−415	82.5	−342	+122	−220	+126	−290
AVERAGES OF ANNUAL ESTIMATES							
14 1919-28	+1,181		+1,738	+18	+1,756	+20	+1,201
15 1924-33	−328		−126	+29	−97	+29	−299
16 1929-38	−194		−37	+122	+85	+126	−68

* The estimate for 1914-23 used in the summary tables and equal to the average of 1914-18, derived by the method used for lines 1-13, and of 1919-23, derived by the method used for lines 14-16, is $1,822 million in current prices and $1,334 million in 1929 prices.

Column 1
Col. 9 of Table II 10.

Column 2
BLS wholesale price index for all commodities adjusted to a 1929 base.

Column 3
LINES 1-13: col. 1 multiplied by col. 2.

LINES 14-16: averages of annual estimates calculated from Table I 11 by deducting col. 6 from col. 8.

Column 4
The estimates for the decades in 1919-38 are not strictly comparable with those covering the preceding years, owing to a difference in the procedure by which the net change in silver bullion was estimated. The series has been treated as continuous, however.

LINES 1-9: net changes in total stocks of gold, of silver bullion held in mints and assay offices, and of silver coin, minus the net change in gold stocks due to international flow. The total net change for each period is derived, then reduced to an average per year basis.

The total net change in gold stocks for each period is estimated as the difference

Table II 11 concluded:

COLUMN 4 *(concl.)*

between the values in the terminal years (*Annual Report of the Director of the Mint*).

The total net change for each period in fine ounces of silver bullion held in mints and assay offices (the difference in stocks as of June 30 in the year preceding the period and that in the year terminating it) is multiplied by the price per fine ounce of silver at New York (average of annual prices for the period). Quantity and price data are from *ibid*.

The total net change for each period in the dollar value of stocks of silver coin (the difference in value as of June 30 in the year preceding the period and that in the year terminating it) is multiplied by the bullion value of the silver dollar at the average price of silver (average of annual prices for the period). Dollar values and price data are from *ibid*.

The total net change for each period in gold stocks due to the inflow and outflow of gold is derived from annual data on imports and exports recorded for 1869-78 in the *Statistical Abstract, 1913*, p. 461, and for other years in 'The Balance of Trade of the United States', by C. J. Bullock, J. H. Williams, and R. S. Tucker (*Review of Economic Statistics*, July 1919).

LINE 10: for the total net change in gold stocks and the net change due to international flow, the procedure is that indicated in the note to lines 1-9. For the total net change for the period in stocks of silver bullion and of silver coin, estimates for 1914-18 and 1919-23 are added. For 1914-18, the procedure is that indicated in the note to lines 1-9; for 1919-23, annual estimates in *Commodity Flow and Capital Formation*, Vol. One, Table VII-11, are added. Finally, the total net change for the period is reduced to an average per year basis.

LINES 11-13: same as lines 14-16.

LINES 14-16: averages of annual estimates in Table I 11, col. 6.

COLUMN 5

Col. 3 plus col. 4.

COLUMN 6

LINES 1-9: components of col. 4 converted to 1929 prices and added. The net change in gold stocks is the same in 1929 prices as in current. Net changes in stocks of silver bullion and in stocks of silver coin are derived by the method followed in estimating the net changes in current prices, the 1929 price being substituted for the average price for each period (see note to col. 4, lines 1-9).

LINE 10: components of col. 4 converted to 1929 prices and added. The net change in gold stocks is the same in 1929 prices as in current. Net changes in stocks of silver bullion and of silver coin are averages of estimates for 1914-18 and 1919-23. For 1914-18, the procedure (identical with that for later years) is that indicated in the note to lines 1-9; for 1919-23, annual estimates in *Commodity Flow and Capital Formation*, Vol. One, Table VII-11, are averaged.

LINES 11-13: same as lines 14-16.

LINES 14-16: averages of annual estimates in Table I 11, col. 6.

COLUMN 7

Col. 1 plus col. 6.

Table II 12

Net Changes in Claims Against Foreign Countries
Averages per Year by Decades, 1869-1938

(all columns except 3 in millions of dollars; + indicates an excess of exports over imports or of additions to claims over reductions in claims; —, an excess of imports over exports or of reductions over additions)

	NET BALANCE OF MDSE. & SILVER MOVEMENT Current Prices	FULL NET BALANCE OF CLAIMS Current Prices	PRICE INDEX 1929:100	FULL NET BALANCE OF CLAIMS 1929 Prices
	(1)	(2)	(3)	(4)
DECADE ESTIMATES				
1 1869-78	+42	−116	83.0	−140
2 1874-83	+146	−67	71.2	−94
3 1879-88	+93	−43	63.6	−68
4 1884-93	+89	−41	59.0	−69
5 1889-98	+237	−0.81	53.8	−1.51
6 1894-1903	+441	−47	54.6	−86
7 1899-1908	+513	−59	62.1	−95
8 1904-13	+495	−57	68.4	−84
9 1909-18	+1,430	+984	85.4	+1,152
10 1914-23		+1,887	110.6	+1,706
AVERAGES OF ANNUAL ESTIMATES				
11 1919-28		+968	125.6	+770
12 1924-33		+365	95.9	+380
13 1929-38		+202	83.7	+241

Column 1
Averages of annual estimates calculated as the difference between exports and imports of merchandise and silver (recorded annually in Bullock, Williams, and Tucker, *op. cit.*).

Column 2
LINES 1-8: col. 1 divided by the ratio of the net balance of merchandise and silver movement to the full net balance of claims (computed from data recorded in *ibid.*). The full net balance of claims is the sum of the net balances in the following commodity and service items, whenever reported: merchandise trade, interest charges, freight charges, charter of vessels, tourist expenditures, immigrant remittances, and miscellaneous. Since data for this ratio are not reported for the exact periods covered in col. 1, the ratios for those periods in the source material most closely approximating those in col. 1 are used. For some decades better conformity in the coverage of the ratio and of col. 1 is achieved by dividing col. 1 into shorter periods. The sum of the full net balance of claims for these shorter periods yields decade estimates, which are reduced to a per year basis. The ratios used, the years they cover, and the periods to which they are applied are listed herewith.

PERIOD TO WHICH RATIO IS APPLIED	YEARS COVERED BY RATIO	RATIO
1869-78		
1870-73 (fiscal years)	1850-73 (fiscal years)	.5455
1874-79 (fiscal years)	1874-95 (fiscal years)	−2.1728
1874-83 (1875-84, fiscal years)	1874-95 (fiscal years)	−2.1728
1879-88 (1880-89, fiscal years)	1874-95 (fiscal years)	−2.1728
1884-93 (1885-94, fiscal years)	1874-95 (fiscal years)	−2.1728

Table II 12 concluded:

COLUMN 2 *(concl.)*

PERIOD TO WHICH RATIO IS APPLIED	YEARS COVERED BY RATIO	RATIO
1889-98		
1890-95 (fiscal years)	1894 (fiscal year)	3.9507
1896-99 (fiscal years)	1896-1914 (fiscal years)	−8.665
1894-1903		
1895 (fiscal year)	1894 (fiscal year)	3.9507
1896-1904 (fiscal years)	1896-1914 (fiscal years)	−8.665
1899-1908 (1900-09, fiscal years)	1896-1914 (fiscal years)	−8.665
1904-13 (1905-14, fiscal years)	1896-1914 (fiscal years)	−8.665
1909-18		
1910-14 (fiscal years)	1909	−1.5647
1914-18	actual net claims reported	

LINE 9: average of 1909-13 and 1914-18. For 1909-13 the procedure is that indicated in the note to lines 1-8; 1914-18 is an average of annual data reported in the source cited in the note to col. 1.

LINE 10: averages of 1914-18 and 1919-23. For 1914-18, see note to line 9; 1919-23 is an average of annual estimates in Table I 11, col. 9.

LINES 11-13: averages of annual estimates in Table I 11, col. 9.

COLUMN 3

LINES 1-9: BLS wholesale price index for all commodities adjusted to a 1929 base.

LINES 10-13: col. 2 divided by col. 4.

COLUMN 4

LINES 1-9: col. 2 divided by col. 3.

LINE 10: average of 1914-18 and 1919-23. For 1914-18 the procedure is that indicated in the note to lines 1-9 (for col. 2, see the note to col. 2, line 9; for col. 3, the source is that cited in the note to col. 3, lines 1-9); 1919-23 is an average of annual estimates in Table I 11, col. 9.

LINES 11-13: averages of annual estimates in Table I 11, col. 9.

TABLE II 13: Gross Capital Formation, Averages per Year by Decades, 1869-1938 (millions of dollars)

	CURRENT PRICES					1929 PRICES				
	Gross Producer Durable (1)	Gross Construction (2)	Net Changes in Inventories (3)	Net Changes in Claims Against Foreign Countries (4)	Gross Capital Formation (5)	Gross Producer Durable (6)	Gross Construction (7)	Net Changes in Inventories (8)	Net Changes in Claims Against Foreign Countries (9)	Gross Capital Formation (10)

DECADE ESTIMATES

#	Year										
1	1869-78	362	702	380	-116	1,328	479	1,496	443	-140	2,278
2	1874-83	459	841	462	-67	1,694	752	1,920	616	-94	3,192
3	1879-88	551	1,162	386	-43	2,056	1,027	2,679	563	-68	4,202
4	1884-93	585	1,662	265	-41	2,472	1,236	3,921	395	-69	5,483
5	1889-98	617	1,862	231	-1	2,709	1,422	4,690	388	-2	6,499
6	1894-1903	839	2,036	482	-47	3,311	1,823	4,992	844	-86	7,573
7	1899-1908	1,285	2,708	399	-59	4,332	2,580	5,848	599	-95	8,932
8	1904-13	1,660	3,512	570	-57	5,684	3,144	6,873	799	-84	10,733
9	1909-18	2,767	3,784	787	984	8,323	3,881	6,609	914	1,153	12,556
10	1914-23	4,567	5,141	1,822	1,887	13,417	4,670	6,114	1,334	1,706	13,824

AVERAGES OF ANNUAL ESTIMATES

11	1919-28	5,650	8,528	1,756	968	16,901	5,479	8,310	1,201	770	15,760
12	1924-33	5,129	8,303	-97	365	13,699	5,335	8,504	-299	380	13,920
13	1929-38	4,356	5,274	85	202	9,917	4,774	5,797	-68	241	10,743

COLUMN 1
LINES 1-6: Table II 4, col. 7, lines 1-6.
LINES 7-10: Table II 6, line 9.
LINES 11-13: Table II 4, col. 7, lines 14-16.

COLUMN 2
LINES 1-8: Table II 5, col. 9, lines 1-8.
LINES 9-13: ibid., lines 14-18.

COLUMN 3
LINES 1-9: Table II 11, col. 5, lines 1-9.
LINE 10: ibid., footnote to line 10.
LINES 11-13: ibid., lines 14-16.

COLUMN 4
Table II 12, col. 2.

COLUMN 5
Sum of col. 1-4.

COLUMN 6
LINES 1-6: Table II 4, col. 5, lines 1-6.
LINES 7-10: Table II 6, line 11.
LINES 11-13: Table II 4, col. 5, lines 14-16.

COLUMN 7
LINES 1-8: Table II 5, col. 7, lines 1-8.
LINES 9-13: ibid., lines 14-18.

COLUMN 8
LINES 1-9: Table II 11, col. 7, lines 1-9.
LINE 10: ibid., footnote to line 10.
LINES 11-13: ibid., lines 14-16.

COLUMN 9
Table II 12, col. 4.

COLUMN 10
Sum of col. 6-9.

TABLE II 14

Consumption and Net Production, Producer Durable Commodities and Construction, Averages per Year by Decades, 1869-1938
(millions of dollars)

	CONSUMPTION OF PRODUCER DURABLES 1929 Prices (1)	NET PRODUCER DURABLES 1929 Prices (2)	Current Prices (3)	CONSUMPTION OF CONSTRUCTION 1929 Prices (4)	NET CONSTRUCTION 1929 Prices (5)	Current Prices (6)
DECADE ESTIMATES						
1 1869-78	274	204	155	720	776	365
2 1874-83	401	351	215	840	1,080	473
3 1879-88	579	448	241	1,008	1,670	726
4 1884-93	807	429	204	1,293	2,627	1,115
5 1889-98	1,026	396	172	1,550	3,140	1,247
6 1894-1903	1,230	593	274	1,947	3,044	1,243
7 1899-1908	1,544	1,037	518	2,329	3,519	1,631
8 1904-13	2,010	1,134	600	2,844	4,029	2,061
9 1909-18	2,524	1,356	970	3,344[a]	3,953[b]	2,268[b]
10 1914-23	3,142	1,529	1,493	4,132	1,982	1,644
AVERAGES OF ANNUAL ESTIMATES						
11 1919-28	3,878	1,601	1,592	4,866	3,444	3,547
12 1924-33	4,497	838	930	5,058	3,446	3,513
13 1929-38	4,472	301	315	5,227	570	637

[a] Consumption, comparable with construction in Table II 5, line 14, and used in the summary tables, is $1,984 million in current prices and $3,442 million in 1929 prices.

[b] Net construction, comparable with Table II 5, line 14, and used in the summary tables, is $1,801 million in current prices and $3,167 million in 1929 prices.

COLUMN 1

LINES 1-10: extrapolated from line 11 by averages of annual estimates derived for any given year as the arithmetic mean of the flow (before inventory change) of producer durable commodities for the thirteen preceding years. Annual estimates of the flow are calculated by multiplying output adjusted for the business use of passenger cars (see notes to Table II 4, col. 1 and 2, and Table II 6, line 1) by the mark-up ratio described in the note to Table II 4, col. 3.

LINES 11-13: averages of annual estimates derived by apportioning total consumption of capital goods excluding war (Table I 16, col. 10) between producer durable commodities and construction on the basis of the distribution of the series underlying col. 1 and 4, lines 1-10, extended through the 1919-28 decade.

COLUMN 2

LINES 1-6: col. 5 of Table II 4 minus col. 1.

LINES 7-10: line 11 of Table II 6 minus col. 1.

LINES 11-13: col. 5 of Table II 4, lines 14-16, minus col. 1.

COLUMN 3

LINES 1-9: col. 2 multiplied by col. 6 of Table II 4 (i.e., col. 7 of Table II 4, lines 1-6, and line 9 of Table II 6 minus the product of col. 1, lines 1-9, and col. 6 of Table II 4, lines 1-9).

LINE 10: average of 1914-18, derived by the method used for lines 1-9, and of 1919-23, derived by the method used for lines 11-13.

LINES 11-13: difference between the flow of producer durables at final cost (Table II 4, col. 7, lines 14-16) and consumption, estimated by a procedure analogous to that by which the values in 1929 prices (see notes to col. 1, lines 11-13) were derived.

Column 4

LINES 1, 3-9: line 11 minus consumption of war construction (Table I 10, col. 6) extrapolated by estimates derived for any given decade as the arithmetic mean of new construction for the five preceding decades and the current decade, the two terminal decades being given half weight. New construction for 1869-78 and later decades is shown in Table II 5. The value for 1869-78, in 1929 prices, is extrapolated for 1819-28, 1829-38, 1839-48, 1849-58, and 1859-68 by an index combining (a) net changes in population in places of 2,500 and over (weighted 5), (b) net changes in population of places under 2,500 (weighted 2) (both derived from *Population Trends in the United States,* p. 20), and (c) net changes in national income adjusted by the cost of living (weighted 3) (from *National Income in the United States, 1799-1938* by R. F. Martin). The value of new construction, 1834-43, is by straight line interpolation between values for 1829-38 and 1839-48. The values for 1844-53, 1854-63, and 1864-73 are interpolated between those for 1839-48, 1849-58, 1859-68, and 1869-78 by decade averages, at 5-year intervals, of the value of building permits per capita in 1913 prices, for varying numbers of cities, derived from unpublished estimates prepared by J. R. Riggleman.

LINE 2: interpolated between lines 1 and 3 with col. 1 as index.

LINE 10: estimate for 1914-23 comparable with lines 1-9 plus consumption of war construction estimated by the procedure indicated for Table I 10, col. 5.

LINES 11-13: averages of annual estimates. See notes to col. 1, lines 11-13, for the method of deriving consumption of construction excluding war consumption (for the latter see Table I 10, col. 6).

Column 5

Col. 7 of Table II 5 minus col. 4.

Column 6

LINES 1-9: col. 5 multiplied by col. 8 of Table II 5 (i.e., col. 9 of Table II 5 minus the product of col. 4, lines 1-9, and col. 8 of Table II 5, lines 1-9).

LINES 10-13: difference between total new construction (Table II 5, col. 9) and consumption, estimated by a procedure analogous to that by which the values in 1929 prices (see notes to col. 4 and col. 1, lines 10-13) were derived.

TABLE II 15

Net Capital Formation, Averages per Year by Decades, 1869-1938

(millions of dollars)

	CURRENT PRICES					1929 PRICES				
	Net Producer Durables (1)	Net Construction (2)	Net Changes in Inventories (3)	Net Changes in Claims against Foreign Countries (4)	Net Capital Formation (5)	Net Producer Durables (6)	Net Construction (7)	Net Changes in Inventories (8)	Net Changes in Claims against Foreign Countries (9)	Net Capital Formation (10)
DECADE ESTIMATES										
1 1869-78	155	365	380	−116	784	204	776	443	−140	1,284
2 1874-83	215	473	462	−67	1,082	351	1,080	616	−94	1,952
3 1879-88	241	726	386	−43	1,309	448	1,670	563	−68	2,615
4 1884-93	204	1,115	265	−41	1,543	429	2,627	395	−69	3,382
5 1889-98	172	1,247	231	−1	1,650	396	3,140	388	−2	3,922
6 1894-1903	274	1,243	482	−47	1,952	593	3,044	844	−86	4,395
7 1899-1908	518	1,631	399	−59	2,488	1,037	3,519	599	−95	5,059
8 1904-13	600	2,061	570	−57	3,174	1,134	4,029	799	−84	5,878
9 1909-18	970	1,801	787	984	4,542	1,356	3,167	914	1,153	6,590
10 1914-23	1,493	1,644	1,822	1,887	6,846	1,529	1,982	1,334	1,706	6,550
AVERAGES OF ANNUAL ESTIMATES										
11 1919-28	1,592	3,547	1,756	968	7,863	1,601	3,444	1,201	770	7,016
12 1924-33	930	3,513	−97	365	4,711	838	3,446	−299	380	4,365
13 1929-38	315	637	85	202	1,239	301	570	−68	241	1,044

COLUMN 1
Table II 14, col. 3.

COLUMN 2
LINES 1-8: Table II 14, col. 6, lines 1-8.
LINE 9: *ibid.*, footnote b to line 9.
LINES 10-13: *ibid.*, lines 14-17.

COLUMNS 3 & 4
See Table II 13, notes to col. 3 and 4.

COLUMN 5
Sum of col. 1-4.

COLUMN 6
Table II 14, col. 2.

COLUMN 7
LINES 1-8: Table II 14, col. 5, lines 1-8.
LINE 9: *ibid.*, footnote b to line 9.
LINES 10-13: *ibid.*, lines 14-17.

COLUMNS 8 & 9
See Table II 13, notes to col. 8 and 9.

COLUMN 10
Sum of col. 6-9.

TABLE II 16

Gross and Net National Product,* Averages per Year by Decades, 1869-1938

(millions of dollars)

	CURRENT PRICES					1929 PRICES				
	FLOW OF GOODS TO CONSUMERS	CAPITAL FORMATION		NATIONAL PRODUCT		FLOW OF GOODS TO CONSUMERS	CAPITAL FORMATION		NATIONAL PRODUCT	
		Gross	Net	Gross	Net		Gross	Net	Gross	Net
	(1)	(2)	(3)	(4)	(5)	(6)	(7)	(8)	(9)	(10)
DECADE ESTIMATES
1 1869-78	5,706	1,328	784	7,033	6,489	8,056	2,278	1,284	10,334	9,340
2 1874-83	7,230	1,694	1,082	8,924	8,312	11,649	3,192	1,952	14,842	13,601
3 1879-88	8,632	2,056	1,309	10,688	9,941	15,260	4,202	2,615	19,462	17,875
4 1884-93	9,410	2,472	1,543	11,882	10,953	17,660	5,483	3,382	23,143	21,042
5 1889-98	10,021	2,709	1,650	12,730	11,671	20,248	6,499	3,922	26,747	24,170
6 1894-1903	12,398	3,311	1,952	15,709	14,350	25,356	7,573	4,395	32,929	29,751
7 1899-1908	17,252	4,332	2,488	21,584	19,740	32,265	8,932	5,059	41,197	37,324
8 1904-13	23,099	5,684	3,174	28,783	26,273	39,114	10,733	5,878	49,847	44,992
9 1909-18	31,799	8,323	4,542	40,122	36,341	43,970	12,556	6,590	56,526	50,560
10 1914-23	48,478	13,417	6,846	61,895	55,324	50,719	13,824	6,550	64,543	57,269
AVERAGES OF ANNUAL ESTIMATES
11 1919-28	64,298	16,901	7,863	81,199	72,160	62,031	15,760	7,016	77,791	69,047
12 1924-33	65,428	13,699	4,711	79,127	70,139	68,900	13,920	4,365	82,820	73,265
13 1929-38	60,036	9,917	1,239	69,952	61,274	71,002	10,743	1,044	81,745	72,045

* Peacetime concept, see Part I.

COLUMN
1 Table II 8, col. 5.
2 Table II 13, col. 5.
3 Table II 15, col. 5.
4 Col. 1 plus col. 2.
5 Col. 1 plus col. 3.

COLUMN
6 Table II 8, col. 10.
7 Table II 13, col. 10.
8 Table II 15, col. 10.
9 Col. 6 plus col. 7.
10 Col. 6 plus col. 8.

TABLE II 17

Gross and Net National Product,* Per Capita and Per Gainfully Occupied, Averages per Year by Decades, 1929 Prices, 1869-1938

	POPULATION (thousands)	GAINFULLY OCCUPIED	GROSS NATIONAL PRODUCT		NET NATIONAL PRODUCT	
			Per Capita (dollars)	Per Gainfully Occupied (dollars)	Per Capita (dollars)	Per Gainfully Occupied (dollars)
	(1)	(2)	(3)	(4)	(5)	(6)
DECADE ESTIMATES						
1 1869-78	43,541	14,440	237	716	215	647
2 1874-83	48,847	16,740	304	887	278	812
3 1879-88	54,762	19,528	355	997	326	915
4 1884-93	61,152	22,729	378	1,018	344	926
5 1889-98	67,625	25,580	396	1,046	357	945
6 1894-1903	74,269	28,311	443	1,163	401	1,051
7 1899-1908	81,540	31,792	505	1,296	458	1,174
8 1904-13	89,646	35,954	556	1,386	502	1,251
9 1909-18	97,743	39,329	578	1,437	517	1,286
10 1914-23	104,963	41,927	615	1,539	546	1,366
AVERAGES OF ANNUAL ESTIMATES						
11 1919-28	112,841	44,904	689	1,732	612	1,538
12 1924-33	120,619	47,953	687	1,727	607	1,528
13 1929-38	125,963	50,307	649	1,625	572	1,432

* Peacetime concept; see Part I.

COLUMN

1 Table II 9, col. 1.

2 Estimates for 1870, 1880, 1890, 1900, 1910, 1920, and 1930 prepared by Daniel Carson for 'Labor Supply and Employment' (WPA, National Research Project, Nov. 1939, mimeo.) and revised in 'Industrial Composition of Manpower in the United States, 1870-1940', a paper prepared for the Conference on Research in Income and Wealth, 1945. The decennial figures were interpolated on the basis of total population, by decades through 1914-23, annually for 1919-38.

3 Col. 9 of Table II 16 divided by col. 1.

4 Col. 9 of Table II 16 divided by col. 2.

5 Col. 10 of Table II 16 divided by col. 1.

6 Col. 10 of Table II 16 divided by col. 2.

PART III

The Share of Services in the Flow of Goods to Consumers

This Part presents the evidence upon which we based the level of and decade changes in the ratio of consumers' outlay on services to their total outlay. The main body of evidence consisted of sample data on family expenditures before 1914. But the samples were scanty and noncomparable; and had to be adjusted in several ways before they could be linked with the more comprehensive data for recent decades. The discussion below summarizes the general characteristics of the sample data, the procedures by which they were adjusted and combined, and the conclusions. The more detailed aspects of the data and of the adjustments are treated in the Appendixes.

A Share of Total Outlay Expended for Services, Low Income Urban Consumers, 1870-1914

1 *Character of the Data*

From *Studies of Family Living in the United States and Other Countries* [1] we selected sources that contained consumer expenditure samples large enough to be representative, similar enough in coverage to warrant comparison, and taken at intervals sufficiently far apart to indicate long term changes in the pattern of consumers' outlay. Little material was found that met all these requirements, and much of that utilized is deficient on one count or another. Almost all the information usable for the purpose of establishing long term changes in the composition of consumers' expenditures is for urban families in low income groups.

a CONSUMER GROUPS COVERED

The samples are not uniform in respect of the income level of the persons canvassed. Many are described merely as 'workingmen's returns' or 'returns from wage earners of the minimum class'. But some returns from persons in somewhat higher income groups are included.

Another source of divergence among the samples is the weighting by occupational or industrial affiliation. We followed two procedures: (1) When the data are not shown by occupational or industrial groups, all complete returns were added and the percentage shares calculated directly from the total, on the

[1] F. M. Williams and C. C. Zimmerman (Department of Agriculture Miscellaneous Publication 223, Washington, D.C., Dec. 1935).

assumption that the sample was so selected as to weight each occupation and industry properly. (2) When data for only selected occupational or industrial groups are shown, per capita absolutes were computed for each. All were assigned equal weights, rather than the weight of the size of the sample as under (1), and combined. The number of returns for the years to be compared and for the occupations combined were usually so disparate that it did not seem justifiable to weight by the size of the sample.

Still another problem of weighting was encountered in combining the 1918 data for sample cities to get averages for a state. The percentage distribution of expenditures varies appreciably from city to city for specific items. Though when total service shares are compared this territorial variation is apparently not large, it seemed desirable to allow for it by weighting each city either by the size of its population or by the population of all cities in the state for which the sample city, by reason of its size, could be considered representative. As these more laborious methods yielded results only slightly different from those obtained by weighting by the size of the sample, they were discarded in favor of the latter.

b DERIVING TOTAL OUTLAY

The total outlay figure from which the percentage shares are calculated is usually the sum of expenditures for each service and commodity reported on returns regarded as complete. Occasionally, the percentage shares are computed from composite or built-up totals—the sum of averages for each type of expenditure. In the first method the persons reporting each item are identical; in the second they are not and each average may be based upon data from a different number of returns. The disparity in number may not be great and the group reporting one type of expenditure may differ only slightly from that reporting another type. For food, clothing, fuel and light, it is doubtful that any serious error is introduced. But for rent and sundries, coverage is commonly less complete. Consequently, averages for them are based upon data from appreciably fewer returns; and in the composite total they are compared with those based upon wider coverage. Whenever used, the composite totals are labeled and should be regarded with less confidence than the direct totals.

Most of the samples are reported on a yearly basis, but some monthly data are used. They may yield slightly distorted results since they do not allow for seasonal variations in cost of living expenditures. They may also fail to register nonrecurrent expenditures, such as for illness or vacations. No correction for this possible bias could be made.

Since we are interested in the distribution of expenditures rather than in the disposition of income, savings as such are disregarded. To be consistent, we should have excluded also expenditures for life insurance, part of which are savings. But as we had to follow the most common procedure, all items except savings, reported or segregable as such, are included, when reported.

c VARIATIONS IN THE COVERAGE OF COMPONENTS
The several components of consumers' outlay vary in coverage. The extent to which each major item is affected is summarized briefly.
Food: Variations in the composition of this item are probably minor, but there are some. For example, if candy is not regarded as a necessity, it may not appear under any category in a budget study to determine the cost of living. But if total expenditures are shown, those for candy will be included under food, or, if food is regarded in its narrower sense—to keep body and soul together—under sundries.
Clothing: As dry goods are frequently included with clothing, it was assumed that they always are. Quite possibly, however, they are sometimes omitted or are regarded as sundries. In the 1918 data the clothing item includes shoe shines and repairs, and cleaning, pressing, and repairing. Whether these services are similarly classified in the other samples cannot be ascertained.
Rent: The sample data rarely cover returns from home owners. Rent paid is the item most commonly reported. Only occasionally do the corresponding expenditures by home owners—for taxes, repairs, and insurance—appear; but even then coverage of outlays is incomplete. The bias arising from such exclusion of home

owners' expenditures may be negligible, but should be borne in mind.

The composition of rent is variable. It may include heat or light, both or neither.

Fuel and light: To the extent that rent includes heat and light, the percentage of total expenditures spent on commodities is understated.

The 1918 source material indicates that persons living in flats and apartments spend less on fuel and light than persons living in houses. Our samples, including, as they do, few returns from home owners, may show too low a percentage share for fuel and light, especially since during the period under consideration the trend was to flats and apartments.

Sundries: This item (comprising all expenditures other than for food, clothing, rent, fuel and light) is subject to greater variation than any other, because of the diversity in the treatment of its components, and because criteria for necessities and luxuries differ. Even when supposedly all expenditures are reported, its composition depends upon the detail in which the information is requested. Because items not mentioned specifically may be overlooked, a questionnaire calling merely for 'sundries' or 'all other expenses' yields a much lower figure than one that itemizes each type of expense.

d THE PERCENTAGE DISTRIBUTION

When the sample was large, the percentage distributions were accepted as published. Whenever feasible, however, the sample data were reviewed to guard against the inclusion of incomplete returns. Many published estimates rested on returns that did not have entries for all items, e.g., home owners' returns on which the rent category had been left blank, and no compensating entry made for taxes, repairs, insurance, and depreciation. Another item commonly not reported is sundries. It was not easy to determine whether this item was zero or was not reported. If the questionnaire called for only a single entry, a blank was regarded as a failure to report. If sundries were called for in great detail, it was assumed that when some were entered, the omission of others signified no expenditure for them.

e ASSIGNMENT TO COMMODITIES AND SERVICES

Our rating of the various items as services or commodities is necessarily arbitrary because a single category may represent outlays for both; e.g., education may cover expenditures for newspapers, magazines, and books as well as for schooling proper. Since we have little material upon which to allocate this item, and since schooling seems to be reported only rarely, the entire expenditure for education was regarded as a commodity outlay. In the case of medicine and medical attendance, however, the services of the physician were considered as outweighing the outlay on medicine, and the item was rated as a service outlay. For all such 'mixed' categories, the decision favored the type of expenditure regarded as predominant.

Sundries is the only 'mixed' category we attempted to distribute between services and commodities. The procedure is outlined in Appendix A which contains also a description of the 1890/91 and 1918 United States samples that provided the basis for the apportionment. The coverage of sundries being less comprehensive for the early years than for the later, the scope of the 1890/91 sample was assumed more representative of the samples for the years before 1900/01, and that of the 1918 sample more representative of the samples for 1900/01 and subsequent years.

2 Summary of Evidence

a PER YEAR CHANGE IN THE TOTAL SERVICE SHARE FOR STATE SAMPLES

A review of the results for the several states (Table III 1) reveals a marked tendency for the total service share to increase over time. Of the 24 entries recording the per year change in the share of services in total consumers' expenditures (col. 3), only 5 are negative, and even the declines in them are smaller, absolutely, than the increases in the 19 positive.

Consistent as the estimates are in indicating a decided uptrend in the proportion of consumers' outlay on services, there is divergence among the samples in the size of the rise. Some averaging process must obviously be resorted to in order to establish the rise that could be considered most representative for low income urban dwellers as a whole.

TABLE III 1
Total Service Share for State Samples, Low Income Urban Consumers
Various Dates, 1870-1914

	YEARS FOR WHICH SAMPLE DATA ARE COMPARED (1)	TOTAL SERVICE SHARE AS % OF TOTAL OUTLAY (2)	PER YEAR CHANGE IN TOTAL SERVICE SHARE (%) (3)
Connecticut	1887/88	16.22	
	1900/01	30.04	+1.063
Illinois	1878/79	28.09	
	1883/84	26.41	−0.336
	1900/01	24.97	
	1914	37.02	+0.893
Kansas	1888/89	31.10	
	1900	31.49	+0.035
	1907	35.34	+0.550
Maine	1890/91	28.46	
	1899/1900	34.21	+0.639
	1900/01	21.79	
	1914	34.47	+0.939
Massachusetts	1870	25.21	
	1883	27.41	+0.169
	1874/75	20.35	
	1901	23.91	+0.134
	1890/91	26.52	
	1900/01	32.46	+0.594
	1914	33.24	+0.058
Missouri	1880	19.63	
	1888/89	23.58	+0.465
	1880	28.15	
	1900/01	33.53	+0.262
Nebraska	1889/90	24.35	
	1912	37.07	+0.565
New Jersey	1877/78	24.46	
	1885/86	23.23	−0.154
	1900/01	30.47	
	1914	35.23	+0.353
Ohio	1878	27.88	
	1885/86	27.14	−0.099
	1900/01	27.65	
	1914	35.30	+0.567
Pennsylvania	1875	24.78	
	1879	24.42	−0.090
	1886/87	28.15	+0.497
	1890/91	34.08	
	1900/01	32.29	−0.179
	1914	33.60	+0.097
Wisconsin	1885	25.06	
	1895	26.51	+0.145
	1900/01	26.83	
	1914	32.42	+0.414

Column 2 is derived from the sample studies summarized in Appendixes A and B.

b MEDIAN AND ARITHMETIC MEAN CHANGES IN THE TOTAL
   SERVICE SHARE FOR STATE SAMPLES

As the first experiment in averaging, changes were arrayed for each of three periods, 1870-85, 1885-1900/01, 1900/01-14, and the medians determined (Table III 2, line 2). When a change covered years in more than one period, it was included in the period in which the greater number of years lay or in both periods as seemed more appropriate. The cases were too few, however, to yield medians that could be regarded as representative.

TABLE III 2

Medians and Arithmetic Means of Per Year Changes in Total Service Share, Low Income Urban Consumers Fifteen-year Periods (percentages)

	1870-1885	1885-1900/01	1900/01-1914
1 No. of items	8	9	9
2 Median	+0.022	+0.262	+0.550
3 Arithmetic mean	+0.073	+0.362	+0.493

Based on Table III 1, col. 3.

Simple arithmetic means of the changes were then computed (Table III 2, line 3). In both median and mean the per year rise is progressively bigger. The small number of items underlying them and the large difference between them led us to consider other methods of summarizing the data.

c MEDIAN TOTAL SERVICE SHARE FOR STATE SAMPLES

The extreme variation in the *changes*, not only from state to state but also for the same state, suggests that pairs of percentage shares for the same state do not warrant temporal comparisons. Even when data are for the same state and when methods of collection are apparently identical from year to year, it is more than possible that differences in coverage or concept appreciably distort the comparisons. In a wide grouping of samples, all for approximately the same period, such differences may partly cancel. Hence there may be more merit in bringing together all percentage shares for a given period regardless of the size, type, or territorial coverage of the sample from which they are com-

TABLE III 3

Median Total Service Share, Low Income Urban Consumers
Ten- and Fifteen-year Periods
(shares as percentages of total expenditures)

A TEN-YEAR PERIODS

	1870–1880	1880–1889/90	1889/90–1900/01	1900/01–1914
Approx. midpoint of period	1875	1885	1895	1907
No. of items	7	10	15	20
Median total service share	24.78	26.94	29.89	32.44
Total change in median total service share from preceding period		+2.16	+2.95	+2.55
Per year change		+0.216	+0.295	+0.212

B FIFTEEN-YEAR PERIODS

	1870–1885	1885–1900/01	1900/01–1914
Approx. midpoint of period	1877/78	1893	1907
No. of items	10	21	20
Median total service share	25.14	27.65	32.44
Total change in median total service share from preceding period		+2.51	+4.79
Per year change		+0.162	+0.342

Based on Table III 1, col. 2, excluding samples covering selected occupations (Illinois for 1878/79 and 1883/84, Maine for 1890/91 and 1899/1900, Massachusetts for 1890/91, and Missouri for 1880 and 1888/89) and including 3 samples (Kansas for 1900/01, Illinois for 1883/84, and Maine for 1890/91) which could not be utilized in estimating the per year changes in that table.

puted (except those for selected occupations),[2] determining the mean or median, and computing the per year change from one period to the next.

A great advantage of this procedure is that we can calculate the median and mean for each period from many more cases than in averaging *changes*. Reference to Tables III 3 and III 4, which give medians and means of *shares*, indicates that the cases are almost twice as many as in Table III 2. It is mainly for this reason that we averaged shares rather than changes in shares, to get the basis for estimating the movement of the ratio of services to total outlay for the decades before 1914.[3]

Two groupings were made: one for 10-year, the other for 15-

[2] The percentage share for mining families in Missouri for 1880, for example, is so much lower than that for the entire sample that it was disregarded, together with the comparable figure for 1888/89.

[3] Even with this larger number of cases, we had to include data for the terminal years twice—once as of the beginning of the period, again as of the end of the preceding period.

Table III 4
Positional Means[a] of Total Service Shares, Low Income Urban Consumers
Ten- and Fifteen-year Periods
(shares as percentages of total expenditures)

	A TEN-YEAR PERIODS			
	1870-1880	1880-1889/90	1889/90-1900/01	1900/01-1914
Approx. midpoint of period	1875	1885	1895	1907
No. of items	7	10	15	20
Positional mean of total service shares	24.82	26.58	29.19	32.60
Total change in positional mean of total service shares from preceding period		+1.76	+2.61	+3.41
Per year change		+0.176	+0.261	+0.284

	B FIFTEEN-YEAR PERIODS		
	1870-1885	1885-1900/01	1900/01-1914
Approx. midpoint of period	1877/78	1893	1907
No. of items	10	21	20
Positional mean of total service shares	25.44	27.68	32.60
Total change in positional mean of total service shares from preceding period		+2.24	+4.92
Per year change		+0.145	+0.351

[a] Based on the three or four middle items in the array of data utilized in Table III 3.

year periods (Table III 3). In both, the simple medians reveal a continuous upward movement of the total service share in consumer outlay. We eventually discarded the 10-year in favor of the 15-year periods, since the cases in the former were so few as to make for erratic movements of medians and of means. But they have been retained in Tables III 3 and III 4 as evidence that the upward trend of the service share characterizes the full period covered by the sample data.

Since the cases are few, positional means, i.e., arithmetic means of the three or four middle cases, are likely to provide more representative measures of central tendency than medians (Table III 4). The slightness of the difference between these positional means and the medians indicates the 'dense' grouping of items around the median value. In the subsequent analysis positional means rather than medians were used.

d MOVEMENT OF SERVICE SHARE COMPONENTS

So far we have concerned ourselves with the movement of the total service share alone. Lacking in detail though the budget

TABLE III 5

Components of Total Service Share for State Samples
Low Income Urban Consumers, Various Dates, 1870-1914

	YEARS (1)	% SHARE OF TOTAL OUTLAY	
		Rent (2)	Other Services (3)
Connecticut	1887/88	12.81	3.41
	1900/01	21.41	8.63
Illinois	1883/84	17.46	9.27
	1900/01	16.20	8.77
	1914	23.37	13.65
Kansas	1888/89	17.84	13.26
	1900	15.50	15.99
	1900/01	16.19	13.70
	1907	16.98	18.36
Maine	1890/91	17.15	10.09
	1900/01	14.89	6.90
	1914	22.89	11.58
Massachusetts	1870	14.67	10.54
	1874/75	16.73	3.62
	1883	21.37	6.04
	1900/01	20.95	11.51
	1901	14.84	9.07
	1914	21.39	11.85
Missouri	1880	17.62	10.53
	1900/01	15.66	17.87
Nebraska	1889/90	21.41	2.94
	1912	22.94	14.13
New Jersey	1877/78	17.89	6.57
	1885/86	17.13	6.10
	1900/01	20.08	10.39
	1914	23.12	12.11
Ohio	1878	17.00	10.88
	1885/86	18.41	8.73
	1900/01	14.11	13.54
	1914	22.29	13.01
Pennsylvania	1875	17.42	7.36
	1879	14.68	9.74
	1886/87	19.11	9.04
	1890/91	24.01	10.07
	1900/01	20.89	11.40
	1914	21.84	11.76
Wisconsin	1885	14.18	10.88
	1895	17.37	9.14
	1900/01	14.31	12.52
	1914	19.98	12.44

From the sources indicated for the total service shares in Table III 1, with the exception of Kansas, 1900/01: from the source indicated for Illinois for that year; Illinois, 1883/84: for 26 occupations rather than the 2 covered in Table III 1; Maine, 1890/91: for 27 occupations rather than the 4 covered in Table III 1.

TABLE III 6

Positional Means[a] of Service Shares, Low Income Urban Consumers
Fifteen-year Periods
(shares as percentages of total expenditures)

	1870-1885 (1)	1885-1900/01 (2)	1900/01-1914 Preliminary (3)	Final[b] (4)
1 Rent	17.15	17.22	20.48	18.98
2 Other services	9.22	10.18	12.04	11.54
3 Total services (1 + 2)	26.37	27.40	32.52	30.52

[a] Based on the three or four middle items in the array of data derived from Table III 5. For the number of items in each period see Table III 4, Part B.
[b] The share of rent reduced 1.5 percent and that of other services 0.5 percent.

samples are, two major components—rent and 'other' services —can nevertheless be distinguished. The upward trend characterizing the movement of the total service share is true also of the shares of rent and of other services measured separately (Table III 5).

The reason for analyzing rent and other services separately lies not only in the interest that may attach to the movement of each, but also in the different effect of any possible undercoverage of the basic data on the total service share when measured as a whole and as the sum of rent and of other services. In samples where sundries are understated, such understatement augments the percentage shares of all other items, including rent. Nevertheless, the resulting exaggeration of the share of rent does not offset the overstatement of the total commodity share, in comparison with the total service share. We therefore grouped the rent and the other service shares separately, ascertained the positional mean of each, and added the two (Table III 6, col. 1-3).

As was to be expected, the period most affected is 1870-85, the service share calculated as the sum of the shares of rent and of other services being 26.37 percent as against 25.44 percent derived directly (in Table III 4). During that period sundries tended to be understated because the sample questionnaires were less detailed and stressed necessary cost of living components rather than total consumer expenditures. Clearly, the estimates in Table III 6 are freer from bias than those in Table III 4.

The share of rent changes little from 1870-85 to 1885-1900/01.

From 1885-1900/01 to 1900/01-14, however, it rises decidedly. The share of other services increases considerably from 1870-85 to 1885-1900/01, and even more from 1885-1900/01 to 1900/01-14.

A part of the increase from 1885-1900/01 to 1900/01-14 might be due to overstatement of the service shares in 1914, since the latter were extrapolated from 1918 on the basis of changes in price levels alone; i.e., compensating changes in quantity and quality were not allowed for. Changes in the service shares from 1914 to 1919, as derived from the over-all estimates of consumers' expenditures by W. H. Lough,[4] and from 1935-39 to June 15, 1942, as evidenced by sample data for wage earners and clerical workers,[5] indicate that variations in the pattern of consumer expenditure due to changes in both prices and quantity and quality are markedly different from those due to changes in prices alone. To allow for the possible inflationary effect of using 1918 as a base, we reduced the share of rent for 1900/01-14 1.5 percent, that of other services 0.5 percent (Table III 6, col. 4).[6] With these adjustments, the ratios of Table III 6 are used below to indicate the trend in the share of services in the total outlay of low income urban consumers.

B   EXPENDITURE PATTERNS FOR LOW INCOME URBAN CONSUMERS AND FOR ALL URBAN, RURAL NONFARM, AND RURAL FARM CONSUMERS, 1935/36 AND 1941, AND THE RELATION ASSUMED FOR 1870-1914

The few studies of expenditures by consumers other than urban for 1870-1914 are inadequate for our purposes. For 1935/36 and 1941, however, reports by the National Resources Planning Board, the Bureau of Labor Statistics, and the Bureau of Agricultural Economics provide data for rural farm, rural nonfarm, and urban families. For 1922/24, there is additional material for

[4] *High-Level Consumption* (McGraw-Hill, 1935).
[5] 'Cost of Living Indexes in Wartime' by F. M. Williams, F. R. Rice, and E. D. Schell, *Journal of the American Statistical Association*, Dec. 1942.
[6] These adjustments are discussed in more detail in Appendix A.

farm families, collected under the supervision of the Department of Agriculture (see App. D).

1 *Major Differences between the Source Material for the Early and Later Years*

a CONSUMER INCOME GROUP COVERED

Most of the sample urban data for the early years were for families with incomes of $1,200 or less. The reports for 1935/36 and 1941, however, cover expenditures by families at all income levels. When comparisons were attempted between the early and the later years, income groups up to $1,500 were selected for the latter as most nearly approximating those up to $1,200 for the former.

b INCLUSION OF IMPUTED VALUES

In none of the earlier studies used were expenditures in kind or imputed values included. In those for the later years they are of some importance. The farm consumer gets a far greater proportion of his living from his house and farm than the urban consumer, or even the rural nonfarm consumer. Values assigned to housing, food, fuel and ice may be a source of discrepancy in the expenditure patterns for these three groups of consumers.

The reports vary in their coverage of these non-money items, that for 1922/24 showing the imputed value of housing alone; the 1935/36 report covers, in addition, the value of home-produced food for rural nonfarm families, and the value of food, fuel and ice for rural farm families. In the 1941 study the items included in non-money income are still more numerous, comprising in addition to housing, fuel, and food, furnishings and clothing received from a relief agency, or as gifts, or as pay.

c DETAIL OF PRESENTATION

For the urban material for the early years, the so-called 'mixed' categories, such as education, and medical attendance and medicine, were not apportioned between services and commodities, but were assigned the rating that seemed to cover the preponderant portion of the expenditure. For 1935/36, when the source material is detailed, most of these categories can be distributed.

2 Relative Size of the Service Shares for Urban, Rural Nonfarm, and Rural Farm Consumers

The report for 1935/36 [7] is our best guide in determining the relative size of the service shares for low income urban consumers and for all urban, rural nonfarm, and rural farm consumers (Table III 7).

TABLE III 7

Service Shares for Urban, Rural Nonfarm, and Rural Farm Consumers Income Groups up to $1,500 and All Income Groups, 1935/36

(shares as percentages of total expenditures)

	Income Groups up to $1,500 (1)	All Income Groups (2)
A URBAN		
1 Housing	20.63	18.71
2 Other services	11.00	17.35
3 Total services	31.63	36.06
B RURAL NONFARM		
4 Housing	16.19	14.93
5 Other services	12.42	16.40
6 Total services	28.61	31.33
C RURAL FARM		
7 Housing	10.41	12.26
8 Other services	9.32	11.11
9 Total services	19.73	23.37

COLUMN

1 *Family Expenditures in the United States* (National Resources Planning Board, Washington, D. C. 1941), pp. 51-65, 120. Expenditures by families receiving some relief during year excluded.

2 *Ibid.*, pp. 13, 69, 70. Expenditures by families receiving some relief during year included.

See Appendix D for rating of expenditures as service or commodity outlays.

The percentage share expended for housing by all urban consumers is almost 2 percent lower than that expended by urban consumers in the income groups up to $1,500. For the latter, however, the share for other services is 6 percent less.

The same relation holds, generally, for rural nonfarm consumers, though the differences in level between the shares for the low income groups and for all are less marked; the share for housing is approximately 1 percent lower for all income groups,

[7] *Family Expenditures in the United States* (National Resources Planning Board, Washington, D. C., 1941).

that for other services, 4 percent higher. When the shares for all rural nonfarm consumers are compared with those for all urban consumers we find that for the latter the share for housing is about 4 percent higher, the share for other services only 1 percent higher.

The share of expenditure for both housing and other services is about 2 percent higher for all rural farm consumers than for those in the low income groups. The service shares for farm consumers are markedly lower than for urban, however; for housing, 6.5 percent, for other services, about 6 percent.

3 Changes in the Relative Size of the Service Shares for Urban, Rural Nonfarm, and Rural Farm Consumers

To estimate long term changes in the service shares for all consumers, we need data that tell us whether the trends for all urban consumers and for all rural consumers were the same as those established for urban families in the low income groups (in Sec. A).

The only material for this purpose is that of the three sample studies mentioned at the beginning of Section B. Unfortunately, the two field studies, for 1935/36 and 1941, differ markedly in coverage, detail, and, most important, in the cyclical characteristics of their periods—1941 was a year of conspicuous cyclical expansion and 1935/36 a much less favorable cyclical phase. The 1922/24 data on farm expenditures cannot be compared with the much more plentiful data for 1935/36 or even 1941. Consequently, while we analyzed and compared the three samples as best we could, the conclusions are subject to too many qualifications to admit of inferences concerning long term changes or to merit detailed presentation. For example, the comparison of the 1935/36 and the 1941 samples, after categories had been regrouped to assure the greatest possible comparability, shows that the share expended for housing (including fuel, light, and refrigeration, which cannot be segregated) by urban consumers declined from 26.4 to 22.1 percent for income groups up to $1,500, and from 21.8 to 17.6 percent for all income groups. The total service share for the low income groups declined from 41.0 to 39.7; for all income groups from 42.7 to 38.8. While both the rent and total service shares thus moved fairly alike for the low income and for all urban consumers, this is obviously not too secure a basis upon which to assume a similarity of long term changes in the service shares in the flow of goods to low income and to all urban consumers in the past. Yet were there *no* similarity in movement between 1935/36 and 1941, it could still be assumed for the longer term trends.

Whatever the limitations of these recent sample data, they do indicate that the shares of rent and of other services moved more or less parallel for low income and all urban consumers; and for urban and rural consumers. And, the assumption we are adopting, for lack of specific information to the contrary—viz., that the longer term changes in the shares of rent and of other services for all urban consumers are similar to those established for the low income groups, and that they are also similar as between urban and the two groups of rural consumers—is plausible, but no more. Under it we combine the two items of information we have—longer term trends in the shares for low income urban consumers and differences in the 1935/36 levels of the shares between low income urban consumers and all urban consumers and between urban and rural consumers—into an estimate for all consumers.

4 Service Shares for All Consumers, 1870-1914

The minor rise in the rent share from 1870-85 to 1885-1900/01 is due almost entirely to the growth of the urban population (Table III 8). The rise from 1885-1900/01 to 1900/01-14 is due not only to the continued rapid growth of the urban population but also to increases in the rent share for all three groups of consumers. The movement of the latter is not unlike that of Carl Snyder's rent index, which practically does not change from 1875 to 1895, then rises gradually from 1895 to 1913.[8]

The rise in the share of other services, while assumed to be proportionately the same for all consumer groups, is affected by the greater gain in the urban population. Consequently, the rise for all groups is somewhat greater than that for any one group.

[8] *Business Cycles and Business Measurements* (Macmillan, 1927), p. 291.

Table III 8
Service Shares for All Consumer Groups,* 1870-1914
(shares as percentages of total expenditures)

	1870-1885 (1)	1885-1900/01 (2)	1900/01-1914 (3)
A Rent			
1 Share for low income urban consumers	17.15	17.22	18.98
2 Share for all urban consumers	15.34	15.41	16.98
3 Weight for all urban consumers	14,212	24,354	38,701
4 Share for all rural nonfarm consumers	11.73	11.78	12.98
5 Weight for all rural nonfarm consumers	9,302	12,963	16,839
6 Share for all rural farm consumers	9.47	9.51	10.48
7 Weight for all rural farm consumers	24,042	28,956	31,191
8 Share for all consumers	11.67	12.12	13.87
B Other Services			
9 Share for low income urban consumers	9.22	10.18	11.54
10 Share for all urban consumers	15.14	16.16	17.54
11 Weight for all urban consumers	14,212	24,354	38,701
12 Share for all rural nonfarm consumers	14.28	15.24	16.54
13 Weight for all rural nonfarm consumers	9,302	12,963	16,839
14 Share for all rural farm consumers	9.96	10.63	11.54
15 Weight for all rural farm consumers	24,042	28,956	31,191
16 Share for all consumers	12.35	13.56	15.19
C Total Services			
17 Share for low income urban consumers	26.37	27.40	30.52
18 Share for all urban consumers	30.48	31.57	34.52
19 Share for all rural nonfarm consumers	26.01	27.02	29.52
20 Share for all rural farm consumers	19.43	20.14	22.02
21 Share for all consumers	24.02	25.68	29.06

* An alternative series was calculated by extrapolating the positional means of the service shares for low income urban consumers for 1900/01-14 (Table III 6) by the arithmetic means of the per year changes in the components of the total service shares underlying Table III 2. The shares for the other consumer groups were estimated by the procedure outlined in this table.

	1870-1885	1885-1900/01	1900/01-1914
Rent	10.79	12.66	14.33
Other services	11.12	12.65	15.33
Total services	21.91	25.31	29.66

LINE

1 Table III 6, line 1.

2 Col. 3, assumed to be 2 percent lower than line 1 (see Table III 7, line 1), extrapolated by line 1.

3, 5, 7, 11, 13, & 15 Representing thousands of persons. Census reports provide estimates for urban and rural population at ten-year intervals from 1870 to 1930, and indicate the apportionment of rural population between farm and nonfarm in 1930 and 1920. *The Agricultural Situation* for June 1939 shows the apportionment for 1910. Rural nonfarm population for the years before 1910 was estimated on the basis of its 1910 relation to total population, as the relation has varied little since. Interpolations for 1885 and 1914 are along a straight line. It was not thought worth while for the present purpose to correct for the lack of uniformity in Census dates.

4 Col. 3, assumed to be 4 percent lower than line 2 (see Table III 7, col. 2, lines 1 and 4), extrapolated by line 2.

Table III 8 concluded:
LINE

6 Col. 3, assumed to be 6.5 percent lower than line 2 (see Table III 7, col. 2, lines 1 and 7), extrapolated by line 2.

8 Average of line 2, weighted by line 3; line 4, weighted by line 5; and line 6, weighted by line 7.

9 Table III 6, line 2.

10 Col. 3, assumed to be 6 percent higher than line 9 (see Table III 7, line 2), extrapolated by two-thirds the rate of change in line 9. The lower rate was assumed after consideration of the rate of change from 1935/36 to 1941.

12 Col. 3, assumed to be 1 percent lower than line 10 (see Table III 7, col. 2, lines 2 and 5), extrapolated by line 10.

14 Col. 3, assumed to be 6 percent lower than line 10 (see Table III 7, col. 2, lines 2 and 8), extrapolated by line 10.

16 Average of line 10, weighted by line 11; line 12, weighted by line 13, and line 14, weighted by line 15.

17 Table III 6, line 3.

18 Sum of lines 2 and 10.

19 Sum of lines 4 and 12.

20 Sum of lines 6 and 14.

21 Sum of lines 8 and 16.

C Movement of the Total Service Share for All Consumers, 1869-78 to 1929-38

1 *The Final Series*

The estimates of consumers' outlay on services, derived by deducting net capital formation and consumers' outlay on commodities from national income, go back only to 1919. The ratio of service outlay to total outlay, as computed from these series for 1919-28, is extrapolated to 1909-18 on the basis of the movement of the service share computed from Lough's over-all estimates of consumer expenditures for 1909, 1914, and 1919-28.[9]

[9] The marked differences in the percentage composition of Harold Barger's recent series on consumers' outlay (*Outlay and Income in the United States, 1921-1938;* National Bureau of Economic Research, 1942) and Lough's is to be attributed in part to differences in concept, in part to the fact that Barger could take account of material Lough could not. Barger's use of our commodity series renders his outlay series more comparable to ours than Lough's, but since it begins in 1921 it is useless as a means of extending our data back. In the light of Barger's series, Lough's estimates appear subject to considerable correction, especially for the later years, but the revision need not appreciably alter the *movement* of the service share from 1909-18 to 1919-28.

From 1909-18 to 1869-78 extrapolation is by the sample series in Table III 8 (Table III 9).

The total service share rises steadily from 1869-78 to 1914-19. The violent price changes during the war caused a decline that offset the rise in the early part of the 1909-18 decade. Resumed after the war, the rise continues through 1929-38.

The upward trend characterizes the shares of both rent and other services, but the rise in the former is much more moderate than that in the latter. While the paucity of underlying data does not warrant full confidence in the exact magnitude of the difference shown between the trends in the shares of the two major components of services, the difference is confirmed by whatever nonquantitative evidence comes to mind. It is 'other' services that include such rapidly growing items of consumers' demand as repairs and maintenance of consumer durable goods; expenditures on education, amusement, and travel; and outlays on medical and other professional services.

From sources and by methods discussed in Part II, we have a series of decade estimates of the flow of finished commodities at final cost to consumers. Converting percentages of total outlay derived in this Part (Table III 9) to percentages of commodity flow to consumers, and applying them to the estimates of such commodity flow in current prices, we get a series of estimates of the value of services not embodied in new commodities, at cost to consumers in current prices, for the overlapping decades 1869-1938 (Table III 10, col. 1-3).

The problems involved in the adjustment of this series for price changes were mentioned in Part II. We present here the series in 1929 prices without further comment, for convenience of reference by students who may wish to have at hand the estimates that distinguish the two major components of the total service category in consumers' outlay.

2 *An Over-all Check*

The reader who has patiently followed the discussion of the character of the sample budget data and the account of the various statistical manipulations that were tried, employed, or discarded in the process of constructing the final series of ratios (Table III 9) is probably left with an impression that the basic

TABLE III 9
Service Shares for All Consumers, 1869-1938*
(shares as percentages of total expenditures)

		SAMPLE DATA EXTRAPOLATING SERIES			LOUGH			FINAL SERIES		
	Rent (1)	Other Services (2)	Total Services (1+2) (3)	Rent (4)	Other Services (5)	Total Services (6)	Rent (line 13 extrapolated by col. 1 & 4) (7)	Other Services (line 13 extrapolated by col. 2 & 5) (8)	Total Services (7+8) (9)
1 1869-78	11.55	12.03	23.58				12.41	13.80	26.21
2 1874-83	11.70	12.43	24.13				12.57	14.25	26.82
3 1879-88	11.84	12.83	24.67				12.72	14.71	27.43
4 1884-93	12.00	13.22	25.22				12.89	15.16	28.05
5 1889-98	12.29	13.67	25.96				13.20	15.68	28.88
6 1894-1903	12.81	14.21	27.02				13.76	16.30	30.06
7 1899-1908	13.42	14.77	28.19				14.42	16.94	31.36
8 1904-13	14.02	15.33	29.35				15.06	17.58	32.64
9 1909-14	14.38	15.67	30.05	12.99	19.56	32.55	15.45	17.97	33.42
10 1914-19				10.25	19.99	30.24	12.19	18.37	30.56
11 1909-18				10.95	19.94	30.89	13.03	18.32	31.35
12 1914-23							13.21	18.30	31.51
13 1919-28				11.86	21.95	33.81	14.11	20.17	34.28
14 1924-33							14.59	23.24	37.83
15 1929-38							14.13	23.88	38.02

* An alternative series was derived for 1869-1913 by extrapolating 1909-14 (col. 7 & 8) by the series in the footnote to Table III 8.

	RENT	OTHER SERVICES	TOTAL SERVICES			RENT	OTHER SERVICES	TOTAL SERVICES
1869-78	10.54	12.76	23.30		1899-98	12.84	14.34	27.18
1874-83	11.08	12.46	23.54		1894-1903	13.31	15.50	28.81
1879-88	11.68	12.40	24.08		1899-1908	13.94	16.52	30.46
1884-93	12.30	13.11	25.41		1904-13	14.84	17.43	32.27

COLUMNS 1 & 2

LINE

Averages of annual estimates derived by straight-line interpolation and extrapolation of the series in Table III 8.

COLUMNS 4 & 5

Derived from *High-Level Consumption* (McGraw-Hill, 1935), pp. 28, 236-46. The data in his Table 3 were adjusted to exclude immigrant remittances and to include direct taxes (shown for Census years in his Appendix A and estimated for non-Census years by straight-line interpolation).

9 Percentage of average value for 1909 and 1914.

10 Percentage of average value for 1914 and 1919.

11 Percentage of average value for 1909, 1914, and 1919.

13 Distribution of col. 6 on the basis of the apportionment of the average value for the odd years, 1919-29.

COLUMN 6

LINE

9-11 Col. 4 plus col. 5.

13 Derived from *ibid.*, from average value for 1919-28.

COLUMN 7

12 Weighted average of 1914-19 (line 10) and 1919-23, calculated from the source indicated for lines 13-15.

13-15 Gross rents (Table III 10, col. 1) divided by flow of goods to consumers (Table II 8, col. 5).

COLUMN 8

12 See note to col. 7, line 12.

13-15 'Other' services (Table III 10, col. 3 minus col. 1) divided by flow of goods to consumers (Table II 8, col. 5).

Table III 10
Total Outlay on Services, Current and 1929 Prices, 1869-1938
(averages per year, millions of dollars)

		CURRENT PRICES			1929 PRICES		
		Rent	Other Services	Total Services	Rent	Other Services	Total Services
		(1)	(2)	(3)	(4)	(5)	(6)
1	1869-78	708	787	1,496	1,292	1,066	2,358
2	1874-83	909	1,030	1,939	1,680	1,625	3,305
3	1879-88	1,098	1,270	2,368	2,015	2,232	4,246
4	1884-93	1,213	1,427	2,640	2,214	2,687	4,900
5	1889-98	1,323	1,571	2,894	2,392	3,226	5,618
6	1894-1903	1,706	2,021	3,727	3,025	4,219	7,244
7	1899-1908	2,488	2,922	5,410	4,238	5,546	9,784
8	1904-13	3,479	4,061	7,540	5,611	6,930	12,540
9	1909-18	4,143	5,826	9,970	6,404	7,915	14,319
10	1914-23	6,406	8,871	15,277	*	*	17,647
11	1919-28	9,072	12,971	22,043	*	*	22,393
12	1924-33	9,543	15,207	24,750	*	*	25,210
13	1929-38	8,486	14,337	22,823	*	*	25,591

* Not estimated.

Column 1
LINE

1-9 The flow of commodities to consumers (Table II 7, col. 1) multiplied by the share of rent in total outlay (Table III 9, col. 7), divided by the share of commodities in total outlay (100 percent minus Table III 9, col. 9).

10 Average of 1914-18 estimated by the procedure indicated for lines 1-9, and of 1919-23, from the source indicated for lines 11-13.

11-13 Averages of annual estimates of gross rents underlying the series on net rents in *National Income and Its Composition*.

Column 2

1-9 The flow of commodities to consumers (Table II 7, col. 1) multiplied by the share of 'other' services in total outlay (Table III 9, col. 8), divided by the share of commodities in total outlay (100 percent minus Table III 9, col. 9).

10 See note to col. 1, line 10.

11-13 Col. 3 minus col. 1.

Column 3

1-10 Col. 1 plus col. 2.

11-13 Table II 7, col. 3.

Column 4

Col. 1 divided by the index described in the note to col. 5 of Table II 7.

Column 5

Col. 2 divided by the index described in the note to col. 5 of Table II 7.

Column 6

1-9 Col. 4 plus col. 5.

10 See note to col. 1, line 10.

11-13 Table II 7, col. 5.

data are extremely scanty and unreliable and that our procedures were beset with pitfalls. A perusal of the Appendixes to this Part will do little to restore his confidence.

It is, therefore, important to have some check by which we may judge whether the results are subject to too wide a margin of error to use in deriving longer term trends in the percentage shares accounted for by services not embodied in new commodities. We turned again to the underlying sample budget data, studying the ratios to total expenditures of the outlay in two commodity categories: food and clothing. The idea was to derive a series of percentage shares of total expenditures accounted for by outlays on food and clothing, and compare the result, in the form of estimated outlay on food and clothing in current prices, with the series that would be derived from the basic production data on food and clothing destined for ultimate consumption (from Shaw's study).[10]

To make the check as close as possible, the data and procedures employed to derive shares of food and clothing in total outlay were kept strictly identical with those used to derive shares of services. The same state and national sample budget data were used; the percentage shares were grouped for the same periods and positional means selected; the shift from shares based on budget data, for low income urban families, to percentages estimated for all consumers, urban and rural, was by the same methods and using the same basic data and population weights that were used for the service shares; and, finally, the linking to the recent decades and the interpolations within the earlier 15-year periods were by procedures strictly analogous to those employed in Table III 9. Indeed, the only difference from methods used in connection with service shares was the omission of the adjustment in the shares for 1900/01-14 for the effect of the extrapolation from 1918 to 1914: the tests showed no need for such an adjustment in the shares of food and clothing.

After the ratios of food and clothing to total consumers' outlay (in current prices) were derived, they were applied to the estimates of this total already available to get dollar values of the flow of food and clothing to consumers in current prices (Table III 11, col. 1).

[10] I am indebted to Solomon Fabricant for suggesting this over-all check.

TABLE III 11

Two Estimates of the Flow of Food and Clothing
to Consumers, 1869-1928
(averages per year, dollar figures in millions, current prices)

DECADE	ESTIMATES BASED ON		DIFFERENCE AS % OF COL. 2	INDEXES, 1904-13:100	
	Sample Budget Data (1)	Production Data (Shaw) (2)	(3)	Col. 1 (4)	Col. 2 (5)
A Food					
1 1869-78	2,001.1	2,141.2	−6.5	28.2	27.6
2 1874-83	2,495.1			35.1	
3 1879-88	2,929.9	2,856.0	+2.6	41.2	36.9
4 1884-93	3,140.8			44.2	
5 1889-98	3,284.8	3,467.4	−5.3	46.2	44.8
6 1894-1903	3,982.6	4,339.7	−8.2	56.0	56.0
7 1899-1908	5,423.5	5,867.8	−7.6	76.3	75.7
8 1904-13	7,107.4	7,747.2	−8.3	100.0	100.0
9 1909-18	10,338.5	10,787.9	−4.2	145.5	139.2
10 1914-23	15,091.6	15,078.9	+0.1	212.3	194.6
11 1919-28	17,999.2	17,876.4	+0.7	253.2	230.7
B Clothing					
12 1869-78	1,077.4	1,102.3	−2.3	32.5	32.7
13 1874-83	1,325.3			40.0	
14 1879-88	1,535.4	1,439.6	+6.7	46.4	42.8
15 1884-93	1,621.5			49.0	
16 1889-98	1,664.1	1,649.5	+0.9	50.2	49.0
17 1894-1903	1,970.1	1,903.7	+3.5	59.5	56.6
18 1899-1908	2,606.3	2,617.6	−0.4	78.7	77.8
19 1904-13	3,312.5	3,366.0	−1.6	100.0	100.0
20 1909-18	4,595.1	4,536.5	+1.3	138.7	134.8
21 1914-23	7,333.6	7,195.0	+1.9	221.4	213.8
22 1919-28	9,372.8	9,140.0	+2.5	283.0	271.5
C Food & Clothing					
23 1869-78	3,078.5	3,243.5	−5.1	29.5	29.2
24 1874-83	3,820.4			36.7	
25 1879-88	4,465.3	4,295.6	+4.0	42.9	38.7
26 1884-93	4,762.3			45.7	
27 1889-98	4,948.9	5,116.9	−3.3	47.5	46.0
28 1894-1903	5,952.7	6,243.4	−4.7	57.1	56.2
29 1899-1908	8,029.8	8,485.4	−5.4	77.1	76.4
30 1904-13	10,419.9	11,113.2	−6.2	100.0	100.0
31 1909-18	14,933.6	15,324.4	−2.6	143.3	137.9
32 1914-23	22,425.2	22,273.9	+0.7	215.2	200.4
33 1919-28	27,372.0	27,016.4	+1.3	262.7	243.1

Column 1

LINE

1-9, 12-20, The flow of goods to consumers (Table II 8, col. 5) multiplied by the percentage share of consumer expenditure on food or clothing, estimated by the procedure outlined for rent and other services in Table III 9.

10 & 21 Average of 1914-18, estimated by the procedure indicated for lines 1-9, 12-20, and of 1919-23 from the source indicated for line 11 or 22.

11 Average of annual estimates of flow, before inventories, in *Commodity Flow and Capital Formation*, Vol. One, Table V-4, line 3, and Table V-8, line 1.

SHARE OF SERVICES

LINE

22 Average of annual estimates of flow, after inventories, of dry goods and clothing, estimated by multiplying the flow of semidurables (Table I 2, col. 2) by the share of dry goods and clothing destined for domestic consumption (*ibid.*, Table II-5, lines 7-11) in the value of all semidurables destined for domestic consumption (*ibid.*, line 14), the latter adjusted by an unpublished estimate of tires used for business purposes.

23-33 Sum of lines 1 and 12, 2 and 13, etc.

COLUMN 2

1-11 Average of annual estimates of value destined for domestic consumption (*Value of Commodity Output since 1869,* Tables I 1 and I 2, groups 1a and 1b) raised by the 1919-28 ratio of flow, before inventories, to the value destined for domestic consumption (col. 1, line 11, divided by the corresponding value destined for domestic consumption from *Commodity Flow and Capital Formation,* Vol. One, Table V-4, line 4, and Table V-8, **line 1).**

12-22 Average of annual estimates of value destined for domestic consumption (*Value of Commodity Output since 1869,* Tables I 1 and I 2, groups 6, 7, and 8) raised by the 1919-28 ratio of flow, after inventories, to the value destined for domestic consumption (for sources of the data for this ratio see the note to col. 1, line 22).

23-33 Sum of lines 1 and 12, 2 and 13, etc.

The totals against which the derived series are tested are based upon the flow of food and clothing into domestic consumption, at manufacturers' prices, as estimated by Shaw from Census and other data. These series differ from estimates of flow at final cost to consumers in two respects: they neither include transportation and distributive margins nor allow for changes in finished inventories. The latter item is minor, particularly for decade averages, and was disregarded in estimating the food series in both columns 1 and 2. The former is taken account of by raising the Shaw series by a constant relative mark-up. For food this mark-up is calculated from the National Bureau of Economic Research annual series for 1919-28. For clothing, it is estimated from the National Bureau of Economic Research series for the entire semidurable group for 1919-28, from which the change in finished inventories also is derived (Table III 11, col. 2).

In observing the two estimates it must be kept in mind that they are independent with respect to *movements over time* but not with respect to absolute level in the last two decades in the table, viz., 1914-23 and 1919-28. The absolute totals in 1919-28 are derived from the same body of data, and the slight differences are due to the differences between Shaw's classification of commodities and ours. In 1914-23 there is also dependence upon the same data, since Lough's work, used to extrapolate the ratios underlying column 1, relies heavily on census of production data utilized by Shaw. But with respect to movement during the decades before 1914-23 the two estimates are completely independent: that in column 1 is based on family budget samples, that in column 2 on production census data.

In view of this independence, the close agreement of the two estimates for the decades before 1914 is encouraging. For food the estimates in column 1 tend to fall somewhat short of those in column 2, suggesting that the sample budget data underestimate somewhat the shares of total outlay devoted to food—as compared with production data. But the percentage differences are quite minor; and no sustained trend in them is apparent. For clothing, the estimates in column 1 tend to exceed somewhat those in column 2, suggesting that the sample budget data slightly overestimate the shares of total outlay devoted to clothing—as compared with production data. But the percentage differences are quite moderate and no sustained trend is apparent. When food and clothing are combined (Table III 11, Part C), the differences tend to cancel out; and the series based on sample budget data approximates closely that based on production data, the greatest difference between the two being slightly over 6 percent and the discrepancies for most decades running below 5 percent.

The use of sample budget data to derive the long term movement of the share of consumers' outlay accounted for by services should have yielded estimates subject to a not much wider margin of error than estimates based on direct use of production data. Naturally, the latter are subject to errors of their own; and no part of the comparison in Table III 11 is a test of our assumption concerning transportation and distributive margins.[11] All we can infer from the evidence of Table III 11 is that the scanty and

[11] The check in Table III 11 may be treated as in a sense reciprocal. If it tends to confirm our use of sample budget data, it also tends to confirm the assumption concerning the 'spread' between manufacturers' prices and final cost to consumers. So far as sample budget data have an independent statistical validity of their own, the fact that they yield results so close to those obtained by the use of production data *plus* the assumption of a constant relative mark-up from manufacturers' values provides a basis for inferring that the error involved in that assumption cannot be large.

deficient sample budget data, treated and combined as they have been, yield estimates not much different from those that would have been derived from production census data were they available for services not embodied in new commodities.

The significance of the comparison in Table III 11 as a test of the series derived in Table III 9 should not be exaggerated. Sample budget data may be far more reliable in measuring the shares of food and clothing than of those of services, even after all the adjustments made to get proper estimates of service shares. There may be an error in our series in column 2 due to the assumption of a constant relative spread between manufacturers' values and final costs that parallels and hence offsets some error in the sample budget data relating to shares of food and clothing. Yet there is no evidence of its existence. It is legitimate to conclude that the over-all check does indicate that the series of service shares in total consumers' outlay, based on family budget samples, reveal a trend not much different from that which would have been shown by evidence comparable in its comprehensiveness and accuracy with production census and other data that underlie our estimates of commodity flow for the decades before 1914.

APPENDIX A

United States Reports on Consumers' Expenditures for Years before 1919

The data for 1918 were used only after extrapolation to 1914. The reasons and the procedure followed are set forth in Parts 2 and 3 of this Appendix.

1 Tabular Summary of Sources and Characteristics of United States Sample Data for Years before 1919

	1890/91	1890/91	1900/01[d]	1918
SOURCE	7th An. Report, Com. of Labor	Retail Prices and Wages (52d Cong., 1st Sess., Senate Comm. Report, Vol. 8, No. 986, Pt. 3, pp. 2040-97)	18th An. Report, Com. of Labor	Cost of Living in the United States (BLS Bulletin 357)
Persons covered by returns	'Normal' families (i.e., families with a husband, wife, & not more than 5 children, none over 14, who had no boarders or dependents) in the textile & glass industries	Workingmen, incl. those receiving income from boarders, wife, children, etc.[b]	Wage workers & salaried workers in the principal industrial centers earning not more than $1,200 a year, with 'normal' families (i.e., families composed of a husband at work, a wife, not more than 5 children, none over 14, & no dependents, boarders, lodgers, or servants)	Wage earners & salaried workers representing proportionately the wage earners & the low or medium salaried families of the locality, with families having as a minimum a husband, wife, & at least 1 child who is not a boarder or lodger, no boarders or over 3 lodgers, either outsiders or children living as such.[e]
Total returns	[a]	232	11,156	12,096[f]

No. of returns utilized in state comparisons:				
Connecticut			387	100
Illinois			699	
Kansas			95	27
Maine			190	213
Massachusetts	191		1,189	
Missouri			447	58
New Jersey			501	192
Ohio			963	194
Pennsylvania		91c	1,666	
Wisconsin			250	128
Expenditures reported & rating as commodity (C), service (S), or 'mixed' category (S & C)				
Food (C)	*	*	*	*
Clothing (C)	*	*	*	*
Rent (S)	*	*	*	*
Fuel (C)	*	*	*	**j
Lighting (C)	*	*	*	**j
Sundries (S & C)	–	*	*	–
Furniture & furnishings (C)	–	–	–	–
Insurance (S)	–	*	–	*
Life	–	–	–	**j
Accident & health	–	–	–	–
Life, other than members of family	–	–	–	*

– Not reported.   * Reported separately.   ** Reported, but not separately.

Tabular Summary continued:

SOURCE	1890/91 7th An. Report, Com. of Labor	1890/91 Retail Prices and Wages (52d Cong., 1st Sess., Senate Comm. Report, Vol. 8, No. 986, Pt. 3, pp. 2040-97)	1900/01ᵈ 18th An. Report, Com. of Labor	1918 Cost of Living in the United States (BLS Bulletin 357)
Contributions, dues, gifts, etc. (S)				
Church	—	*	1	*
Labor organizations	—	*	1	*
Lodges, clubs, societies, etc.	—	*	1	*
Charity	—	*	1	*
Patriotic purposes	—	—	—	*
Gifts	—	*	1	*
Street-car fares (S)				
To work	—	—	—	*
To school	—	—	—	*
Other	—	—	—	*
Travel (S)	—	*	1	*
Amusements, vacations, etc. (S)				
Movies	—	—	—	*
Plays, concerts, etc.	—	—	1	*
Other amusements	—	—	1	*
Excursions	—	—	1	*
Vacations	—	—	1	*
Education & uplift (C)				
Newspapers	—	**g	1	*
Magazines	—	—	—	*
Books	—	**g	1	*
Schools, tuition, books, etc.	—	—	1	*
Music	—	—	—	*

Postage (S)	*	—	—
Sickness & disability (S)	—	—	**h
Physician, surgeon, oculist (S)	*	—	—
Medicine (C)	*	—	—
Nurse (S)	*	—	—
Hospital (S)	*	—	—
Dentist (S)	*	—	—
Eyeglasses (C)	*	—	—
Other sickness (S)	*	—	—
Undertaker (S)	*	—	**h
Cemetery (S)	*	—	**h
Liquor (C)	*	—	*
Tobacco (C)	*	—	*
Insurance, personal property (S)	*	—	*
Taxes, personal property & poll (S)	*	—	*
Tools (C)	*	—	—
Cleaning supplies, soap, etc. (C)	*	—	—
Toilet articles & preparations (C)	*	—	—
Barber (S)	*	—	—
Telephones (S)	*	—	—
Moving (S)	*	—	—

— Not reported.   * Reported separately.   ** Reported, but not separately.

Tabular Summary concluded:

SOURCE	1890/91 7th An. Report, Com. of Labor	1890/91 Retail Prices and Wages (52d Cong., 1st Sess., Senate Comm. Report, Vol. 8, No. 986, Pt. 3, pp. 2040-97)	1900/01ᵃ 18th An. Report, Com. of Labor	1918 Cost of Living in the United States (BLS Bulletin 357)
Automobiles, motorcycles, bicycles (C)	—	—	—	*
Servant & day wages (S)	—	—	—	*
Other miscellaneous items (S & C)	—	*	i	*

— Not reported.   * Reported separately.   ** Reported, but not separately.

The items are not strictly comparable from sample to sample, the greatest difference occurring in 'other miscellaneous items' which may include any of or all the expenditures not specifically covered.

ᵃ Because it covers persons in selected industries only, this report was not utilized except as indicated below, for Massachusetts. Even in this instance, its use has been questioned.

ᵇ Location of workingmen reporting is:

City	Number	City	Number
Savannah, Ga.	20	Cleveland, Ohio	19
Indianapolis, Ind.	17	Altoona, Pa.	17
Dubuque, Iowa	12	Harrisburg, Pa.	14
Manchester, N. H.	11	Philadelphia, Pa.	60
Auburn, N. Y.	23	Richmond, Va.	27
Syracuse, N. Y.	12		

ᶜ The only state with a sample large enough to warrant consideration in the state comparisons.

ᵈ Some of the reports are for the year ending in 1900, some for the year ending in 1902, but the majority, for the year ending in 1901.

ᵉ For other details regarding the selection of persons canvassed, see *Cost of Living in the United States*, p. 2.

ᶠ Distribution of those reporting is by the following income groups:

Income	Number	Income	Number
Under $900	332	$1,800-2,100	1,594
$900-1,200	2,423	2,100-2,500	705
1,200-1,500	3,959	2,500 & over	353
1,500-1,800	2,730		

Where these data are used by states in comparison with those for 1900/01, which were confined to returns of wage workers and salaried workers earning not more than $1,200 a year, data for families with an income of $1,200 or more were omitted.

ᵍ Expenditure reported is for books and newspapers.

ʰ Expenditure reported is for illness and death.

ⁱ Specifically included with sundries.

ʲ Expenditure reported is for fuel and light.

SHARE OF SERVICES

2 *Extrapolation to 1914 of the BLS Sample Data for 1918*

Extrapolation to 1914 was carried through for each state sample on the basis of changes in the service shares for a city sample. Average yearly expenses per family for each type of outlay in 1918 were taken from Table 3 of *Cost of Living in the United States*. The corresponding outlay in 1914 was estimated by dividing that in 1918 by 1 plus the percentage increase indicated in Table H (*ibid.*) for each item from December 1914 to December 1918. These outlay estimates were added, percentage shares of the total calculated, and the change from 1914 to 1918 in the service shares computed.

TABLE A 1

Extrapolation to 1914 of the United States Sample for 1918
(shares as percentages of total expenditures)

EXPENDITURE	1914 EXTRAPOLATED FROM 1918 BY CHANGES IN LIVING COSTS	1918 *Cost of Living in the United States* *
	(1)	(2)
Food	35.3	38.2
Clothing	13.4	16.6
Rent	19.6	13.4
Fuel & light	5.8	5.3
Furniture & furnishings	4.1	5.1
Miscellaneous	21.8	21.3

* Bureau of Labor Statistics Bulletin 357.

For the two state samples for which city samples were lacking, extrapolation was by the change in the service shares for *all* cities in the United States sample comprising the index in Table K (*ibid.*). The extrapolators for each state sample are shown below, and the results of the extrapolation for the United States sample in Table A 1.

State	*Extrapolator*
Illinois	Chicago
Maine	Portland
Massachusetts	Boston
New Jersey	U. S. sample
Ohio	Cleveland
Pennsylvania	Philadelphia
Wisconsin	U. S. sample

Most striking of the changes in the shares of the various items is the decline in the share of rent from 1914 to 1918. This is due less to a decrease in the expenditure for rent than to the increased outlay on commodities caused by the precipitous rise in prices.

"During the early war period rents did not rise at the same time nor to the same degree as the prices of most commodities, chiefly in consequence of rent laws enacted at the time." [1] These rent laws, together with other influences not usually present or present in exaggerated degree (e.g., shortages of materials and goods created by diversion to military purposes) compel us to characterize 1914-18 as an abnormal period and preclude its use in estimating the long term movement.

3 Adjustment of the Extrapolation to 1914

The extrapolation from 1918 to 1914 was felt to be in error because constant weights were used. When the consumption of an item is substantially curtailed owing to the war, or one item is substituted for another, extrapolation that takes account of the changes in prices alone is inadequate. To gauge the extent of our error and to provide a possible means of correcting for it, our 1914-18 extrapolations were compared with similar extrapolations for 1935-39 to 1942, and with the 1914-19 change in Lough's estimates.

'Cost of Living Indexes in Wartime' (*Journal of the American Statistical Association,* Dec. 1942) shows percentage shares of expenditures for 1935-39 and June 15, 1942, as well as the percentage increase in groups of items from August 1939 to August 1942. Extrapolation of the percentage shares for June 15, 1942 by the percentage changes in living costs from August 1942 to August 1939 yielded an estimate for 1939. The latter is compared with that for 1935-39 which reflects the quantities and prices for a period in which the cost of living was substantially the same as in 1939. This procedure is of course extremely arbitrary, both for the extrapolation of June by the August to August change and for its identification of 1939 with the entire period 1935-39. Variations in the cost of living during 1935-39 do not seem big enough, however, to impair the results seriously (Table A 2). Although the direction of the change is in general the same for both lines 4 and 5, the amount differs considerably. The difference in the service shares in line 5 is appreciably less than

[1] *Changes in Cost of Living, 1914-1936,* M. Ada Beney (National Industrial Conference Board, 1936), p. 47.

TABLE A 2

Changes from 1935-39 to 1942 in the Percentage Shares of
Total Expenditures
Based on Extrapolated and on Observed Values

	FOOD	CLOTHING	RENT	FUEL & LIGHT	FURNITURE & FURNISHINGS	MISC.
1 June 15, 1942, 'Cost of Living Indexes in Wartime' [a]	35.9	11.4	16.8	5.8[b]	3.6	26.5
2 1939, extrapolated from June 15, 1942 by changes in living costs	31.6	10.8	19.3	6.3[b]	3.5	28.4
3 1935-39, 'Cost of Living Indexes in Wartime' [a]	33.9	10.5	18.1	6.4[b]	4.2	26.9
4 Change, 1939 to June 15, 1942 (1 − 2)	+4.3	+0.6	−2.5	−0.5	+0.1	−1.9
5 Change, 1935-39 to June 15, 1942 (1 − 3)	+2.0	+0.9	−1.3	−0.6	−0.6	−0.4

[a] F. M. Williams, F. R. Rice, and E. D. Schell (*Journal of the American Statistical Association*, Dec. 1942).
[b] Fuel, electricity, and ice.

in line 4 where changes in prices alone are considered. Consequently it is more than likely that the difference in the service shares between 1914 and 1918 in Table A 1 is also exaggerated.

As a check, our percentage shares for 1914 and 1918 were compared with those derived from Lough's estimates of consumers' outlay for 1914 and 1919 (Table A 3). The relation between the actual and the estimated change in the shares is similar to that observed in Table A 2. The decline in the total service share in Lough's estimates from 1914 to 1919 is less than four-tenths of that in our sample data from 1914 to 1918, a difference too large to be attributed wholly to the difference of one year in the interval compared or to the difference in coverage—Lough's estimates purport to cover expenditures by all consumers, whereas ours cover only low income urban consumers. It seems reasonable to assign a portion of it to our failure to adjust for changes in the quantity and quality of goods consumed arising from the change in prices. Therefore, we lowered the rent share for our sample states 1.5 percent, the 'other' service share 0.5 percent. Although the correction should properly be applied to

TABLE A 3

Estimated Changes from 1914 to 1918 in Service Shares,
Computed from Urban Sample Data
Compared with Changes from 1914 to 1919, Computed from
Comprehensive Totals
(shares as percentages of total expenditures)

	RENT	OTHER SERVICES	TOTAL SERVICES
SEVEN SAMPLE STATES [a]			
1 1918, *Cost of Living in the U.S.*	14.45	12.25	26.70
2 1914, extrapolated from 1918 by changes in living costs	22.13	12.34	34.47
3 Change, 1914-18 (1 − 2)	−7.68	−0.09	−7.77
ALL STATES			
4 1914, Lough [b]	12.75	19.36	32.11
5 1919, Lough [b]	8.91	20.33	29.24
6 Change, 1914-19 (5 − 4)	−3.84	+0.97	−2.87

[a] Illinois, Maine, Massachusetts, New Jersey, Ohio, Pennsylvania, and Wisconsin.
[b] Derived from data in *High-Level Consumption,* Table 3, adjusted by the deduction of immigrant remittances and the addition of taxes shown in Appendix A.

the 1914 data for each state, it was made in the positional mean for 1900/01-14 since the latter was felt to be affected by the 1914 data.

4 Apportioning the Undistributed Sundry Item in the State Samples between Services and Commodities by the 1890/91 and 1918 United States Samples

As indicated in Section A Ie, the undistributed sundry item in the state samples for the years before 1900/01 is divided on the basis of the apportionment of the 1890/91 United States sample; in the state samples for 1900/01 and subsequent years, on that of the 1918 United States sample.

Before the 1890/91 and 1918 United States samples could be so utilized, their expenditures on 'other miscellaneous items' had to be divided between services and commodities. All the specific sundry service and commodity items were added, the ratio of each sum to the total was determined, and this ratio applied to the undistributed sundry item.

In applying the ratios taken from the 1890/91 and 1918 samples, allowance was made for the relative coverage of the undistributed sundry item in the state samples. From the per capita absolute for total sundry expenses in the United States

SHARE OF SERVICES

sample was deducted the sum of the absolutes for items covered separately in the state sample. The percentage distribution of the balance between services and commodities was then determined and applied to the state sample figure for unallocated sundries.

Because furniture is included with sundries the United States data by states for 1900/01 had to be adjusted before sundries proper were allocated. Furniture was estimated by its 1918 ratio to furniture and other sundries and deducted.

APPENDIX B

State Reports on Urban Consumers' Expenditures
Tabular Summary of Sources and Characteristics of the Sample Data

SOURCE	CONNECTICUT 4th An. Report, Bureau of Labor Statistics 1887/88	5th An. Report, Com. of Labor Statistics 1888/89	KANSAS 16th An. Report, Bureau of Labor 1900	23d An. Report, Bureau of Labor and Industry 1907	ILLINOIS 1st Biennial Report, Bureau of Labor Statistics 1878/79	3d Biennial Report, Bureau of Labor Statistics 1883/84	MAINE 5th An. Report, Com. of Industrial & Labor Statistics 1890/91	14th An. Report, Com. of Industrial & Labor Statistics 1899/1900
No. of returns utilized	43	b	e	f	j	j	p	p
Expenditures reported & rating as (C), (S), or (S & C)								
Food (C)	—	—	*	*	*	—	*	*
Groceries	*a	*	—	—	—	*	—	—
Meat	—	*	—	—	*k	*	—	—
Clothing (C)	*	*	*	*	**l	**	*	*
Boots & shoes	—	—	—	—	**l	**	—	—
Dry goods	—	—	—	—	**l	**	—	—
Rent (S)	*	*	*	*	*	**	*	*
Fuel (C)	*	*	*	*	**m	*	**m	**m
Lighting (C)	—	—	—	—	**m	*	**m	**m
Sundries (S & C)	*	*	*	*	*	*	*	*
Furniture & furnishings (C)	—	—	—	—	—	—	—	—

Insurance (S)	—	—	—	—	—	|*
Life	—	—	***g	***g	|*	|*
Accident	—	—	***g	***g	—	**q
Religion (S)	—	|*	—	—	—	|*
Trade unions (S)	—	—	—	**i	|*	—
Societies (S)	—	—	—	—	—	|*
Charity (S)	—	—	—	—	—	**q
Care of parents (C)	—	—	—	—	—	—
Street car fares (S)	—	—	—	—	—	—
To work	—	—	—	—	—	—
Travel (recreation) (S)	—	**c	—	—	—	—
Amusements (recreation) (S)	—	—	—	—	—	—
Vacation (S)	—	—	—	—	—	—
Musical instruments (C)	—	**c	—	—	—	—
Education (C)	—	—	—	|*	—	—
Newspapers (C)	—	—	—	—	—	—
Books (C)	—	—	—	**n	—	—
Music & music lessons (C)	—	—	—	**n	—	—
Medicine & medical attendance (sickness) (S)	—	|*	|*	—	|*	—
Funeral expenses (S)	—	—	—	|*	**r	—
Liquors (C)	—	**d	|*	—	|*	**r
Tobacco (C)	—	**d	**h	**o	—	—
Insurance, fire (S)	—	—	***	**o	—	—
Taxes (S)	—	—	—	—	—	—
Road (S)	—	—	**h	—	—	—
Repairs (S)	—	—	—	—	—	—
Improvement & tools (C)	—	—	|*	—	|*	—
Soap (C)	—	—	—	—	—	—
Personal expenses (C)	—	—	|*	—	—	—
House girl (help) (S)	—	**d	—	—	—	—
Care of house (C)	—	|*	—	—	—	—
Boarding (C)	—	**d	|*	—	—	—
Interest (S)	—	—	—	|*	—	—
Laundry (S)	—	—	—	—	—	—
Food for cows, chickens, etc. (C)	—	—	—	—	|*	|*

—Not reported. * Reported separately. ** Reported, but not separately.

Appendix B continued:

SOURCE	MASSACHUSETTS				MISSOURI		NEBRASKA	
	1870 2nd An. Report, Labor & Industries Dept. on Statistics of Labor	1874/75 6th An. Report, Labor & Industries Dept. on Statistics of Labor	1883 15th An. Report, Labor & Industries Dept. on Statistics of Labor	1901 32nd An. Report, Labor & Industries Dept. on Statistics of Labor	1880 2nd An. Report, Com. of Labor Statistics	1888/89 11th An. Report, Com. of Labor Statistics	1889/90 2nd Biennial Report, Bureau of Labor & Industrial Statistics	1912 13th Biennial Report, Bureau of Labor & Industrial Statistics
No. of returns utilized	10	397^t	16	152	13^y / 89^z	77^y	27^bb	ee
Expenditures reported & rating as (C), (S), or (S & C)								
Food (C)	—	*	—	—	—*a	*aa	*	*
Groceries	*a	—	**s	**v		—/*	—	—
Meat	—	—	*	**v	—	*	—	—
Clothing (C)	*	*	**	*	*	*	*	*
Boots & shoes	—	—	**	—	*	—	—	—
Dry goods	—	—	**	—	*	—	—	—
Rent (S)	*	*	*	*	*	*	*	*
Fuel (C)	**m	*	**	**m	*	u	*kk	*dd
Lighting (C)	**m	—	—	**m	—	u	*	—
Sundries (S & C)	*	*	*	*	*	*u	—	**ee
Furniture & furnishings (C)	—	*u	—	*	—	*u	*	**ee
Insurance (S) Life	—	*u	—	—	—	—	*	—
Accident	—	—	—	*q	—	—	—	—
Religion (S)	**q	*u	—	**q	—	*u	—	**ee
Trade unions (S)	—	—	—	**w	—	—	—	—

Societies (S)	**q	□ □ □		**w			
Charity (S)		□ □		**q		* *	
Care of parents (C)							
Street car fares (S)						*	
To work	**e	□ □		**jj			
Travel (recreation) (S)				*	*	*	
To work				**jj		*	
Amusements (recreation) (S)	**c			**x		*	
Vacation (S)		□		**x	*		
Musical instruments (C)		□		**x			
Education (C)							
Newspapers (C)				**r			
Books (C)				**r			*
Music & music lessons (C)							
Medicine & medical attendance (sickness) (S)	*				*		*
Funeral expenses (S)							
Liquors (C)							
Tobacco (C)							
Insurance, fire (S)							
Taxes (S)							
Road (S)							
Repairs (S)							
Improvement & tools (C)					*		
Soap (C)							
Personal expenses (C)		□ □					
House girl (help) (S)							
Care of house (C)							
Boarding (C)							
Interest (S)							
Laundry (S)							
Food for cows, chickens, etc. (C)		□				□	

− Not reported.   * Reported separately.   ** Reported, but not separately.

Appendix B continued:

SOURCE	NEW JERSEY		OHIO		PENNSYLVANIA			WISCONSIN	
	1877/78 1st An. Report, Bureau of Statistics of Labor & Industries	1885/86 9th An. Report, Bureau of Statistics of Labor & Industries	1878 3d An. Report, Bureau of Labor Statistics	1885/86 10th An. Report, Bureau of Labor Statistics	1875 4th An. Report, Sec. of Internal Affairs	1879 7th An. Report, Sec. of Internal Affairs	1886/87 15th An. Report, Sec. of Internal Affairs	1885 2nd Biennial Report, Bureau of Labor & Industrial Statistics	1895 7th Biennial Report, Bureau of Labor, Industrial & Census Statistics
No. of returns utilized	73	189	72	87	9	163	39	8	423
Expenditures reported & rating as (C), (S), or (S & C)									
Food (C)	—	*	—	—	—	—	*	*	*
Groceries	—	—	*	—	*s	—*	—	—	—
Meat	*k	—	*k	*	*	—	—	—	—
Clothing (C)	*	*	*gg	*	*	**l	*	*	**l
Boots & shoes	—	—	*	*	*	—*l	—	—	**l
Dry goods	—	—	—	*	*	—	—	—	—
Rent (S)	*	*	**hh	*	*	*	*	*	*
Fuel (C)	*	**m	**m	—	*	*	**m	—	*
Lighting (C)	—	**m	**m	*	*	—	**m	—	—
Sundries (S & C)	*	*	*	*	*	*	*	*	*
Furniture & furnishings (C)	—	—	—	—	—	—	—	*	—
Insurance (S)	—	**ff	—	—	—	—	*	—	—
Life	—	—	—	—	—	—	—	—	—
Accident	—	—	—	—	*	—	—	—	—
Religion (S)	—	—	—	—	—	—	—	—	—

Trade unions (S)
Societies (S)
Charity (S)
Care of parents (C)
Street car fares (S)
 To work
Travel (recreation) (S)
 To work
Amusements (recreation) (S)
Vacations (S)
Musical instruments (C)
Education (C)
Newspapers (C)
Books (C)
Music & music lessons (C)
Medicine & medical attendance (sickness) (S)
Funeral expenses (S)
Liquors (C)
Tobacco (C)
Insurance, fire (S)
Taxes (S)
Road (S)
Repairs (S)
Improvement & tools (C)
Soap (C)
Personal expenses (C)
House girl (help) (S)
Care of house (C)
Boarding (C)
Interest (S)
Laundry (S)
Food for cows, chickens, etc. (C)

— Not reported.   * Reported separately.   ** Reported, but not separately.

Notes to Appendix B

a Expenditure reported is for groceries and provisions.
b Averages of monthly data for 15 occupations. The location of the persons reporting, the number of monthly returns, and the months they cover, are indicated below.

CITY	NO. OF MONTHLY RETURNS UTILIZED	MONTHS COVERED
Blacksmiths		
Atchison	56	Jan.-Sept. 1889
Kansas City	51	Nov. 1888, Jan.-Sept. 1889
Leavenworth	52	Jan.-Sept. 1889
Topeka	32	Jan.-Sept. 1889
Harness-Makers		
Atchison	29	Jan.-Sept. 1889
Topeka	26	Apr.-Sept. 1889
Laborers		
Atchison	51	Jan.-Sept. 1889
Kansas City	52	Nov. 1888, Jan.-Sept. 1889
Leavenworth	62	Nov. 1888, Jan.-Sept. 1889
Topeka	175	Jan.-Sept. 1889
Laborers—Railroad		
Atchison	9	Jan.-Apr. 1889
Kansas City	25	Nov. 1888, Jan.-Apr., June-Sept. 1889
Painters		
Atchison	43	Jan.-Sept. 1889
Kansas City	52	Nov. 1888, Jan.-Sept. 1889
Leavenworth	26	Jan., Apr.-Sept. 1889
Topeka	29	Jan.-Sept. 1889
Printers		
Atchison	46	Jan.-Sept. 1889
Kansas City	52	Nov. 1888, Jan.-Sept. 1889
Leavenworth	46	Jan.-Sept. 1889
Topeka	89	Jan.-Sept. 1889
Street Car Drivers		
Atchison	41	Jan.-Sept. 1889
Leavenworth	30	Jan.-Sept. 1889
Topeka	45	Jan.-Sept. 1889
Conductors—Cable Street Railroad		
Kansas City	19	Nov. 1888, Jan.-Sept. 1889
Topeka	13	Jan., May, July-Sept. 1889
Conductors—Elevated Street Railroad		
Kansas City	16	Jan.-Mar., May-Sept. 1889
Engineers—Elevated Street Railway		
Kansas City	13	Jan.-Mar., May-Sept. 1889
Topeka	14	Apr.-Sept. 1889
Gripmen—Cable Street Railroad		
Kansas City	9	Jan.-July 1889
Cigar Makers		
Leavenworth	32	Jan.-Mar., June-Sept. 1889
Topeka	15	Jan.-May, July 1889
Bricklayers		
Topeka	16	May-Sept. 1889
Shoemakers		
Topeka	24	Jan.-Apr., June, July 1889

SHARE OF SERVICES

CITY	NO. OF MONTHLY RETURNS UTILIZED	MONTHS COVERED
	Tinners	
Topeka	15	Jan., Feb., Apr., May, July, Aug. 1889

For occupations for which there were returns from more than one city, an average for all the cities reporting was computed, equal weight being assigned the per capita for each city.

c Expenditure reported is for education and amusements. The distribution between services and commodities is based on the division of the United States sample for 1890/91 (App. A).

d Expenditure reported is for interest, insurance, taxes.

e Averages of data for 21 occupations. The size of the sample utilized for each occupation is:

Occupation	No. of Returns Utilized
Railway Employees in Train Service	
Brakemen	7
Conductors	11
Locomotive engineers	5
Locomotive firemen	11
Railway Employees in Miscellaneous Trades	
Blacksmiths	2
Boilermakers	4
Agents and operators	6
Machinists	3
Trackmen	4
Miscellaneous	10
Building Trades	
Carpenters	8
Laborers	5
Painters and paper hangers	2
Stone masons and bricklayers	6
Miscellaneous Trades	
Barbers	1
Butchers	6
Leather workers	1
Miners, coal	7
Printers	3
Retail clerks	8
Miscellaneous	12

f Averages of data for 25 occupations. The size of the sample utilized for each occupation is:

Occupation	No. of Returns Utilized
Railway Employees in Train Service	
Brakemen	3
Freight conductors	9
Engineers	5
Firemen	7
Switchmen	4
Railway Employees in Miscellaneous Trades	
Boilermakers	8
Boilermakers' helpers	1
Carmen	18
Machinists	2
Building Trades	
Bricklayers and stone masons	8
Carpenters	19
Electrical workers	7
Hod carriers	1
Painters and paper hangers	4
Stone cutters	1

Notes to Appendix B *(concl.)*

Occupation	No. of Returns Utilized
Miscellaneous Trades	
Barbers	14
Cigar makers	7
Retail clerks	1
Iron molders	5
Laborers (common)	2
Mine workers	12
Powder workers	1
Printers	9
Teamsters	18
Miscellaneous Skilled Vocations	12

g Expenditure reported is for life and accident insurance.
h Expenditure reported is for taxes and repairs.
i Expenditure reported is for books and lodge dues.
j Averages of data for laborers and carpenters. The size of the sample utilized for each occupation is:

OCCUPATION	NO. OF RETURNS UTILIZED	
	1878/79	1883/84
Laborers	11	174
Carpenters	15	49

k Expenditure reported is for meat and vegetables.
l Expenditure reported is for clothing and dry goods.
m Expenditure reported is for fuel and light.
n Expenditure reported is for education, including papers.
o Expenditure reported is for tobacco and liquors.
p Averages of data for laborers, shoemakers, blacksmiths, and machinists. The size of the sample utilized for each occupation is:

OCCUPATION	NO. OF RETURNS UTILIZED	
	1890/91	1899/1900
Laborers	25	3
Shoemakers	58	35
Blacksmiths	7	8
Machinists	18	7

q Expenditure reported is for religion and charity.
r Expenditure reported is for sickness and funeral expenses.
s Separate expenditures for fish and milk included.
t Composite total derived from returns for 397 families.
u Specifically included with sundries.
v Expenditure reported is for groceries, meats, fish, ice, milk.
w Expenditure reported is for (dues to) societies and unions.
x Expenditure reported is for education, newspapers, and periodicals.
y Returns for mine workers utilized in the 1880-88/89 comparison alone.
z Returns for all industries canvassed.
aa Expenditure reported is for food other than meat.
bb Most of the data reported are on a monthly basis but annual data are shown for clothing and house furnishings.
cc Returns for 'wage earners of the minimum class from seven Nebraska industrial centers'. The size of the sample is not stated. All data are monthly.
dd Expenditure reported is for fuel and ice.
ee Expenditure reported is for incidentals including union dues and insurance.
ff Expenditure reported is for society dues and life insurance.
gg Expenditure reported is for clothing, etc.
hh Expenditure reported is for rent, taxes, or repairs.
ii Expenditure reported is for education and books.
jj Expenditure reported is for amusements and travel for recreation.
kk Separate expenditure for oil included.

Appendix C
Appraisal of the Sample Data and of the Comparisons

Changes in the service shares from one period to another may be due to the incomparability of the basic data as well as to a genuine shift in the pattern of consumer expenditures. It is impossible to determine the relative influence of these two factors. Careful scrutiny of each sample, together with consideration of the movement of the per capita expenditure from sample to sample, however, afford a better basis for judging the comparability of the data, so that we are able to surmise the extent of the true change in the service shares. We proceed, therefore, to examine each sample, pointing up aspects that may affect their comparison. An A or B beside a year indicates whether the sample material is tabulated in Appendix A or B.

CONNECTICUT
1887/88 (B) and 1900/01 (A)
Of 611 reports for 1887/88, 568 had to be discarded either because of incompleteness or because returns for several families were combined, making it impossible to ascertain whether all items were reported for each family. (Inclusion of these combined returns depresses the share of rent—evidence, probably, that rent was often not reported.) The 1900/01 report includes no returns for persons with incomes over $1,200; for 1887/88, data were included for persons with incomes up to $1,400. In the earlier sample only 12 industries are covered; in the later years presumably far more.

ILLINOIS
1878/79 (B) and 1883/84 (B)
Of the 38 occupational groups covered by the report for 1878/79, only two—laborers and carpenters—are utilized in our comparison. Had we summarized the entire report, our conclusions might be different, but the period between the two sample years was so short that the time and labor did not seem warranted. Enlarging the sample in 1883/84 to cover all 26 occupations reported yields a total service share of 26.73 percent, only slightly higher than that for laborers and carpenters—26.41 percent.

The drop in the total service share from 28.09 percent in 1878/79 to 26.41 percent in 1883/84 is due to the decline in 'other' service items from 10.76 to 7.41 percent, which offsets the rise in the share of rent from 17.33 to 19.00 percent. Comparison of the per capita absolutes leads to the belief that coverage of items other than food, fuel and light, clothing, and rent is far less complete for 1883/84 than for 1878/79. Since 'all other' and 'sundries' are not described in the source material, this belief cannot be confirmed, but there appears to be justification for attributing at least a part of the drop in the total service share to the less complete coverage of service items in the later year.

1900/01 (A) and 1918 (A)

The 1918 sample, comprising returns for 3 cities (69 for Chicago, 19 for Danville, and 12 for Pana), is only 14 percent of that for 1900/01. Although the disparity in size and territorial coverage is appreciable, the comparability of the samples is not seriously affected. The 1918 material is extrapolated to 1914 by the movement of the shares for rent and other services for Chicago.

From 1900/01 to 1914 the rent share rose from 16.20 to 23.37 percent; that of other services from 8.77 to 13.65 percent. Even were a part of these rises due to inconsistencies between the two samples, the movement would still be definitely upward.

KANSAS

1888/89 (B), 1900 (B), and 1907 (B)

From the source material for 1888/89 it is not clear how the published figures were arrived at, but considerable computation was evidently required to raise the partial data to the coverage finally indicated. We had to recompute the average expenses for illness, interest, insurance, taxes, education, and society dues—dividing by total returns rather than by the number showing the particular type of expense. When boarding is mentioned, as well as expenses for groceries and meat, these items are also divided by total returns. The sum of these per capitas is the total per capita outlay for food. We are not justified in disregarding the rent element involved in the payments for board, but comparison of the per capitas for board with those for groceries and meat seems to indicate that the item is essentially a payment for food rather than for food and lodging.

The omission of returns for October and December may affect the comparison with the 1900 and 1907 samples.

The rise in the total service share from 31.10 percent in 1888/89 to 31.49 percent in 1900 is due to the increase in the share of 'other' services from 13.26 to 15.99 percent; the share of rent declines from 17.84 to 15.50 percent. The increase of 3.85 percent in the total service share from 1900 to 1907 is due chiefly to 'other' services, which rose from 15.99 to 18.36 percent. The shares for 1888/89, computed as they are from monthly data, are probably not comparable with those for 1900 and 1907, computed from annual data. This may well account for the surprising difference in the per year increases in the share of services: 0.035 percent from 1888/89 to 1900, and 0.550 percent from 1900 to 1907.

Maine
1890/91 (B) and 1899/1900 (B)

The sample for 1899/1900 is far smaller than that for 1890/91, yet comparison of the per capita absolutes in the two years fails to reveal any serious disparity. However, though enlarging the sample for 1899/1900 to cover all 7 occupations canvassed causes practically no change in the percentage share for services, the total service share for 1890/91 is lowered more than 1 percent —from 28.46 to 27.24 percent—if all 27 occupations are used. The shares based on the 4 occupations should not, therefore, be compared with percentage shares for other states purporting to represent complete occupational coverage.

The rise in the total service share from 28.46 to 34.21 percent is due to the increase in the share of rent from 17.35 to 20.45 percent as well as in the share of other services from 11.11 to 13.76 percent. Since it was feared that these increases might have been the accidental effect of the small, and therefore doubtful, samples, they were checked against those for shoemakers—the one occupational group for which our 1899/1900 sample is of appreciable size. They tally closely.

1900/01 (A) and 1918 (A)

The sample for 1918 is only one-seventh of that for 1900/01 and is for a single city, Portland. However, the data are apparently not out of line with those for states for which the samples are larger and more representative.

The total service share for 1914, extrapolated from 1918 on the basis of the movement of the share for all income groups in Portland, is 34.47 percent, an annual increase from 1900/01 to 1914 of 0.939 percent—slightly higher than that for Illinois.

MASSACHUSETTS

1870 (B) and 1883 (B)

Not only are the samples extremely small, but inspection of the per capita absolutes in the two years casts grave doubt upon their comparability. Fuel and light are reported in 1870, but the item on the 1883 schedule is for fuel alone. Since the 1883 figure is appreciably lower than the 1870, there is reason to suspect that light is not covered in the later year. On the other hand, the very much higher rent figure in 1883 may include light. The markedly larger figure for sundries in 1883 may indicate the inclusion of furniture, education, etc., which were reported separately in 1870.

The total share of services is 25.21 percent in 1870 and 27.41 percent in 1883. Rent rises from 14.67 to 21.37 percent; other services decline from 10.54 to 6.04 percent. In an alternative distribution it was assumed that the expenditure for fuel and light in 1883 was the same as in 1870. The amount thus added to the 1883 figure for fuel was deducted from the figure for rent, on the ground that the rent figure, rising out of all proportion to other items, included expenses for lighting. It was further assumed that in 1883 sundries excluded furniture, education, etc., and hence was comparable with sundries proper in 1870. These adjustments reduced the percentage shares for services, but the increase from 1870 to 1883 was even larger—from 21.03 to 24.11 percent. The movement of the components seemed more reasonable than that yielded by the unadjusted data, rent rising from 17.15 to 18.07 percent and other services from 3.88 to 6.04 percent. But these alternative distributions were disregarded because they widen the difference between the total service shares in the two years.

1874/75 (B) and 1901 (B)

Although the fuel item reported in 1874/75 purports to be for fuel alone, comparison of the per capita absolutes in the two years seems to indicate that light is included. The statement in the source that "only about one-third of this (the sundries) item is specifically accounted for" does not necessarily mean that there is undercoverage, but it does indicate that in many instances sundries were estimated as a whole rather than by items and that in this lump estimate certain items may possibly have been undervalued. When rent was not reported for 1901, 'other expenses' were substituted, inasmuch as apparently they usually represented payments by home owners. In the few cases where both rent and 'other expenses' were reported on the same schedule, the latter was regarded as a miscellaneous item.

The rise from 20.35 percent in 1874/75 to 23.91 percent in 1901 is due entirely to the rise in the 'other' service share from 3.62 to 9.07 percent, since rent declines from 16.73 to 14.84 percent. The very marked rise in the share for sundries can be regarded as an indication either of greater proportionate outlay on services not embodied in new commodities or of greater coverage in the later year. Probably both factors were at work.

1890/91 (A), 1900/01 (A), and 1918 (A)

The sample for 1900/01 is much bigger and presumably, therefore, of wider territorial coverage than the fairly large samples for 1890/91 and 1918. In using the 1890/91 sample for comparison, we assume that the data on workers in cotton, woolen, and glass mills vary little, at least in percentage distribution, from those in other industries. The marked difference in per capita rents in 1890/91 and 1900/01, however, may indicate that the assumption is invalid.

The rise in the total service share from 26.52 percent in 1890/91 to 32.46 percent in 1900/01 is due to the rise in the share of rent from 15.38 to 20.95 percent, as the share of other services rises only slightly—from 11.14 to 11.51 percent. When we extrapolate the 1918 shares of rent and of other services to 1914 by the movement of the shares for Boston, the total service share becomes 33.24 percent, as against 32.46 percent for the 1900/01 sample, or a yearly increase of 0.058 percent.

It seems unlikely that this low annual gain would follow that of +0.594 percent for 1890/91-1900/01. Surprising also is the wide disparity between the percentage shares calculated from the Massachusetts source material for 1901 and the United States source material for 1900/01. It seems to be due to the groceries and provisions item, the per capita absolute computed from the Massachusetts report being $415 and that from the United States material $258. The higher per capita is consistent with those for other years based on Massachusetts reports, while the lower tallies with those for 1890/91 and 1918 with which it is compared. The low per capita rent in 1890/91 mentioned above may be evidence of incomparability in the 1890/91 and 1900/01 samples.

Missouri

1880 (B) and 1888/89 (B)

Fuel in 1888/89 was estimated on the basis of the 1880 ratio of fuel to the sum of items other than rent, food, and clothing.

The total service share rises from 19.63 percent in 1880 to 23.58 percent in 1888/89: rent from 10.01 to 12.75 percent, and other services from 9.62 to 10.83 percent. Part of these rises may be due to undercoverage of expenditures for food in 1888/89. According to the source, many of the families canvassed had a small garden, pigs, chickens, etc.; sometimes a cow. Though there is no way of determining how much home-grown products contributed to the food supply, it is unlikely that the addition of their value would raise the commodity share sufficiently to offset the very pronounced rise in the service shares.

1880 (B) and 1900/01 (A)

The rise in the total service share from 28.15 percent in 1880 to 33.53 percent in 1900/01 is due entirely to the increase in sundries. The declining shares of all other items, despite the substantial rise in the per capita absolutes, may be evidence of greater coverage of sundries in the later year.

SHARE OF SERVICES 175

NEBRASKA
1889/90 (B) and 1912 (B)

Both samples are derived from monthly data. Per capita expenditures are $696 in 1912 and $379 in 1889/90. This 84 percent increase is not distributed equally, as food, e.g., increases only 39 percent, rent, 97 percent, and street car fares, more than 1,500 percent. The sample for the earlier year shows no specific entry for laundry, nor does it include a miscellaneous category in which laundry might be covered. It is impossible, on the other hand, to determine what the later sample includes under 'incidental'; i.e., whether house furnishings, musical instruments, and the other items not specifically listed are taken care of or disregarded. Since, with the exception of contributions, the items unaccounted for in the later year are all in the commodity category, there may be a bias in favor of services. This may explain, in part at least, the very large increase in the share of 'other' services, from 2.94 percent in 1889/90 to 14.13 percent in 1912, as rent rises only moderately—from 21.41 to 22.94 percent.

The service shares for 1918, computed from data for 19 families in Grand Island, and 8 in Omaha (*Cost of Living in the United States*), and extrapolated to 1914 by the movement of the cost of living for 32 cities in the United States (*ibid.*), yields a total service share of 36.11 percent, less than 1 percent smaller than that calculated from the Nebraska data for 1912. Although the shares for these two years cannot be regarded as comparable, their closeness suggests that the figure for 1912 is not much too high.

NEW JERSEY
1877/78 (B) and 1885/86 (B)

The decline in the total service share from 24.46 to 23.23 percent reflects a decline in both rent (from 17.89 to 17.13 percent) and other service items (from 6.57 to 6.10 percent). The comparability of the sundry category in the two years is suspect, for while the per capita absolutes of all other items rise appreciably, that for sundries declines.

As data for consecutive years are more likely to be comparable than those for widely separated years, percentages were calculated for 1878/79 and 1884/85 also. These indicate a slight rise in the total service share from 1877/78 to 1878/79 and from 1884/85 to 1885/86. The decline from 1877/78 to 1885/86 cannot be dismissed on the evidence of these short term changes, though they lend weight to the surmise that the decline may be due to vagaries in the sample.

1900/01 (A) and 1918 (A)

The 1918 sample, comprising returns for 3 cities (12 for Dover, 35 for Newark, and 11 for Trenton), is only one-tenth of that for 1900/01. This appreciable disparity in size and territorial coverage may affect the results of the comparison of the percentage shares in the two years.

The shares for rent and other services in 1918 are extrapolated to 1914 by the change in the cost of living for 32 cities in the United States as derived from *Cost of Living in the United States*, yielding a total service share of 35.23 percent, an annual increase from 1900/01 of 0.353 percent.

OHIO

1878 (B) and 1885/86 (B)

The source material does not indicate what the category 'clothing, etc.' in 1878 comprises. It may be the equivalent of clothing, boots and shoes, and dry goods, as reported in 1885/86. The composition of 'other expenses' and of 'sundries' is likewise unknown.

If it is assumed that the two samples are comparable, the total service shares are 27.88 percent in 1878 and 27.14 percent in 1885/86; rent rises from 17.00 to 18.41 percent; other services decline from 10.88 to 8.73 percent. The per capita absolutes, however, suggest that recreation and education were not covered in the 1885/86 sample and that dry goods and trade union dues were disregarded in 1878. Without these items, total service shares are 27.14 percent in 1878 and 28.21 percent in 1885/86; rent rises from 17.64 to 19.67 percent; other services decline from 9.50 to 8.54 percent, owing to the drop in the expenses for illness. Perhaps the one conclusion we are justified in drawing is that there is no pronounced change in the pattern of consumers' outlay.

1900/01 (A) and 1918 (A)

Although the 1918 sample is only one-fifth that for 1900/01, it is fairly representative, covering returns for 192 families (117 in Cincinnati, 25 in Cleveland, 47 in Columbus, and 3 in Steubenville). When the 1918 shares are extrapolated to 1914 by the movement of the shares for Cleveland, the total service share becomes 35.30 percent, an annual increase of 0.567 percent from 1900/01. Rent rises from 14.11 percent in 1900/01 to 22.29 percent in 1914; other services decline slightly—from 13.54 to 13.01 percent.

PENNSYLVANIA

1875 (B), 1879 (B), and 1886/87 (B)

The samples differ appreciably in size and may not be comparable for the three years. Expenditures for recreation are not specifically mentioned in the 1875 sample, and religion is apparently not covered in the 1879 sample. The 1886/87 sample, on the other hand, mentions society dues and life insurance, but not education, recreation, or religion. As sundries or 'other' expenses are not described, it cannot be determined whether they include these items. It was assumed that the data are comparable so far as coverage is concerned, since discrepancies are presumably minor. Rent per capita, however, suggests that there is some disparity in concept, since rent in 1879 seems unreasonably low, and is the primary cause for the fall in the total service share from 1875 to 1879, and the rise from 1879 to 1886/87. The rent shares for these three years are 17.42, 14.68, and 19.11 percent respectively; other services rise from 7.36 to 9.74 percent and drop from 9.74 to 9.04 percent.

1890/91 (A), 1900/01 (A), and 1918 (A)

The great disparity in the size of the three samples and in the territorial coverage may account for the big differences the comparison reveals. The sample for 1890/91—91 families, of which 17 reside in Altoona, 14 in Harrisburg, and 60 in Philadelphia—may give too much weight to the high rent figures in Philadelphia. The 1918 sample, covering returns for 4 cities (31 for Chambersburg, 56 for Pittsburgh, 40 for Scranton, and 67 for Philadelphia and Camden, N. J.), is bigger, and is not as greatly influenced by the returns for any one city.

The total service share declines from 34.08 percent in 1890/91 to 32.29 percent in 1900/01, because of the drop in the share of rent from 24.01 to 20.89 percent; the share of other services rises from 10.07 to 11.40 percent. The total service share for 1914, extrapolated from 1918 on the basis of the changes in the component shares for Philadelphia, is 33.60 percent, an annual increase of 0.097 percent from 1900/01.

WISCONSIN

1885 (B) and 1895 (B)

It was assumed that expenditures for fuel in 1885 are included with miscellaneous expenditures and are the same as in 1895.

Despite the great disparity in the size of the two samples, there is surprising agreement in the per capita absolutes and in the level of expenditures. The earlier sample, though small, may therefore be regarded as fairly representative. In sundries alone does the very much higher per capita in 1885 indicate more complete coverage. A widening of the scope of this item for 1895 would, however, tend to raise the service share, thereby accentuating the rise from the 1885 level. If, on the other hand, undue emphasis was placed on the miscellaneous items in the 1885 sample, as may occur when samples are small, we should, perhaps, assume a lower share of the service items in 1885 rather than a higher in 1895. Therefore, the difference between the shares for the two years tends to be the same whichever alternative is assumed. The total service share in 1895 tallies so closely with that for 1900/01 that overstatement in 1885 seems more likely than understatement in 1895.

The rise in the service share from 25.06 percent in 1885 to 26.51 percent in 1895 is due entirely to the rise in rent from 14.18 to 17.37 percent; the share of other services declines from 10.88 to 9.14 percent.

1900/01 (A) and 1918 (A)

The sample for 1918, comprising returns for 128 families (31 in Green Bay, 53 in Milwaukee, and 44 in Chippewa Falls), though only half that for 1900/01, is nevertheless large enough to merit consideration.

SHARE OF SERVICES

The shares for rent and other services in 1918 are extrapolated to 1914 by the change in the cost of living for 32 cities in the United States as derived from *Cost of Living in the United States*, yielding a total service share of 32.42 percent, an annual increase from 1900/01 of 0.414 percent.

APPENDIX D

United States Reports on Consumers' Expenditures since 1919
Tabular Summary of Sources and Characteristics of the Sample Data

	1922/24[a]	1935/36	1941
SOURCE	*The Farmer's Standard of Living* (Dept. of Agriculture, Bull. 1466)	*Family Expenditures in the United States* (National Resources Planning Board, Washington, D. C., 1941)	'Family Spending and Saving in Wartime' (preliminary releases by the Bureau of Home Economics, Dept. of Agriculture; 'Income and Spending and Saving of City Families in Wartime', *Monthly Labor Review*, Sept. 1942)[b]
Persons covered by returns	Farm families of selected localities in 11 states.[c] Each family had an adult man operating the farm and an adult woman as homemaker. It included parents & children who were at home, or, who, while away at school or elsewhere, were supported from the family purse.	'Normal' families in 6 types of community: farms, rural nonfarm areas, small cities, middle-sized cities, large cities, & metropolises. A normal family was one containing a husband & a wife, with or without other persons. 7 broad occupational groups were represented: wage earner, clerical, independent business, salaried business, independent professional, salaried professional, & farming.[d]	Families & single consumers in farm & rural nonfarm areas, & in cities [e]
Total returns	2,886	54,000	3,060[f]
Expenditures reported & rating as '(C), (S), or (S & C)[g]			
Food (C)	*	*	*
Clothing (C)	**h	**	**p
Cleaning, pressing (S)	**h	**	**p
Housing (S)	*i	*	**q
Household operation	–j	–*	–q
Fuel, light, refrigeration (C)	**j	**	**q
Paid household service (S)	**j	*	***r

Telephone (S)   **r
Laundry sent out (S)   **r
Other (S & C)   **r
Furnishings (C)   **k
Transportation
  Automobile
    Purchase (C)
    Operation
      Gasoline (C)   **j
      Oil (C)
      Insurance (S)
    Other items (S & C)
  Other (S & C)   **j
Medical care   *l
  Physician, dentist, oculist, other
    specialist (S)
  Medicine, drugs (C)
  Other medical care (S & C)
Recreation
  Movies & other paid admissions (S)   **m
  Sports, games (S & C)
  Radio purchase (C)
  Other recreation (S & C)
Personal care
  Services (S)   **n
  Toilet supplies (C)   **n
Tobacco (C)   **m
Education (S)
Reading (C)   *o
Other items (S)
Gifts
  To individual (C)   **n
  To church (S)   **m
  Other (S)
Personal taxes (S)

— Not reported.   * Reported separately.   ** Reported, but not separately.

NOTES TO APPENDIX D

a Data are for one year in 1922/24.
b Final estimates, published since this study went to press, appear in *Family Spending and Saving in Wartime,* BLS Bulletin 822.
c Distribution of families studied is:

	NUMBER OF FAMILIES		NUMBER OF FAMILIES
New Hampshire	40	Alabama	558
Vermont	86	Missouri	178
Massachusetts	81	Kansas	406
Connecticut	110	Iowa	472
Kentucky	370	Ohio	383
South Carolina	202		

d A much more detailed description is given in the source.
e A more detailed description is given in the final report (see note b, above).
f Given in the final report (see note b, above).
g When the rating is indicated as (S & C) an equal division between services and commodities was made. For 1922/24 the apportionment of the so-called 'mixed' categories between services and commodities is based upon the relation in 1935/36. For 1941, and for 1935/36 when comparison is with 1941, the rating for these mixed categories is:
Clothing, including cleaning and pressing (C)
Housing, including fuel, light, and refrigeration (S)
'Other' household operation (S)
Automobile (C)
Other transportation (S)
Medical care (S)
Recreation: for urban and rural nonfarm families (S); for rural farm families (S & C)
Personal care (S & C)
Gifts (S & C)

h Expenditure reported is for clothing, including sewing, dry cleaning, pressing, and shoe repairing.
i Rent, estimated at 10 percent of the total value of the house, plus taxes, insurance, improvements, repairs, and depreciation.
j Expenditure reported is for automobile (including license, tax, operation, repairs, and depreciation); fuel; household labor (hired); ice and water; insurance on furnishings and equipment; laundry work done outside; postage, stationery, express, freight and drayage; travel by bus, trolley, and train; supplies for cleaning, laundry, and miscellaneous purposes; telephone.
k Furnishings and portable equipment (including repairs) plus musical instruments.
l Expenditure reported is for doctors, etc., eye glasses, medicine, and travel to hospitals or for treatments.
m Expenditure reported is for advancement and covers education, contributions to church organizations, concerts, vacations, etc.
n Expenditure reported is for personal care and covers barbers, hairdressers; candy, etc.; gifts to family and friends; jewelry, including repairs; tobacco; toilet articles.
o Expenditure reported is for exceptional items, emergencies, etc.
p Expenditure reported is for clothing which includes cleaning and pressing.
q For urban families the expenditure reported is for housing, fuel, light, and refrigeration.
r Expenditure reported is for 'other' household operation.

PART IV

Reproducible Wealth
Its Growth and Industrial Distribution
1880-1939

Part IV

The purpose of the analysis is partly to test the validity of the wealth estimates when compared with cumulated totals of capital formation based on commodity flow data; partly to attempt a distribution of capital formation by categories of industrial users. We first discuss the character of the wealth estimates that can be had for this purpose; then present the detailed basic and summary tables.

A CHARACTER OF THE ESTIMATES

1 *Scope*

The first official estimate of wealth in the United States was prepared for 1850. And the first estimate distributed by categories was for 1880. The 1890 estimate was similarly classified; and the 1900, 1904, 1912, and 1922 in considerably greater industrial detail.

In preparing its 1922 estimate, the Bureau of the Census defined wealth as the material wealth or value of tangible property within the continental United States, including, in addition, all vessels of the United States Navy and merchant marine. It decided to adhere closely to the methods previously used by the Census in computing wealth, and presented totals and their components for the selected years back to 1880.[1] The increment in these estimates should reflect, therefore, the accumulation of consumer commodities and capital formation and yield some information on the industrial distribution of the latter. But the data are not strictly comparable for the entire period and for several wealth categories no trustworthy conclusions can be reached.

The value of consumer goods in households was one category we had to omit. The 1922 estimate was based upon a questionnaire survey asking for the total fair value of household equipment and wearing apparel in use. In making estimates for earlier years attention was concentrated on production, imports, and exports with assumed periods of usefulness and rates of depreciation.[2] Because the methods for 1922 and preceding years differed and because the basis of the estimates for the years before

---

[1] "The chief merit of the method actually followed by the census of 1922 in evaluating the wealth of the people of the United States is its continuity with the methods used in earlier censuses" (*Estimated National Wealth*, Bureau of the Census, 1924, p. x).

[2] See *Wealth, Debt, and Taxation: 1913* (Bureau of the Census, 1915), I, 19-20, and *Wealth, Debt, and Taxation* (Special Report of the Census Office, 1907), pp. 25-6.

1922 was inadequate, an attempt to compile a comparable and acceptable series of values for this category was deemed hopeless. This omission did not affect the primary purpose of our study—to distribute capital formation by industrial categories—but it did preclude the possibility of presenting a series on *total* commodity wealth. Consequently, the definition of wealth used here was narrowed to omit commodity stocks in households.

Further exclusions had to be made to obtain data satisfactory for our purposes. For only two of the four components of capital formation, producer durable equipment and new construction, could the wealth estimates be used. For changes in claims against foreign countries they are useless, since they include the value of all property in the United States regardless of ownership. Nor are the Census of Wealth data on inventories usable. Although inventories were estimated for each wealth report, they were actually based on diverse and crude assumptions; so that the resulting series cannot be considered adequate.[3] The estimates of changes in both claims and inventories prepared in connection with the commodity flow and capital formation study were used here whenever necessary; but unfortunately, this left us with the distribution by channel of industrial destination only for the output of producer durable goods and for construction.

[3] E.g., for stocks of manufactured products in 1922 "it was assumed that 25 percent of the year's production of foodstuffs and kindred products and two-thirds of other products were in stocks at the close of the year" (*Estimated National Wealth*, p. 15).

In 1912 "it was assumed that one-twelfth of the value of foodstuffs and one-half of other products for domestic use were in the possession of the merchants, and the value of materials and products in possession of the factories was assumed to be an amount equal to one-sixth of the gross products of the year 1912" (*Wealth, Debt, and Taxation: 1913*, I, 19).

In 1900 "it allows for the value of materials and products in the possession of the factories an amount equal to two months' 'gross products' of 1900, and for the manufactured goods in the possession of merchants an amount equal to one-half the annual 'net products' of the factory output, exclusive of hand trades" (*Wealth, Debt, and Taxation*, Special Report of the Census Office, p. 24).

In 1890 "the Eleventh Census Report on Wealth, Debt, and Taxation, Part II, expressly states that it includes an estimate for the value of the products of manufactures in the hands of factory owners" (*ibid.*). But no explanation of the derivation is given.

In 1880 "three-quarters of the annual product of agriculture and manufactures and of the annual importation of foreign goods, assumed to be the average supply in the hands of producers or dealers," is reported (*Estimated National Wealth*, Table 3).

Even for producers' equipment and construction the wealth estimates cannot be used as reported. Some of their limitations we can merely list; for others we have attempted to adjust.

OMISSIONS

The coverage of the wealth estimates is narrower than that of the two corresponding components of capital formation in that they exclude the value of (a) streets and roads and (b) United States Navy and other military equipment.

a) *Streets and roads:* The Bureau of the Census omitted this item from its wealth estimates since "in most cities a part or all of the cost of such improvements is assessed against property presumably benefited by the improvement, such presumption doubtless being taken into account by officials in determining assessed valuations for purposes of taxation".[4]

Carried to its logical conclusion this argument is hardly valid. It would mean excluding irrigation enterprises from the national wealth just because farm land in the 'dry' states is not fertile unless irrigated; and electric power or electrical equipment just because the latter is virtually worthless without the former.

The reason for omitting streets and roads here is lack of data. For 1922 the Federal Trade Commission estimated the value of land and improvements in streets and roads to be $21,850 million —$9,100 million as the value of land and $12,750 million, of improvements.[5] But these estimates cannot be extrapolated to preceding decades on even a crude basis.

b) *United States Navy and other military equipment:* Since 1900 the Bureau of the Census has stated in its wealth reports that the value of the Navy is included, but only for 1912 and 1922 does it give separate figures. That for 1912, $402 million, is "the reported cost of the vessels of the United States Navy in active commission, the cost of light vessels and tenders of the Lighthouse Service, the cost of the vessels of the Revenue-Cutter Service, and the value of the floating equipment of the War Department. No depreciation is shown for the vessels of the United States Navy, as the Navy Department carries its vessels at cost".[6]

[4] *Ibid.,* p. 6.
[5] *National Wealth and Income,* 69 Cong., 1st Sess., Senate Doc. 126, pp. 28, 34, 40-3.
[6] *Wealth, Debt, and Taxation: 1913,* I, 18.

The figure for 1922, $1,446 million, is "the value of the floating equipment of the United States Navy . . . secured from the Navy Department".[7]

If 'in active commission' is understood to be the same category as 'in commission' a considerable part of the fleet appears to be omitted from the wealth estimates. According to the *Statistical Abstract, 1925,* Table 144, the tonnage displacement of vessels 'in commission' was 1,501,315 and of vessels 'out of commission' 745,227 on January 1, 1926. A third category, 'under construction and authorized but not placed', covers some 38 vessels, but for most of these, displacement is not given. Similar data for earlier years are not published in the *Statistical Abstract.*

It is doubtful, therefore, that the 1912 and 1922 data are complete or even comparable in scope. And since it would be difficult, if at all possible, to prepare estimates for the entire period, this item was excluded from our totals. For similar reasons, the value of other military equipment also was omitted.

EXCESSES

The wealth reports include two items that do not fit into the pattern of our purpose: the value of (a) land and (b) motor vehicles.

a) *Land:* The official wealth reports contain estimates of the value of real estate, i.e., the sum of the value of land and of improvements. Since our primary concern is with the value of reproducible wealth, in order to allocate capital formation industrially, we had to estimate the value of improvements separately. The details of this adjustment are given in Section B.

This exclusion of land limits even further the definition of wealth adopted. Theoretically we might have omitted land values from the capital formation analysis and included them in the wealth discussion. Practically, however, it was impossible because of the difficulty of reducing land values to a common and constant base. Data on real estate are reported at market, or book or cost values. While with some statistical ingenuity and arbitrariness the value of land could be segregated from the reported totals, information is not available whereby land values for the various industrial categories can be converted to a constant and

[7] *Estimated National Wealth,* p. 12.

comparable base. Table IV 1 gives the *reported* values of land by industrial groups; but this category is omitted from any summaries intended to show comparable real magnitudes.

Segregation of the value of land, for the purpose of estimating *reproducible* fixed capital, is a difficult statistical operation, and the results are subject to error. *National Wealth and Income,* our primary source for this distribution in 1922, is relied upon heavily and is supplemented by fragmentary material for the earlier years.

There is a distinct possibility that our estimates of land values include some improvements that should properly be included in our estimate of reproducible wealth. For agriculture, for example, in years for which the Census of Agriculture reports land separately, it is stated that the figures include the value of fences, tile drains, and other incidental improvements. Consequently, the value of improvements, net of land, may be understated.

b) *Motor vehicles:* In 1922 the value of motor vehicles was included as a separate category for the first time in the national wealth estimate. It is excluded from our totals for two reasons. First, it is too broad in coverage: we are concerned only with the value of trucks and that portion of the value of passenger cars used solely for business. Second, since motor vehicles are part of capital equipment and would be covered in any report on that item, and since our estimates of equipment for specific industries are based upon such reported totals, motor vehicles, so far as they are capital equipment, are already covered. An additional figure would, therefore, introduce duplication.

2 *Allocation by Type*

Within total reproducible fixed capital, the only allocation possible on the basis of both wealth and capital formation data is that between construction or real estate improvements, on the one hand, and producer durable goods or machinery and equipment, on the other.

While a rough and ready distinction between these two categories of durable capital can be made on the basis of attachment to or separability from a specific location, it is too much to expect the line to be drawn consistently between one Census of Wealth and the next or among industrial categories; or the distinction followed in preparing the capital formation estimates to be identical with that drawn in the responses to or estimates in the

Census of Wealth. Furthermore, for many industrial categories, the Census of Wealth does not itself separate out equipment and improvements from total capital (or from total real estate); and the segregation must be made on the basis of fragmentary data and assumptions of doubtful validity.

For these reasons, the estimates for each major category of reproducible durable wealth are less reliable than for their total; and in the comparison of wealth and capital formation data the over-all totals, rather than the two components of each, should be emphasized.

3 *Allocation by Industry*

The characteristic of the distribution of wealth and capital formation by industries most important to bear in mind is that it is based upon a mixture of two criteria: industrial affiliation of the unit *owning* and *using* the capital item. The significance of this mixture of criteria is not the same for the two major components of reproducible wealth. For equipment the distribution by ownership is probably not very different from that by use: it is unlikely that rented equipment is an appreciable percentage of the total. But for improvements there may well be a substantial discrepancy between the two, e.g., all property owned by real estate firms, or a preponderant part of it, would be redistributed on the basis of use; a considerable part of property used for residential purposes would be redistributed on the basis of ownership.

Ownership is the dominant criterion. Three broad groups can be distinguished by type of ownership: private, public utility, and tax exempt, the last including public and 'socially owned' property (nonprofit institutions, etc.). But for the minor industrial divisions within these major groups the classification is mixed, based in part on ownership and in part on use. The public utility subdivisions are based on ownership throughout the period whereas agricultural and residential property are based on use. For mining, manufacturing, and other industrial property, however, in the early period, when the estimates are derived from capital values, the classification is based on ownership, while in the later period, when the estimates are derived from expenditures, it is based on use.

Another source of difficulty in interpreting the industrial classification is the incomparability of the periods before and after

1922, because Census of Wealth data are used for the former, capital formation data for the latter. The distribution for the earlier years is more detailed; that for the later must use broader categories (see Table IV 12). And in some minor respects full comparability could not be established between the sums of the narrower and the broader industrial divisions.

4 Valuation

Before the Census of Wealth data can be used, the valuation methods must be examined. In computing the 'value' of the several forms of wealth, what price has been assigned to them? Can these values be readily adjusted for changes in the price and value levels from one point of time to another? There is no single answer since the total is the sum of the components and the components have not been valued by similar methods.

As taxable real estate values are based on assessments and the relation of sales values to them, they can be said to approximate the current price of the property. Tax exempt property, on the other hand, is taken at book value, which may be assumed to be original cost modified by resale and revaluation.[8] The value of shipping is stated to be current reproduction cost; that of canals, the cost of construction. The totals, therefore, are sums of items evaluated at either market or book prices.[9] Obviously, any analysis of the uncorrected reported values would have little meaning.

Hence, once the reported values for the several industrial and type categories of wealth had been established, the next major task was to convert them to a common price base. Since we are dealing with both market and book values two sets of indexes had to be calculated: of current prices and of prices underlying book values.

These indexes, used to convert reported values to a constant price base, are rough and subject to a considerable margin of error, especially for periods when changes in the price level were marked. They suffer from the paucity of statistical material, par-

---

[8] See Solomon Fabricant, *Capital Consumption and Adjustment* (National Bureau of Economic Research, 1938), for a discussion of the effect of revaluation of assets on book values.
[9] For more detailed discussion see the wealth reports of the Bureau of the Census and *National Wealth and Income*, Ch. II.

ticularly for the early years; and the index of prices underlying book values has the additional qualification that arbitrary life spans had to be assumed. Furthermore, the price indexes are annual averages whereas the value figures are for particular points of time. When prices are rising rapidly, converting the value at the beginning of the year by the average index for the year leads to an underestimate of the value in constant prices; an opposite bias occurs in periods of rapid price decline. For reasons stated below, two variants of adjustment for price changes were calculated for wealth components reported as valued at current prices. But when all is said and done, the adjustment remains the least satisfactory step in our procedure, and yields results that can be accepted only in their broadest indications.

5 *Gross or Net*

Are the wealth estimates gross or net of depreciation, i.e., do changes in them represent gross or net capital formation? Capital assets in the specific industries are estimated from reported 'capital invested', 'value of road and equipment', 'investment in plant and equipment', 'market value of taxable real estate', and even 'capitalization'. For some items it is expressly stated that depreciation has been allowed for; others, especially the estimates for the early part of the period, undoubtedly include undeducted depreciation, since not until recently has depreciation become an important consideration in business accounting.

The depreciation included in the total can be estimated roughly. For manufacturing, for which the Census instructions since 1890 have specifically stated that depreciation should be deducted, John R. Arnold has estimated that undeducted depreciation fluctuated between 4 and 5 percent from 1899 to 1919, and was smaller in the earlier years, becoming negligible before the Civil War.[10] For several public utilities, depreciation reserves are reported for 1922. The gross and net figures on capital are shown in the accompanying tabulation. Investment in 1922 is overstated by the amounts shown and we can assume less overstatement in the earlier years. For 1912 steam railroads, the one industry for which data are available, report $16,408 million for gross and $16,149 million for net value of road and equipment.

[10] 'Manufacturing Capital and Output, 1839-1931; Main Factors in Their Changes', *The Annalist*, July 7, 1933.

CAPITAL VALUES, 1922 (millions of dollars)

	GROSS	NET
Steam railroads, road and equipment	21,327	19,988
Street railways, road and equipment	5,059	4,878
Telephones, plant and equipment	2,205	1,746
Telegraphs, plant and equipment	361	257*
Electric light and power, plant and equipment	4,229	3,888*

* Total reserves, depreciation and other, deducted.

Although the Census reports are not definite concerning the deduction of depreciation allowances in every case, the assumption that the items reported at market values are net of depreciation is probably valid. On this assumption, at least 60 percent of our totals for the value of real estate improvements and of equipment is net. If we further assume that undeducted depreciation amounts to about 10 percent of the balance, our totals exceed net values by, at most, 5 percent.[11]

6 Comparison with Capital Formation

To test our estimates of the increase in the value of improvements and of equipment derived from the wealth data, we use the estimates of the flow of producer durable goods and total new construction for 1879-1938 from the capital formation study. The comparison in Table IV a, Part 1 shows that for the full period the increase in the wealth items falls $28 billion, or almost 20 percent, short of that indicated by net capital formation data; that this shortage is both absolutely and relatively greater for improvements than for durable equipment; that most of the shortage in improvements occurs during the decade 1912-22; and that the decade-to-decade discrepancies are relatively larger than those for periods of about twenty years.

Of the many reasons that could explain positive or negative discrepancies, the following are important:

a) The wealth data exclude street and road construction, which are covered in the net capital formation data. The net value of street and road construction for 1919-38, the only period for which statistics are available, was $19 billion in 1929 prices.[12] It

---

[11] The 1922 ratio of net to gross derived from the text table is .927. In the earlier years, with smaller depreciation reserves, the ratio would approach unity. Solomon Fabricant's data on gross and net capital assets for transportation and public utility corporations in 1934 yield a ratio of .871 (*op. cit.*, p. 271).

[12] Data underlying estimates in Table I 8.

TABLE IV a

Increase in Wealth Compared with Net Capital Formation, Census Dates, 1880-1922
1929 Prices (millions of dollars)

	1880 to 1890 (1)	1890 to 1900 (2)	1880 to 1900 (3)	1900 to 1912 (4)	1912 to 1922 (5)	1900 to 1922 (6)	1880 to 1922 (7)
1 Wealth Items Adjusted by Current Cost (for Market Valuation) and Past Cost (for Book Valuation)							
Improvements							
1 Wealth increase	21,162	19,868	41,030	47,819	1,076	48,895	89,925
2 Net construction	18,908	31,964	50,872	42,577	21,862	64,439	115,312
Equipment							
3 Wealth increase	6,927	8,338	15,265	18,093	2,627	20,720	35,985
4 Net producer durable equipment	4,406	4,919	9,325	14,237	14,891	29,128	38,453
Improvements and Equipment							
5 Wealth increase	28,089	28,206	56,295	65,912	3,703	69,615	125,910
6 Net construction & equipment	23,314	36,883	60,197	56,814	36,753	93,567	153,765
2 Wealth Items Adjusted by an Average of Current and Past Cost (for Market Valuation) and Past Cost (for Book Valuation)							
Improvements							
7 Wealth increase	20,050	20,486	40,536	50,645	9,659	60,304	100,840
8 Net construction	18,908	31,964	50,872	42,577	21,862	64,439	115,312
Equipment							
9 Wealth increase	6,909	8,792	15,701	18,077	2,120	20,197	35,898
10 Net producer durable equipment	4,406	4,919	9,325	14,237	14,891	29,128	38,453
Improvements and Equipment							
11 Wealth increase	26,959	29,278	56,237	68,722	11,779	80,501	136,738
12 Net construction & equipment	23,314	36,883	60,197	56,814	36,753	93,567	153,765

LINE
1 Derived from line 19 of Table IV 5.
2 & 8 Derived from col. 7 of Table II 15.
3 Derived from line 18 of Table IV 6.
4 & 10 Derived from col. 6 of Table II 15.
5 Sum of lines 1 and 3.
6 & 12 Sum of lines 2 and 4.
7 Derived from line 38 of Table IV 5.
9 Derived from line 36 of Table IV 6.
11 Sum of lines 7 and 9.

does not seem unreasonable to assume that the cumulated total for 1880-1922 was not far different from that figure.[13]

b) The wealth data exclude shipbuilding for the United States Navy and, indeed, net additions to stocks of all military equipment, which, so far as they originate in private production, are included in the net capital formation figures. This item, however, is minor.

c) Undeducted depreciation items, which are included in the wealth estimates, may have constituted a larger percentage of the total in 1880 than in 1922. Even if they did, the effect on the *understatement* of the increase in wealth can be only negligible, since the difference in the percentages would have to be large enough to offset the huge increase in the absolute values of wealth between 1880 and 1922 (from $32 billion to $158 billion, in 1929 prices, as shown in Tables IV 4 and IV 5).

d) A more important factor is that some improvements may be included with land; if they are, part of the net addition to improvements is omitted from the increase in wealth as measured in Table IV a. How much cannot be guessed, even crudely, but it may mean that the increase in the estimates based on the Census of Wealth is substantially less than that based on net capital formation data.

e) As already indicated, the adjustment of wealth data for changes in valuation is most difficult; and the results are subject to wide errors. For the wealth items that are supposed to be valued at market prices, it is not easy to assume that the reports are based upon a wide variety of well sampled current market transactions; and it is impossible to construct accurate indexes of changing market valuation. To measure changes in the market values of improvements and durable equipment in Table IV a, Part 1, we used current construction costs or current prices of durable equipment—a procedure that may be valid for the shorter lived items of durable equipment sold on well organized central business markets but can yield only the crudest approximation for the long

[13] The Federal Trade Commission estimated the value of improvements embodied in public roads and streets to be $12.75 billion as of December 31, 1922 (*National Wealth and Income*, p. 43). This total, based largely on past costs, is, according to the Commission's own statement, an underestimate (see particularly the bottom of p. 41) and should not be adjusted for depreciation. In view of the much lower level of cost underlying this estimate, as compared with the 1929 price level, the assumption in the text does not seem unreasonable.

lived structures, etc. sold on thousands of local markets. For the wealth items supposed to be reported at book value, the cost may not be identical with the original construction or production cost minus the accumulated depreciation; but for lack of better data we adjusted for changes in values on the basis of indexes of past production or construction costs calculated on the assumption of a constant life period.

The errors in these procedures are likely to be biggest for wealth items that are reported as valued at current prices, for periods during which the prices have risen or fallen drastically and quickly, or for items reported at book values for periods during which readjustments in book values (from original costs) are likely to be major. On both counts, 1912-22 is the period for which we could expect the biggest error. For improvements, the use of current construction costs may well have overcorrected the current price wealth items in 1922, since prices of real estate may have risen less than current construction costs—either because of a more sluggish movement or because an easier supply of new construction units had already been anticipated. For durable equipment the change in the wealth items may reflect a writing down of assets in the postwar reconversion process of a type that cannot be reflected in our price indexes; and certainly not in the estimates derived from net capital formation data.

We could not improve or replace our price indexes for capital wealth items reported at book values. But for those valued at market prices, we give an alternative price index in the form of a simple mean of the index of past costs and of current production costs. The assumption is that current market prices underlying the valuation of wealth items do not fully reflect the ups and downs in the current cost of new items, but are rather a cross between past and current costs. The changes introduced are not great; but they do reduce the discrepancy between the two sets of estimates in 1912-22 and lessen the difference between the two totals for 1880-1922 from $28 to $17 billion (Table IV a, Part 2).

The factors discussed so far stress the possible biases and errors in the wealth data. We turn now to those in net capital formation estimates:

f) Net construction and net durable equipment totals allow for the deduction of consumption estimates that include depletion of nonreproducible assets. As these assets are presumably part of the land values changes in them do not enter the values of improvements and durable equipment derived from the wealth data. Consequently, while in calculating net capital formation, it is correct to deduct the calculable consumption of nonreproducible assets, it is not correct to make this deduction in comparing net increases in construction and equipment with net increases shown by the corresponding wealth items.

In the 1920's the ratio of depletion to total consumption was roughly 5 percent (Solomon Fabricant, *Capital Consumption and Adjustment,* Table 30, proportion of depletion to total, the latter excluding automobiles and repairs and maintenance items). Since for most of the period, consumption and net capital formation were about equal (see Table II g), the increase represented by net capital formation should, for comparison purposes, be 5 percent, or about $8 billion, larger than is shown in Table IV a.

g) On the other hand, depreciation, depletion, and fire losses—the only items used in estimating consumption—do not exhaust the types of capital consumption. Items may be discarded before the end of the depreciation period; items may be destroyed by forces other than fire. Hence net capital formation totals tend to be biased upward by an amount that cannot even be guessed, but that may be substantial (as was already suggested with reference to durable equipment for 1912-22).

h) Capital formation is also too high so far as it includes items that may have been charged to maintenance and other current expenses. However, so far as the items are really durable, the wealth reports are an understatement rather than the net capital formation account an overstatement.

i) If too long a life period for improvements and equipment was assumed in calculating consumption, the consumption totals are too low and the net capital formation residuals too high. If, on the contrary, too short a life period was assumed, the consumption estimates are too high and the net capital formation residuals too low.

It is difficult to balance all these factors. Those to which magnitudes have been assigned (a and f) reduce the total discrepancy for 1880-1922 $19 billion and raise it $8. This still leaves a discrepancy of $17 billion in Part 1 of Table IVa, and of $6 billion in Part 2. Of the other factors the ones that lead to an understatement of the wealth figures seem most important (d and e). Of these (d) could well account for a large part or all of the remaining discrepancy in Part 2.

The preceding discussion has also indicated why the differences were so large during the decade 1912-22; and why the discrepancy should have been relatively greater for improvements than for durable equipment. That the differences between the two sets of estimates are relatively, and sometimes absolutely, greater for short periods than for long is due to other factors.

The first is the comparative importance of net changes and of the totals used as diminuend and subtrahend. Under conditions of steady growth or decline, the shorter the period the smaller the total change compared with the initial and terminal quantities. Hence, errors in the latter may greatly affect the net difference, i.e., the total change. The longer the period, on the contrary, the less the relative effect on the net difference of errors in the terminal quantities. This argument is of particular bearing in connection with possible errors in the adjustment of wealth totals for changes in valuation.

The second factor is also more important in short period comparisons. The capital formation data are for overlapping decades (1879-88, 1884-93, 1889-98, 1894-1903, etc.) and in the form of annual averages; from these we calculated the total flow for 1880-90, 1890-1900, 1900-12, and 1912-22. That the dates for the wealth data are June 1 for 1880, 1890, and 1900, and December 31 for 1912 and 1922 also had to be taken into account. We calculated the capital formation for each period as follows:

1880-90: (8.5 × annual average for 1879-88) + (1.5 × annual average for 1889-98)
1890-1900: (8.5 × annual average for 1889-98) + (1.5 × annual average for 1899-1908)
1900-12: (8.5 × annual average for 1899-1908) + (4 × annual average for 1909-18)
1912-22: (1 × annual average for 1904-13) + (9 × annual average for 1914-23)

Other combinations of decade figures would have yielded different results. For example, if the estimates for 1912-22 were the sum of 6 times the annual average for 1909-18 and 4 times the annual average for 1919-28, improvements would have totaled $32,779 million, and equipment $14,540 million, instead of $21,862 million and $14,891 million. And were annual estimates available, the differences might well be reduced.

For these reasons we used, in subsequent analyses, longer time spans—subdividing the full period for which wealth and capital formation could be estimated into three twenty-year spans. Also, for reasons stated above, we considered the capital formation estimates more reliable in general than changes in wealth totals reduced to constant and comparable valuation; and used the wealth estimates only to suggest the distribution of capital formation by industrial destination for long periods when the capital formation estimates themselves did not give the information.[14]

[14] We also tried to compare the totals for real estate and equipment based upon the *Census of Wealth for 1922* with the values of fixed assets based upon the capital stock tax returns summarized in *Statistics of Income, 1924*, pp. 41-76. The comparison is difficult since the date for which the capital stock tax returns are reported is not identical with that of the *Census of Wealth;* the returns are not complete for all corporations; do not include fixed assets in the hands of unincorporated enterprises; and may well be based upon a definition and valuation of fixed assets that differ materially from the contents and valuation base of real estate and of durable equipment in the *Census of Wealth*. Before making the comparison we had to adjust the corporate data for undercoverage and for exclusion of noncorporate assets. These adjustments could be made for the capital stock tax returns data as of the end of 1923, and cover adequately four major divisions— mining, manufacturing, public utilities, and other industries (construction, trade, service, finance, and miscellaneous).

For these four categories, the value of real estate and equipment based on the *Census of Wealth* is estimated to be $96.3 billion at the end of 1922; that based on the corporate data, $86.4 billion at the end of 1923. If we allow for an addition to assets during 1923, the estimate based on the wealth data is roughly 15 percent higher than that based on the corporate data. However, for mining and manufacturing combined the two estimates are quite close ($35.5 billion from wealth data and $34.8 from corporate data). The major discrepancy is in the public utility group ($37.2 billion from the wealth data and $30.8 from corporate data) for which the wealth estimates are based upon a careful consideration of the valuations as checked by various regulatory commissions; and for which the reporting of assets as part of corporate income statistics has not been too complete, even in recent years. The discrepancy for 'other' industries, while sizable ($23.6 billion from wealth data and $20.8 from corporate data), cannot be assigned too much significance, because in so many subdivisions, corporations constitute a small proportion of the total; and hence the 'blow up' from corporate to total bases may easily be deficient.

While, in the nature of the case, the comparison cannot be conclusive there seems on the surface little reason to infer a sizable error in the wealth estimates. They may not reflect upward or downward revaluations of assets as promptly as corporate data. But they are sufficiently grounded on various censuses (agriculture, manufacturing, mining, utilities, etc.) and other comprehensive data to yield an estimate perhaps more indicative of the general order of magnitude than a set derived by raising the totals on corporate assets to cover all durable reproducible commodity wealth.

B Basic Tables

Three groups of tables are presented below:

1) *Tables IV 1-IV 7:* estimates of the value of improvements and equipment and data basic to them. Estimates of reproducible wealth are given for June 1, 1880; June 1, 1890; June 1, 1900; December 31, 1912; December 31, 1918; and December 31, 1922. To each table are appended notes giving sources and methods and, in some cases, alternatives the reader may consider preferable.

Although the value of land is excluded from our estimates, Table IV 1, which gives estimates for the *Census of Wealth* dates, is presented in the belief that it may be of interest to some students.

Table IV 7 gives (unless otherwise noted) the wealth totals at the initial date of the period for which additions to reproducible wealth are available, January 1, 1919.

2) *Tables IV 8 and IV 9:* estimates of changes in the value of improvements and equipment, based upon capital formation, 1919-38. Gross and net additions to construction and equipment are given in current and 1929 prices.

3) *Tables IV 10-IV 13:* summary tables. The entries are either transcribed or derived from the preceding tables in this Part or Part II.

TABLE IV 1

Value of Land, Census Dates, 1880-1922 (millions of dollars)
Based on Reported Valuation

		VALUATION BASE	1880 (1)	1890 (2)	1900 (3)	1912 (4)	1922 (5)
1	Agriculture	Market	8,158	10,623	13,058	31,574	41,541
2	Mining	Book	364	818	1,189	2,109	3,362
3	Manufacturing	Book	320	776	1,027	1,700	4,328
4	Other industrial	Market	1,293	2,844	3,507	5,382	9,382
5	Residential	Market	3,170	7,687	10,513	18,455	36,011
6	Total taxable, excl. public utilities		13,305	22,748	29,294	59,220	94,624
7	Tax exempt	Book	1,152	2,170	3,307	6,689	11,065
8	Steam railroads	Book	886	1,494	1,741	2,602	3,202
9	Street railways	Book	15	41	157	434	455
10	Pullman, express, etc.	Book	4	7	8	9	38
11	Telephone	Book	1	3	14	34	66
12	Telegraph	Book	4	6	6	7	11
13	Shipping & canals	Book	145	176	237	454	511
14	Electric light & power	Book	0	9	46	222	424
15	Waterworks	Book	12	12	13	14	18
16	Irrigation	Book	1	3	5	18	28
17	Pipe lines	Book	0.5	2	8	18	25
18	Total public utilities		1,069	1,753	2,235	3,812	4,778
19	Total land		15,526	26,671	34,836	69,721	110,467

The derivation of the value of land is given in the notes to Table IV 2.

TABLE IV 2

Value of Real Estate Improvements, Census Dates, 1880-1922
(millions of dollars)
Based on Reported Valuation

		VALUATION BASE	1880 (1)	1890 (2)	1900 (3)	1912 (4)	1922 (5)
1	Agriculture	Market	2,039	2,656	3,557	6,889	11,169
2	Mining	Book	91	201	325	644	1,120
3	Manufacturing	Book	363	879	1,450	3,450	8,772
4	Other industrial	Market	1,374	2,491	3,173	6,044	8,320
5	Residential	Market	3,361	6,736	9,527	20,676	31,904
6	Total taxable, excl. public utilities		7,228	12,963	18,032	37,703	61,285
7	Tax exempt	Book	626	1,237	2,061	4,258	7,164
8	Steam railroads	Book	3,376	5,794	7,054	10,672	13,220
9	Street railways	Book	104	288	1,131	3,156	3,339
10	Pullman, express, etc.	Book	4	7	9	10	44
11	Telephone	Book	9	33	178	455	882
12	Telegraph	Book	43	70	72	94	144
13	Shipping & canals	Book	145	176	237	454	511
14	Electric light & power	Book	0	44	223	1,100	2,113
15	Waterworks	Book	209	225	242	261	325
16	Irrigation	Book	27	60	97	325	495
17	Pipe lines	Book	10	42	141	323	450
18	Total public utilities		3,927	6,739	9,384	16,850	21,523
19	Total improvements		11,781	20,939	29,477	58,811	89,972

LINE 1

COL. 1 AND 2: The value of farm real estate is reported in the *Census of Agriculture*. The value of improvements is assumed equal to 20 percent of the total value of real estate (the average of the ratio of improvements to real estate in 1900—21%, 1912—18%, and 1922—21%).

COL. 3: The value of improvements is reported in the *Census of Agriculture*.

COL. 4 AND 5: Obtained directly from the Bureau of Agricultural Economics. The figures reported are for March 1 of the following year but are assumed correct for the end of the given year.

LINE 2

COL. 1: The 1880 wealth estimate includes the item "Mines (including petroleum wells) and quarries together with one-half the annual product reckoned as the average supply in the hands of producers or dealers" reported to amount to $781 million. One-half of the value of product, the sum of the value of product for precious metals, nonprecious metals, quarries, and petroleum reported in the 1880 *Census Compendium,* is subtracted, leaving $641 million as the value of capital invested.

The 1880 *Census of Mines* also reports separately the value of real estate, plant, and working capital for nonprecious mines, and on the assumption that the percentage distribution shown is representative of the entire mining industry, the value of real estate in 1880 is computed. The further apportionment of the value of real estate between the value of land and of improvements is based on the 1890 ratio of buildings to real estate (see the notes to col. 2).

Several other estimates of total capital invested are possible. The 1902 *Census of Mines* reports $1,449 million for capital invested in 1880 (more than double the figure we use). However, the 1890 *Census* reports $369 million for value of product in 1880; and if we subtract from the wealth estimate for 1880 one-half of this we get a smaller estimate of capital invested than the one we use. The 1902

REPRODUCIBLE WEALTH

Census reports $252 million for value of product in 1880; using this subtrahend, we get a slightly larger estimate of capital invested.

A somewhat different apportionment of total capital among real estate, equipment, and working capital is also possible if we use the nonprecious mining distribution for the total *excluding* petroleum and accept the 1880 *Census of Mines* figures for petroleum: $2 million for buildings, $4 million for machinery, and $27 million for total capital.

COL. 2: The 1890 *Census Abstract* reports capital invested in the mining industry as $1,292 million. The *Minerals Census* for 1890 classifies capital invested in specific mineral industries, $1,276 million, into four groups: land, building and fixtures, tools, etc., and cash and miscellaneous. The ratio of building and fixtures to the total is applied to total capital invested. The resulting estimate of 'building' is probably too high because of the inclusion of 'fixtures' but no correction could be made for this item.

Here also alternative estimates could have been made from other data. The 1890 wealth estimate for "Mines and quarries including product on hand" is $1,291 million but on the assumption that one-half of the annual product is included (following the procedure used for 1880) investment would be reduced to about $1,000 million.

The value of product reported in the 1890 *Census Abstract* as comparable with 'capital invested', which we accept, is $419 million. The same source gives $587 million as the total value of product. Had we used this figure the capital invested figure would have been increased 40 percent. We did not, because later *Census of Mines* reports do not show it. E.g., the 1902 *Census* gives (without explanation) $411 million and $438 million as the 1890 value of product, and the 1919 *Census* accepts the latter.

The 1902 *Census* gives "capital invested" figures for 1890 as $1,288 million and $1,311 million (also without explanation). The 1919 *Census* reports the latter but qualifies it as "for producing mines". These figures are not very different from those we adopted.

COL. 3: Total capital invested is estimated by multiplying the value of product by the ratio of capital invested to it. The value of product is interpolated between 1890 and 1902 (see the notes to col. 2 for 1890 and the *Census of Mines and Quarries* for 1902) by means of the Bureau of Mines data on value of product (see *Mineral Resources*). The ratio of capital invested to value of product is interpolated along a straight line between 1890 and 1909 (see the notes to col. 2 for 1890 and the *Census of Mines and Quarries* for 1909).

The value of real estate is estimated by multiplying total capital invested by the ratio of the value of real estate to it. The ratio of the value of real estate to capital invested is interpolated along a straight line between 1890 and 1922 (see the notes to col. 2 for 1890 and to col. 5 for 1922).

The value of improvements is the product of the value of real estate and the ratio of the value of improvements to it. This ratio also is interpolated along a straight line between 1890 and 1922 (see the notes to col. 2 for 1890 and to col. 5 for 1922).

An alternative for the value of mining real estate is the estimate in the 1900 wealth report, $687 million; our estimate is $1,514 million. Our estimate for 1890 is $1,019 million, and the ratio for 1900 of the value of real estate (wealth estimate) to the value of product is much lower than in other years. Consequently, the wealth estimate seems unreasonably low and was disregarded.

COL. 4: The value of improvements in 1912 is estimated by a procedure analogous to that for 1900 (see the notes to col. 3) except that the ratio of capital invested to value of product is interpolated along a straight line between 1909 and 1919. The data basic to this ratio are reported in the *Census of Mines and Quarries* for 1909 and 1919.

Table IV 2 continued:

LINE 2 (*concl.*)

COL. 5: For the value of real estate we accepted Robert R. Doane's estimate of $4,482 million which he bases on the Federal Trade Commission's figure of $6 billion but corrects in the light of state distributions (see *The Anatomy of American Wealth;* Harper, 1940; pp. 209, 217-8). This reduction seems reasonable, especially since the F.T.C. figure is based on *Statistics of Income* data, which include all fixed assets, and is therefore an overestimate. For the allocation of real estate between land and improvements we accepted Doane's estimates of 75 percent for land and 25 percent for improvements (in line with our 1890 figures, 80 and 20 percent).

Total capital invested, to which the value of real estate is related in deriving the 1900 and 1912 estimates, is extrapolated from 1919 with the value of product as index. The value of product, reported for 1919 in the *Census of Mines and Quarries,* is extrapolated to 1922 by the Bureau of Mines series.

The Federal Trade Commission estimates the ratio of value of land to value of real estate in mineral counties to be 0.609 (*National Wealth and Income,* p. 35). This ratio is too low for mining *property* since it covers all real estate in those counties.

LINE 3

COL. 1: Total capital invested is reported in the *1900 Census of Manufactures.* The value of buildings is estimated by multiplying capital invested by the ratio of the value of buildings to it for 1879 (Paul Douglas, *Theory of Wages;* Macmillan, 1934; p. 115):

"It seems undeniable that buildings and machinery did not increase as rapidly in comparison with working capital during the eighties as they did during the fifteen years which followed 1889 when buildings advanced from 13.4 to 15.8 per cent, or an increase of 2.4 points, and machinery, etc., from 24.3 to 27.5 points a year, respectively. We have assumed that the growth in the proportions which buildings formed of the total was at approximately only one-quarter of the rate of speed of the nineties and for machinery at only one-fifth. This would give 13.0 per cent as the probable figure for buildings in 1879 and 24.0 per cent as that for machinery, tools, and equipment."

COL. 2: The value of buildings is from the *1900 Census of Manufactures.*

The $3,059 million for "machinery of mills, and production on hand, raw and manufactured" in the wealth estimate for 1890 was not used in our calculations.

COL. 3: The value of buildings is from the *Census of Manufactures.*

The value of real estate, the sum of the value of land and of buildings, from this source, $2,478 million, checks with the value for 1900 in *Wealth, Debt, and Taxation* (Department of Commerce and Labor, 1907), $2,477 million.

The *1914 Census Abstract* reports capital (excluding hand and neighborhood trades) as $8,975 million; but since the original figure, $9,817 million, has broader coverage, we did *not* adjust it to the lower level.

COL. 4: The value of buildings is estimated by multiplying total capital by the ratio of the value of buildings to it. The ratio is interpolated along a straight line between 1909 and 1914 (for the ratio in 1909 and 1914 see Douglas, *op. cit.,* Ch. 5, Table 4). Total capital is estimated by dividing the value of machinery (*Wealth, Debt, and Taxation: 1913,* I) by the ratio of the value of machinery to it (calculated by a method similar to that for the ratio of buildings to total capital).

As a check on these estimates the value of fixed assets also was computed and the percentage distribution of total capital derived. The value of fixed assets is interpolated between 1904 and 1922 with the value of buildings and machinery as index (for 1904, see the *Census of Manufactures,* and for 1922, see the notes to col. 5). The value of land is obtained by subtraction. The percentage distribution of total capital is compared in the accompanying table with that for 1904.

PERCENTAGE DISTRIBUTION OF TOTAL CAPITAL (MANUFACTURING)

	1904	1912
Land	7.7	7.9
Buildings	15.7	16.1
Machinery	27.5	28.5
Other capital	49.0	47.5
Total	100.0	100.0

Total capital in 1912 is estimated to be $21,404 million, a reasonable figure when compared with total capital reported for 1909 and 1914 in the *Census of Manufactures*—$18,428 million and $22,791 million.

COL. 5: The value of buildings is estimated by multiplying total capital by the ratio of the value of buildings to it (Douglas, *op. cit.*, Ch. 5, Table 4). Total capital is derived by extrapolating the 1919 figure (*Census of Manufactures*) by the index of the value of fixed assets (unpublished series prepared by Solomon Fabricant).

Total capital may have a wider margin of error than the other estimates since Douglas' ratios are assumed to have a more or less steady trend and Fabricant's index of fixed assets is used for total capital. Working capital, and therefore total capital, may undergo marked cyclical fluctuations. Unfortunately, no data are available with which to check on this point.

Total fixed assets, essential to the computations for col. 4, are estimated by dividing the sum of the value of buildings and of machinery (for the latter see the notes to Table IV 3, line 3, col. 5) by its ratio to the value of fixed assets. The ratio is derived from data on land and other fixed assets for Missouri (*Missouri Red Book*, 1923).

Lowell J. Chawner's estimates of expenditures for manufacturing plant ('Capital Expenditures for Manufacturing Plant and Equipment—1915 to 1940', *Survey of Current Business*, March 1941) were used to test the accuracy of our estimates. Total capital in 1914 (*Census of Manufactures*), multiplied by Douglas' ratio of buildings to capital yielded an estimate of the value of buildings in 1914. To this total were added Chawner's estimates of plant expenditures for 1915-22, yielding $8,646 million as the 1922 value of buildings, gross of depreciation for 1915-22. Our estimate for 1922, net of depreciation, is $8,772 million.

Several other estimates of the value of capital and some of its components can be compared with our figures. Our estimate of total capital is $53,164 million. The Federal Trade Commission, in *National Wealth and Income*, uses $44,000 million, the 1919 figure, stating that "there was probably comparatively little change for 1922".

The Census figure, $52,611 million (*Estimated National Wealth*, 1924) is derived by extrapolating the 1919 figure to 1921 by the value of land, buildings, and machinery for a sample of 60 corporations, 1919-21, and assuming that the increase from 1921 to 1922 was at the same rate as from 1920 to 1921. An error was introduced in the initial steps by the use of $44,567 million for total capital in 1919 instead of $44,467 million, as reported in the *1920 Census of Manufactures* (VIII, 14).

The difference between our estimate of the value of buildings, $8,772 million, and Douglas', $8,681 million, is also due to the use of an incorrect figure for total capital in 1919, since Douglas uses the data in *Estimated National Wealth*.

Our estimate of the value of land is $4,397 million; of the value of real estate, therefore, $13,169 million. The Federal Trade Commission puts this item at $24,000 million—definitely an overestimate since its basis is *Statistics of Income* corporate data, which include machinery. By applying the 1904 ratio of real estate to capital (.235) to total capital as reported in *Estimated National Wealth*, Doane estimates the value of real estate to be $12,364 million.

An alternative estimate for the value of land is also possible. On the basis of

Table IV 2 continued:

LINE 3 (*concl.*)

a sample of Massachusetts corporations, collected by the National Bureau (Financial Research Program), the 1904 ratio of machinery to fixed assets can be extrapolated and applied to the 1922 machinery figure to yield total fixed assets. The value of land, $5,833 million, is the difference between total fixed assets and the value of machinery and buildings. The percentage distribution of fixed assets on this basis is land, 18.9; buildings, 28.8; and machinery, 52.3; for the estimates we use, the percentage distribution is land, 14.9; buildings, 30.2; and machinery, 54.9. For a sample of Wisconsin corporations the National Bureau also collected some fixed asset data; the percentage distribution for it is land, 17.2; buildings, 36.9; and machinery, 45.9. We accepted the Missouri data as more typical and reliable.

LINE 4

The values of all taxable real estate (excluding public utilities) in the wealth reports for 1880, 1890, 1900, 1912, and 1922 are basic to our estimates.

COL. 1: To the value of taxable real estate as reported is added the value of mining real estate (see the notes to line 2, col. 1) since in the wealth estimate the latter, combined with the product on hand, is shown separately. From the total the value of real estate in agriculture, mining, and manufacturing (see the notes to lines 1-3, col. 1) is subtracted to yield the value of other industrial and residential real estate.

The value of land in total taxable real estate is obtained by multiplying the value of real estate by the ratio of the value of land to it. The ratio is extrapolated from 1900 (see the notes to col. 3) by the ratio for agriculture, mining, and manufacturing combined. The value of other industrial and residential buildings is the difference between the value of real estate and of land.

The value of other industrial real estate is the difference between the value of other industrial and residential real estate and the value of residential real estate (for which see the notes to line 5, col. 1). The value of other industrial buildings is based on the assumption that the ratio of the value of other industrial and residential real estate is applicable to the value of other industrial real estate alone.

COL. 2: The method is analogous to that used for col. 1 except that total taxable real estate as given in the wealth report already includes mining real estate.

COL. 3: To the total value of taxable real estate reported is added the value of tax exempt property used for agriculture and manufacturing since both are presumably covered in the agricultural and manufacturing statistics. The value of other industrial and residential real estate is estimated by the method described for col. 1, with the value of mining real estate given in the wealth report as part of the subtrahend.

The value of land in all taxable real estate is estimated by the method described for col. 1. The ratio of the value of land to the total value of real estate is extrapolated from 1922 (for which see the notes to col. 5) by the comparable ratio for five sample states. The data for the latter ratio in 1922 are the percentages for California, Colorado, Indiana, Minnesota, and West Virginia (*National Wealth and Income*), weighted by the value of taxable property reported for those states (*Estimated National Wealth*); the data for the 1900 ratio are from *Wealth, Debt, and Taxation* (Special Report of the Census Office, Washington, D. C., 1907), Table 2.

From this point on the procedure is the same as that outlined for col. 1.

COL. 4: The method is the same as that for col. 1 except that the ratio of the value of land to the value of real estate for all taxable property is interpolated along a straight line.

COL. 5: The method here too is similar to that for col. 1 except that the value of land included in total taxable real estate as estimated by the Federal Trade Commission (*National Wealth and Income*) is used.

REPRODUCIBLE WEALTH 207

LINE 5

COL. 1 AND 2: The value of residential real estate is estimated by multiplying the value of other industrial and residential real estate (see the notes to line 4, col. 1) by the ratio of the former to the latter. The ratio is extrapolated along a straight line, based on the data for 1900 and 1922.

For the assumption under which the total value of real estate is divided into the value of land and of buildings see the notes to line 4, col. 1.

COL. 3: The method is similar to that for col. 1 except that the value of residential real estate is given separately in *Wealth, Debt, and Taxation*.

COL. 4: The method is similar to that for col. 1 except that the ratio of the value of residential real estate to the total value of taxable real estate is interpolated along a straight line between 1900 and 1922.

COL. 5: The method is similar to that for col. 1 except that the value of residential real estate is from *A Study of the Physical Assets, Sometimes Called Wealth, of the United States, 1922-1933*, prepared by the University of Notre Dame, Bureau of Economic Research (1939).

LINE 6

Sum of lines 1-5.

LINE 7

COL. 1-5: The total value of tax exempt real estate as given for 1922 in the Notre Dame report is extrapolated for the earlier years with the value of tax exempt real estate in the wealth reports as index. The 1900 figure had first to be reduced by the value of tax exempt agricultural and manufacturing real estate, already covered in the estimates for those groups.

To estimate the value of buildings we assumed the same percentage distribution between land and buildings as for taxable real estate. The percentage of the value of land to the value of real estate in 1922 is 60.7, the figure the Federal Trade Commission uses (*National Wealth and Income*, pp. 31-5). The Notre Dame percentage is 24.5 (*A Study of the Physical Assets*, pp. 123-32). *Federal Ownership of Real Estate and Its Bearing on State and Local Taxation* (76 Cong., 1st Sess., House Doc. 111) gives two divisions of federal real estate—one based on cost, the other on assessed valuation—for property owned June 30, 1937. The percentage of land in real estate is 9.0 on the cost basis, and 43.7 on the assessed valuation basis.

LINE 8

Available statistics cover the cost of construction of roads as a whole, and the division into land and equipment in all years is based on the 1922 distribution. The ratio of the value of improvements to the total value of real estate that the Federal Trade Commission reports for 1922 (*National Wealth and Income*) is extrapolated for the other years with the similar ratio for taxable real estate as index. The derivation of the cost of construction is given below for each year.

COL. 1: The cost of construction reported in the *1880 Census of Transportation* is raised to the total by including the Census estimate of such cost not reported.

As the estimate in the wealth report for 1880 is for railroad capital, it includes the value of equipment. It also includes the investments and cash assets of the railroads and is, therefore, too broad in coverage.

COL. 2: The cost of road and equipment is reported in the *1922 Statistics of Railways*. The segregation of equipment is based on the percentage distribution of the total in the *1890 Census Abstract*.

Several other figures for the cost of road and equipment are available. The estimate we use is $8,134 million; the wealth report shows $8,296 million; the *1890 Census Abstract* reports $8,041, of which $7,202 million is for road and $838 million for equipment (the percentage division we apply to the total we use); *Statistics of Railways for 1890* reports $7,755 million, of which $7,333 million is

Table IV 2 continued:

LINE 8 (*concl.*)

for road and $422 million for equipment. As the latter division gives, unreasonably, a lower percentage for equipment than we have for 1880, it was not used.

COL. 3: The cost of road and equipment is reported in the *1922 Statistics of Railways*. The division into real estate and equipment is derived by interpolating the ratio of real estate to the total along a straight line between 1890 and 1922, and applying the resultant ratio to the total for 1900 (see the notes to col. 2 for 1890 and to col. 5 for 1922).

Our total of the cost of road and equipment is $10,263 million whereas the estimate for railroad capital in the wealth report is $9,036 million. Our estimate checks, however, with the total in the *1900 Statistics of Railways*. The latter also reports the cost of road and of equipment separately, $9,675 million and $588 million; but as the percentage of the cost of equipment to the total seems unreasonably low, it was disregarded.

COL. 4: The method is similar to that for col. 3 except that the cost of road and equipment for switching and terminal companies is taken from the *1912 Statistics of Railways*.

The estimate of railroad capital in the wealth report differs from ours in that it is net of depreciation.

COL. 5: To the cost of road and equipment for both railroads and switching and terminal companies (*Statistics of Railways*) we added the cost of road and equipment for private and intrastate companies (*Estimated National Wealth*). The segregation of the values of land, improvements, and equipment is based on the percentage distribution in *National Wealth and Income*.

The difference between our total, $21,327 million, and that in the wealth report, $19,951 million, is due almost entirely to the deduction for depreciation made by the Bureau of the Census.

LINE 9

COL. 1: The only available data are miles of lines reported in the *1890 Compendium of the Census*. The cost of road and equipment is estimated by multiplying the number of miles by average cost per mile, the latter being assumed to be the same as in 1890. Real estate is segregated by multiplying the estimated cost of road and equipment by the 1890 ratio of real estate to the total, extrapolated by the similar ratio for steam railroads. The further division of real estate into land and improvements is based on the 1922 ratio extrapolated by the ratio of land to real estate for taxable real estate.

COL. 2: The total cost of street railways in the *Census Compendium* is divided into animal, electric, cable, and steam railways in the *1890 Transportation Census*. Also given for sample railways (for each of the four types) is the division of the total cost into road and equipment cost. On the basis of these samples (over 50 percent coverage) and total cost a weighted ratio of equipment to total cost is derived and applied to total cost to yield separate estimates of the cost of equipment and of construction. The cost of construction is divided into land and improvements by the method used in obtaining the 1880 estimate.

COL. 3-5: The estimates for road and equipment are taken from the wealth reports except for 1922, when depreciation was deducted. For that year the figure, before depreciation, in the *Census of Electrical Industries* is used. The series, taken from both sources, is, in millions of dollars: 1900, 1,576; 1902, 2,168; 1904, 2,220; 1907, 3,638; 1912, 4,597; 1917, 5,136; 1922, 5,059 (4,878 after deducting depreciation). The 1922 total is divided into land, improvements, and equipment by means of the Federal Trade Commission percentages. For the other years the ratio of equipment to the total is interpolated between 1890 and 1922 by the similar ratio for steam railroads and applied to the total to yield the value of

REPRODUCIBLE WEALTH

equipment and real estate. Real estate for years other than 1922 is distributed by extrapolating the 1922 ratio of land to real estate (derived from the Federal Trade Commission ratios) by the similar ratio for taxable real estate.

LINE 10

COL. 1 AND 2: The total is extrapolated from 1900 by the cost of steam railroad real estate and equipment. The value of real estate is estimated by multiplying the total by the ratio of real estate to it. This ratio (derived for 1922 from Federal Trade Commission data) is extrapolated with the similar ratio for steam railroads as index. The value of improvements is estimated by multiplying the value of real estate by the ratio of improvements to real estate. This ratio, also derived for 1922 from Federal Trade Commission data, is extrapolated with the similar ratio for taxable real estate as index.

COL. 3-5: The total value is given in the wealth reports. The value of improvements is estimated by the methods described in the notes to col. 1 and 2.

Wealth, Debt, and Taxation for 1900 and 1904 states: "The value of Pullman and private cars was ascertained in connection with the estimates of the value of railroads. . . ." The report for 1912 states: "The estimate of the value of cars belonging to the Pullman and other private car companies is based upon the report rendered by the Pullman Company to the Interstate Commerce Commission, which shows the cost of property and equipment, exclusive of land." The report for 1922 states: "The estimated values of cars belonging to the Pullman Company and express companies are based on reports . . . to the Interstate Commerce Commission. . . . The estimated value of privately owned cars . . . is based on the number of such cars as shown in the Equipment Register of January, 1923, and the average value of such cars. . . . The estimated values of the three classes of cars are combined into a single item in this report."

It would seem, therefore, that our estimates are too large in that they include cars owned by other industries and presumably covered under equipment in those industries. On the other hand, they are too small in that they exclude the value of real estate and other equipment owned by the Pullman Company and express companies. Also, if the wealth item is only *cars,* as stated above, we are in error in following the Federal Trade Commission's technique of dividing the total into land, improvements, and equipment.

Some other data are available for 1922 in the Interstate Commerce Commission's published data for the Pullman and express companies—*Preliminary Abstract of Statistics of Common Carriers:*

EXPRESS COMPANIES	(millions of dollars)
Land (cost)	5
Buildings (cost)	10
Equipment (cost)	22
Total (cost)	37
Depreciation	10
Net physical property	27
Equipment (inventory value)	13
" of which cars " "	0.7
PULLMAN COMPANY	
Cost of property and equipment	195
Reserve accounts	74

Similar data are not available for any of the other years for which we have wealth estimates.

LINE 11

For no years do we have statistics other than for total investment in plant and equipment. The value of real estate is estimated by multiplying this total by the ratio of real estate to it. The ratio, derived for 1922 from Federal Trade Commission data (*National Wealth and Income*), is extrapolated with the similar ratio

Table IV 2 continued:

LINE 11 (*concl.*)

for steam railroads as index. The value of improvements is estimated by multiplying the value of real estate by the ratio of improvements to it. This ratio (also derived for 1922 from Federal Trade Commission data), is extrapolated with the similar ratio for taxable real estate as index.

COL. 1: The only investment figure reported is for capital stock and funded debt (given in the *1880 Census of Transportation* and also in the *1912 Census of Telephones*). The *1880 Census* also reports total miles of wire and the miles of wire of companies reporting capital stock and funded debt. The reported figure was raised accordingly.

COL. 2: 'Investment in plant and equipment' is given in the *1927 Census of Telephones* with a note "Partial enumeration only". In the *1912 Census of Telephones* this item is reported as "capital stock and funded debt". Data by which this figure can be stepped up to the total are not available.

COL. 3-5: The estimates of investment in plant and equipment are from the wealth reports. They agree with the *Census of Telephones* figures for 1912 and 1922, and seem reasonable when assembled with the latter figures for earlier years. The combined series is, in millions of dollars: 1900, 400; 1902, 404; 1904, 586; 1907, 820; 1912, 1,081; 1917, 1,258; 1922, 1,746.

LINE 12

The values of land, improvements, and equipment were estimated by the same method as for telephones (see the notes to line 11).

COL. 1: Investment in plant and equipment is assumed equal to 'franchise and construction', $93 million, for land telegraph only (*1880 Census of Transportation*). In a table on world statistics in the same volume 'cost of line and equipment' is given as $18.7 million with a note: "based on the report of the president of the Western Union Telegraph Co. for 1869, and upon other data found in Mr. Lines' report".

COL. 2: No data on investment are reported. We interpolate between 1880 and 1902 on the basis of 'Telegraph lines; stocks owned of leased telegraph companies that are merged in Western Union Co.'s system; franchises; patents, etc.' given by the Western Union Telegraph Co. in its annual reports for 1880, 1890, and 1902.

COL. 3-5: For 1900, 1904, 1912, and 1922 estimates of plant and equipment are given in the wealth reports; for 1902, 1907, 1912, 1917, and 1922 in the *Census of Telegraphs*. For 1912 alone do the two sources check. The series based on the two sources is in millions of dollars: 1900, 212; 1902, 162; 1904, 227; 1907, 210; 1912, 223; 1917, 253; 1922, 361 (*Census of Telegraphs*) and 204 (*Estimated National Wealth*). Since for 1900 and 1904 the description of the derivation in the wealth reports is vague, and since the figures seem out of line with those in the *Census of Telegraphs* we used the *1902 Census of Telegraphs* estimate for 1900. Wireless is included for the first time in 1907.

For 1922 we use the figure reported in the *Census of Telegraphs*. The 1922 estimate in the wealth report is net of depreciation reserves but still seems unreasonably low. The *Census of Telegraphs* reports 'Reserves, depreciation and other' as $94 million; subtracting that from the gross figure, we obtain $267 million; the wealth estimate is $204 million.

LINE 13

The cost of canals (described below) and the value of vessels (see the notes to Table IV 3, line 12) were estimated separately, then combined and raised to the value of total fixed capital before being classified into land, improvements, and equipment.

The total value of fixed capital is estimated by dividing the value of vessels (equipment) by its ratio to the total. The ratio is obtained as the complement of the ratio of real estate to total fixed capital, which is estimated for 1880, taken for 1922 from *National Wealth and Income,* and interpolated along a straight line for other years. The ratio for 1880 is derived as follows:

For steamship traffic the value of vessels is $80 million; of capital invested, $112 million (*1880 Census of Transportation*). Assuming that the difference represents real estate we multiplied its ratio to the comparable value of vessels by the total value of vessels to obtain the value of real estate in shipping. The ratio of real estate to total fixed assets is obtained by dividing the value of real estate in shipping plus the cost of canals by the value of real estate in shipping plus the cost of canals plus the value of vessels.

The real estate value is estimated by subtracting the value of equipment from total fixed capital. It is divided into land and improvements on the assumption that the Federal Trade Commission's distribution (*National Wealth and Income*) is applicable for the entire period.

Canals
COL. 1 AND 2: The cost of operated and of abandoned canals is given in the *1916 Census of Water Transportation*. An alternative estimate for operated canals, $170 million, is given in the *1880 Census Compendium;* our estimate is $184 million.

COL. 3: The estimates of the cost of canals, both operated and abandoned, are interpolated along a straight line between 1890 and 1906 (for 1906 also reported in the *1916 Census of Water Transportation*).

COL. 4: The estimate of the cost of abandoned canals is interpolated between 1906 and 1916 (for 1916 also reported in the *1916 Census of Water Transportation*). The cost of operated canals is estimated by adding $51 million to the 1906 figure. In *Wealth, Debt, and Taxation: 1913,* I, it is stated: "The increase in the valuation reported for 1912 over the valuation shown for 1904 and 1900 is due largely to the construction of the Barge Canal in New York, upon which $50,864,369 has been expended down to October 1, 1912."

COL. 5: For both operated and abandoned canals the 1916 value (*Census of Water Transportation*) is used. In *Estimated National Wealth* it is stated: "the values of canals and investments in canalized rivers were taken from a report of the Bureau of Census for 1916".

The figures in the wealth reports for 1900, 1904, 1912, and 1922 are smaller than those described above, presumably because they exclude the value of real estate in shipping; on the other hand, they include the value of the Navy in 1900 and 1904. The comparison is, in millions of dollars:

SHIPPING AND CANALS

	1900	1904	1912	1922
Wealth estimates	538[a]	846[a]	1,089	1,506
Present estimates	817[b]	...	1,693[b]	2,044[b]

[a] Includes Navy. [b] Includes shipping real estate.

For 1880 the wealth report's figure for telegraphs, shipping, and canals is $419 million. Our total for the two groups is $539 million.

For 1890 the wealth report's figure for telegraphs, telephones, shipping, canals, and equipment is $702 million. Our total for the three groups is $798 million.

LINE 14

The values of land, improvements, and equipment are estimated by the same method as for telephones (see the notes to line 11).

COL. 1: We assumed the investment to be zero since of those companies surviving in 1902 only 7 began operations in 1881, and there are no other figures by which

Table IV 2 continued:

LINE 14 (*concl.*)

we can estimate the investment in 1880. If it was not zero, it was probably very close to it.

COL. 2: The *1902 Census of Electric Light and Power* reports the number of stations in operation in 1890. Plant and equipment is estimated on the basis of the number of stations and the estimated cost of plant and equipment per station. The latter figure, available for 1902 from the *Census,* is extrapolated to 1890 by the similar figure for New York electric light and power stations (also reported for 1890 and 1902 in the *1902 Census*).

COL. 3-5: The estimates are from the wealth reports. They agree with the *Census of Electric Light and Power* figures for 1912 and 1922, and seem reasonable when assembled with the latter figures for earlier years. The combined series is, in millions of dollars: 1900, 403; 1902, 483; 1904, 563; 1907, 1,054; 1912, 2,099; 1917, 2,933; and 1922, 4,229.

LINE 15

The 1922 distribution of total investment into land, improvements, and equipment (*National Wealth and Income*) is applied throughout the period.

COL. 1 AND 2: Total investment in 1880 and 1890 is derived by assuming the same annual increment as held from 1900 to 1904.

COL. 3-5: Total investment is from the wealth reports.

LINE 16

According to the *1930 Census of Irrigation of Agricultural Lands,* "The investment includes cost of construction and cost of acquiring rights. The latter usually consists of filing fees only, . . ." Assuming therefore that improvements make up the preponderant part, we used the Federal Trade Commission percentages for waterworks—5 for land, 90 for improvements, and 5 for equipment—and kept them constant for the entire period.

COL. 1: The value of irrigation enterprises is an extrapolation of the 1890 figure based on the investment in 1930 of companies in business in 1880, 1890, and 1900. While the latter series (*1930 Census of Irrigation*), includes, of course, investments made after the date in question, it was thought to be a better basis for extrapolation than a straight line. The ratio of the percentage change in this series from 1880 to 1890 to the percentage change from 1890 to 1900 was applied to the percentage change in capital invested as reported in 1890 and estimated for 1900.

COL. 2: The estimate is that in the *1912 Census of Wealth, Debt, and Taxation,* which states (p. 18): "These enterprises increased in value from $66,062,275 in 1889 to $360,865,270 in 1912. . . ."

Another estimate for 1890, $30 million, is reported in the *1930 Census of Irrigation.*

COL. 3: The only figure reported is in the *1930 Census of Irrigation.* Since figures are also given there for 1890 and 1910 we used that series as an index to interpolate between the 1890 and 1912 figures in the wealth reports. The 1910 figure is used for 1912 without any adjustment (the former, from the *Census of Irrigation,* is $321 million and the latter, from the *Census of Wealth, Debt and Taxation,* is $361 million).

COL. 4: The estimate is from the wealth report.

COL. 5: The 1920 figure in the *Census of Irrigation,* but excluding government investment, is used.

The figure for 1922 may well be an underestimate. For 1930 the *Census of Irrigation* reports the 'cost of preparing land for irrigation', an item not included in 'investment in irrigation enterprises'. The two figures for 1930 are for investment $1,033 million, and for cost of clearing land $524 million.

LINE 17

The only figure for investment in pipe lines, a rough estimate for 1922 (*Estimated National Wealth*), is extrapolated by mileage figures for interstate pipe lines (Walter Splawn, 'Transportation by Pipe Lines', *Oil and Gas Journal,* Sept. 22, 1938). No data for intrastate mileage are available for these years, but for 1924-38 the ratio of interstate to total mileage is quite stable.

The 1922 Federal Trade Commission percentage distribution into the value of land, improvements, and equipment (*National Wealth and Income*) is applied throughout the period.

LINE 18

Sum of lines 8-17.

LINE 19

Sum of lines, 6, 7, and 18.

TABLE IV 3

Value of Equipment, Census Dates, 1880-1922 (millions of dollars) Based on Reported Valuation

	VALUATION BASE	1880 (1)	1890 (2)	1900 (3)	1912 (4)	1922 (5)
1 Agriculture	Market	407	494	750	1,392	2,292
2 Mining	Book	143	202	399	980	2,001
3 Manufacturing	Book	670	1,584	2,543	6,091	15,949
4 Other industrial	Market	889	1,778	2,227	3,809	5,901
5 Total taxable, excl. public utilities		2,109	4,058	5,919	12,272	26,143
6 Tax exempt	Book	222	438	730	1,507	2,536
7 Steam railroads	Book	418	846	1,468	3,134	4,905
8 Street railways	Book	19	60	288	1,007	1,265
9 Pullman, express, etc.	Book	37	64	82	104	463
10 Telephone	Book	9	36	208	592	1,257
11 Telegraph	Book	46	77	84	122	206
12 Shipping & canals	Market	156	221	343	785	1,022
13 Electric light & power	Book	0	23	134	777	1,692
14 Waterworks	Book	12	12	13	14	18
15 Irrigation	Book	1	3	5	18	28
16 Pipe lines	Book	1	2	8	18	25
17 Total public utilities		699	1,344	2,633	6,571	10,881
18 Total equipment		3,030	5,840	9,282	20,350	39,560

LINE 1

COL. 1-3: Value of farm equipment is reported in the Census of Agriculture.

COL. 4 AND 5: The estimates are those prepared by the Bureau of Agricultural Economics (*Income Parity for Agriculture,* Part II, Sec. 3, Washington, D. C., Aug. 1940). Forty percent of the value of automobiles is included to cover business use of passenger cars.

The figure for 1922 is $2,292 million; that reported in *Estimated National Wealth* is $2,605 million. The latter excludes automobiles and trucks, estimated by the Bureau of Agricultural Economics to be $750 million, of which $358 million was included in our estimate.

LINE 2

COL. 1 AND 2: The method is the same as that described for value of improvements (see the notes to Table IV 2, line 2, col. 1 and 2).

Table IV 3 continued:

LINE 2 (*concl.*)

COL. 3-5: Value of equipment is obtained by multiplying capital other than real estate by the ratio of machinery to it. The derivation of the former is given in the notes to Table IV 2, line 2, col. 3-5; for the latter the 1890 figure is used (see the notes to Table IV 2, line 2, col. 2).

LINE 3

COL. 1 AND 2: The method is the same as that described for value of improvements (see the notes to Table IV 2, line 3, col. 1 and 2).

COL. 3: See the notes to Table IV 2, line 3, col. 3 for the method. Value of equipment, $2,543 million, checks with the value in the wealth report for 1900, $2,541 million.

COL. 4: The value of machinery is given in *Wealth, Debt, and Taxation: 1913*, I.

COL. 5: The estimate is obtained by multiplying total capital (see the notes to Table IV 2, line 3, col. 5) by the ratio of the value of machinery to it (*Estimated National Wealth* and used also by Douglas).

We checked our estimate of the value of machinery in 1922 against Chawner's estimates of expenditures for manufacturing equipment. The method and sources are the same as those for Table IV 2, line 3, col. 5. Our total is $15,949 million; that based on Chawner's data is $15,755 million.

LINE 4

As no estimates for this item are available for any year, we had to make our own. The National Bureau (Financial Research Program) has collected data on fixed assets for Massachusetts nonmanufacturing corporations. The material is available for several years but unfortunately for a varying and small number of corporations. For the largest sample, covering 129 corporations, 1920-21, the ratio of the value of machinery to the value of fixed assets is .274 in 1920 and .270 in 1921. We took .25 for the entire period, 1880-1922. Since the manufacturing ratio of the value of machinery to the value of fixed assets rose only slightly (from .50 in 1880 to .55 in 1922) the assumption of constancy in the ratio for 'other industrial' probably does not introduce a great error. On the basis of the value of real estate (see the notes to Table IV 2, line 4) and this ratio the value of equipment can be estimated.

The data in the Notre Dame report are a possible check on our estimate. Appendix B, Table 8, of *A Study of the Physical Assets, Sometimes Called Wealth, of the United States* gives total commercial and industrial fixed assets, based upon corporate data from *Statistics of Income,* and divided (a) by industry and (b) into land, buildings, and equipment. The figure for all industries other than manufacturing and mining is $22,868 million in 1922; our figure is $23,603 million ($17,702 million for real estate and $5,901 million for equipment).

The Notre Dame division by type of asset, based on the Federal Trade Commission division of real estate and the Census of Wealth estimate of manufacturing machinery, and allowing for no other type of equipment, is questionable. Its ratio of equipment to total commercial and industrial fixed assets is .32. Ours, obtained by combining manufacturing, mining, and 'other industrial', is .40.

LINE 5

Sum of lines 1-4.

LINE 6

For the value of equipment in 1922 we took the Notre Dame estimate and assumed that in the preceding years it was the same percentage of the value of buildings.

LINE 7

The method is the same as for the value of real estate (see the notes to Table IV 2, line 8).

REPRODUCIBLE WEALTH   215

LINE 8
The method is the same as for the value of real estate (see the notes to Table IV 2, line 9).

LINE 9
The method is the same as for the value of real estate (see the notes to Table IV 2, line 10).

LINE 10
The method is the same as for the value of real estate (see the notes to Table IV 2, line 11).

LINE 11
The method is the same as for the value of real estate (see the notes to Table IV 2, line 12).

LINE 12
COL. 1: The value of vessels is from the *1880 Census of Transportation.*

COL. 2: The value of vessels is from the *1890 Census Compendium.*

In the *1916 Census of Water Transportation* the value of vessels is reported as $207 million; in the *1890 Census Compendium,* as $221 million ($215 million plus $6 million for canal boats).

COL. 3: The value of vessels is estimated as the product of the tonnage and the value per ton. Tonnage is interpolated between 1890 and 1906 (for 1890 given in the *Census Compendium* and for 1906 in the *Census of Water Transportation*) by tonnage of the total merchant marine (*1923 Annual Report,* Bureau of Navigation). Value per ton, computed for 1890 and 1906, is interpolated along a straight line. Value figures for 1890 and 1906 are from the sources cited for tonnage.

COL. 4: The value of vessels is estimated as the product of tonnage and value per ton, but both are interpolated along a straight line since the tonnage figures in the Bureau of Navigation report increase from 1906 to 1916 whereas the tonnage figures in the *Census of Water Transportation* decrease.

COL. 5: The value of vessels, the difference between the figure for shipping and canals, excluding the Navy (*Estimated National Wealth*), and the cost of operated canals (see the notes to Table IV 2, line 13, col. 5), $1,022 million, is larger than the 1916 figure, $960 million. If abandoned canals had also been deducted from the total the value of vessels in 1922 would have been lower than in 1916. This seemed unlikely since the tonnage given in the Bureau of Navigation report for 1922 is much bigger than the 1916 tonnage figure, as is the 1926 tonnage than the 1916, both reported in the *1926 Census of Water Transportation.*

LINE 13
The method is the same as for the value of real estate (see the notes to Table IV 2, line 14).

LINE 14
The method is the same as for the value of real estate (see the notes to Table IV 2, line 15).

LINE 15
The method is the same as for the value of real estate (see the notes to Table IV 2, line 16).

LINE 16
The method is the same as for the value of real estate (see the notes to Table IV 2, line 17).

LINE 17
Sum of lines 7-16.

LINE 18
Sum of lines 5, 6, and 17.

TABLE IV 4

Price Indexes (1929:100), Census Dates, 1880-1922

		1880 (1)	1890 (2)	1900 (3)	1912 (4)	1922 (5)
	CONSTRUCTION					
1	Market price, all construction*	79.2	77.7	79.5	97.9	173.2
2a	Market price, residential	42.2	41.4	42.3	52.1	92.2
2b	Market price, residential, 2d variant	43.2	43.6	43.2	50.5	77.5
3a	Market price, other private	41.5	40.7	41.7	51.3	90.8
3b	Market price, other private, 2d variant	42.8	43.2	43.0	50.1	76.8
4a	Market price, farm	41.8	41.0	42.0	51.7	91.5
4b	Market price, farm, 2d variant	43.0	43.4	43.1	50.3	77.2
5	Book value, all construction	44.6	46.2	44.6	49.1	62.8
	EQUIPMENT					
6a	Market price	62.1	49.0	49.8	55.9	94.7
6b	Market price, 2d variant	64.4	50.0	47.3	54.2	96.4
7	Book value	66.6	51.1	44.8	52.5	98.0

* 1913:100

LINE 1

This index, necessary for the extrapolation of lines 2-4 and basic to the computation of line 5, is a weighted average of an index of building materials prices, and of an index of building wage rates. Constant weights for these two components, used for the entire period, are derived from the data for 1919-33 on the cost of materials and the cost of materials and wages and salaries, in 1929 prices (*Commodity Flow and Capital Formation,* Table VI-5, lines 19 and 20).

The construction materials price index is derived from Shaw's unpublished data.

The wage index for 1890 and later years is derived from Paul H. Douglas' figures on full time weekly earnings in the building trades (*Real Wages in the United States;* Houghton Mifflin, 1930, p. 137). The data for the years prior to 1890 are based on wage rates for various occupations in several states (Bureau of Labor Statistics *Bulletin 499*). The occupational groups covered are bricklayers, carpenters, engineers, firemen, hod carriers, masons, painters, plasterers, and plumbers. Linked relatives are based on quotations for two successive years for identical states. The 1890 index is extrapolated to the earlier years by the arithmetic average of the relatives.

LINE 2a

COL. 1-4: The index is extrapolated from 1922 by means of line 1.

COL. 5: The value of residential construction in current prices divided by the value in 1929 prices. The value figures are from Part I, Tables I 7 and I 8, col. 1.

LINE 2b

Average of lines 2a and 5.

LINE 3a

The method is the same as for line 2.

LINE 3b

Average of lines 3a and 5.

LINE 4a

The average of lines 2 and 3 is used here since farm values include both residential and business property.

LINE 4b

Average of lines 4a and 5.

LINE 5

The index of prices underlying book values is based on the construction cost index (line 1) and the assumption of a fifty-year life. The materials price index is extrapolated to 1840 by the index for lumber and building materials (*Wholesale Prices, Wages and Transportation,* Part I, p. 91). The wage data are available back to 1840 in the Bureau of Labor Statistics *Bulletin 499* (see the notes to line 1 for the derivation of the index).

The weights used in computing the index of prices underlying book values are the product of the constant price values of new construction and the estimated percentage of construction in use in a given year. The construction values (see the notes to Tables II 5, col. 7, and II 14, col. 4) are annual averages for the decades from 1829-38 to 1909-18 and annual estimates from 1914 on. The percentage in use is based on the assumption of a fifty-year life so that in 1890, for example, 2 percent of construction in 1841, 4 percent in 1842, etc. are the weights assigned to the price index for those years. The decade averages, however, are for periods whose terminal years do not coincide with the specific years for which the index of prices underlying book values is desired. We were therefore compelled, in deriving the index for 1890, for example, to use average annual construction, 1889-98, in deriving the weights for 1889 and 1890.

The resultant index of prices underlying book values is used to extrapolate the 1922 index (see the notes to col. 5).

COL. 1: Since there are no price data for years before 1840 the index of prices underlying book values in 1880 does not take account of construction for 1831-39.

COL. 5: *Capital Consumption and Adjustment,* Table 35.

LINE 6a

Shaw's price index for producer durable goods is adjusted by minor groups to the 1929 level. His data are available for 1869, 1879, and 1889-1922. Interpolation for 1880 is by the price index for metals and implements excluding pocket knives (*Wholesale Prices, Wages and Transportation,* Part I, p. 92; see also the notes to Table II 6, col. 1).

LINE 6b

Average of lines 6a and 7.

LINE 7

The method is like that used for line 5 except that annual data on the value of production are used and a thirteen-year life is assumed. For the derivation of the values see Table II 4, col. 1. For the price index see the notes to line 6a; extrapolation of the index back to 1868 is on the basis indicated there for the interpolation for 1880.

Table IV 5
Value of Real Estate Improvements, Census Dates, 1880-1922
1929 Prices (millions of dollars)

		1880 (1)	1890 (2)	1900 (3)	1912 (4)	1922 (5)
	A Adjusted by Current Cost (for Market Valuation) and Past Cost (for Book Valuation)					
1	Agriculture	4,878	6,478	8,469	13,325	12,207
2	Mining	206	439	735	1,317	1,783
3	Manufacturing	821	1,919	3,281	7,055	13,968
4	Other industrial	3,311	6,120	7,609	11,782	9,163
5	Residential	7,964	16,271	22,522	39,685	34,603
6	Total taxable, excl. public utilities	17,180	31,227	42,616	73,164	71,724
7	Tax exempt	1,416	2,701	4,663	8,708	11,408
8	Steam railroads	7,638	12,651	15,959	21,824	21,051
9	Street railways	235	629	2,559	6,454	5,317
10	Pullman, express, etc.	9	15	20	20	70
11	Telephone	20	72	403	930	1,404
12	Telegraph	97	153	163	192	229
13	Shipping & canals	328	384	536	928	814
14	Electric light & power	0	96	505	2,249	3,365
15	Waterworks	473	491	548	534	518
16	Irrigation	61	131	219	665	788
17	Pipe lines	23	92	319	661	717
18	Total public utilities	8,884	14,714	21,231	34,457	34,273
19	Total improvements	27,480	48,642	68,510	116,329	117,405
	B Adjusted by an Average of Current and Past Cost (for Market Valuation) and Past Cost (for Book Valuation)					
20	Agriculture	4,742	6,120	8,253	13,696	14,468
21	Mining	206	439	735	1,317	1,783
22	Manufacturing	821	1,919	3,281	7,055	13,968
23	Other industrial	3,210	5,766	7,379	12,064	10,833
24	Residential	7,780	15,450	22,053	40,943	41,166
25	Total taxable, excl. public utilities	16,759	29,694	41,701	75,075	82,218
26	Tax exempt	1,416	2,701	4,663	8,708	11,408
27	Steam railroads	7,638	12,651	15,959	21,824	21,051
28	Street railways	235	629	2,559	6,454	5,317
29	Pullman, express, etc.	9	15	20	20	70
30	Telephone	20	72	403	930	1,404
31	Telegraph	97	153	163	192	229
32	Shipping & canals	328	384	536	928	814
33	Electric light & power	0	96	505	2,249	3,365
34	Waterworks	473	491	548	534	518
35	Irrigation	61	131	219	665	788
36	Pipe lines	23	92	319	661	717
37	Total public utilities	8,884	14,714	21,231	34,457	34,273
38	Total improvements	27,059	47,109	67,595	118,240	127,899

Values in 1929 prices are obtained by dividing the reported values (Table IV 2) by the appropriate price indexes (Table IV 4). Table IV 4, line 4a is used for line 1; Table IV 4, line 5 for lines 2, 3, 7-17, 21, 22, 26-36; Table IV 4, line 3a for line 4; Table IV 4, line 2a for line 5; Table IV 4, line 4b for line 20; Table IV 4, line 3b for line 23, and Table IV 4, line 2b for line 24.

Table IV 6
Value of Equipment, Census Dates, 1880-1922
1929 Prices (millions of dollars)

	1880 (1)	1890 (2)	1900 (3)	1912 (4)	1922 (5)
A Adjusted by Current Cost (for Market Valuation) and Past Cost (for Book Valuation)					
1 Agriculture	655	1,008	1,506	2,490	2,420
2 Mining	215	395	891	1,867	2,042
3 Manufacturing	1,006	3,100	5,676	11,602	16,274
4 Other industrial	1,432	3,629	4,472	6,814	6,231
5 Total taxable, excl. public utilities	3,308	8,132	12,545	22,773	26,967
6 Tax exempt	333	857	1,629	2,870	2,588
7 Steam railroads	628	1,656	3,277	5,970	5,005
8 Street railways	29	117	643	1,918	1,291
9 Pullman, express, etc.	56	125	183	198	472
10 Telephone	14	70	464	1,128	1,283
11 Telegraph	69	151	188	232	210
12 Shipping & canals	251	451	689	1,404	1,079
13 Electric light & power	0	45	299	1,480	1,727
14 Waterworks	18	23	29	27	18
15 Irrigation	2	6	11	34	29
16 Pipe lines	2	4	18	34	26
17 Total public utilities	1,069	2,648	5,801	12,425	11,140
18 Total equipment	4,710	11,637	19,975	38,068	40,695
B Adjusted by an Average of Current and Past Cost (for Market Valuation) and Past Cost (for Book Valuation)					
19 Agriculture	632	988	1,586	2,568	2,378
20 Mining	215	395	891	1,867	2,042
21 Manufacturing	1,006	3,100	5,676	11,602	16,274
22 Other industrial	1,380	3,556	4,708	7,028	6,121
23 Total taxable, excl. public utilities	3,233	8,039	12,861	23,065	26,815
24 Tax exempt	333	857	1,629	2,870	2,588
25 Steam railroads	628	1,656	3,277	5,970	5,005
26 Street railways	29	117	643	1,918	1,291
27 Pullman, express, etc.	56	125	183	198	472
28 Telephone	14	70	464	1,128	1,283
29 Telegraph	69	151	188	232	210
30 Shipping & canals	242	442	725	1,448	1,060
31 Electric light & power	0	45	299	1,480	1,727
32 Waterworks	18	23	29	27	18
33 Irrigation	2	6	11	34	29
34 Pipe lines	2	4	18	34	26
35 Total public utilities	1,060	2,639	5,837	12,469	11,121
36 Total equipment	4,626	11,535	20,327	38,404	40,524

Values in 1929 prices are obtained by dividing the reported values (Table IV 3) by the appropriate price indexes (Table IV 4). Table IV 4, line 6a is used for lines 1, 4, and 12; Table IV 4, line 7 for lines 2, 3, 6-11, 13-16, 20, 21, 24-29, 31-34; Table IV 4, line 6b for lines 19, 22, and 30.

TABLE IV 7: Value of Improvements and Equipment, January 1, 1919 (millions of dollars)

		IMPROVEMENTS			EQUIPMENT		
		Reported Value (1)	Price Index (1929:100) (2)	Value 1929 Prices (3)	Reported Value (4)	Price Index (1929:100) (5)	Value 1929 Prices (6)
1	Agriculture						
	a Adj. by current cost	9,541	102.2	9,336	2,625	122.6	2,141
	b Adj. by av. of current & past cost	9,541	80.2	11,897	2,625	104.1	2,524
2	Mining	1,113	58.3	1,909	1,899	85.5	2,221
3	Manufacturing	7,293	58.3	12,509	13,118	85.5	15,343
4	Other industrial						
	a Adj. by current cost	7,687	98.0	7,844	5,064	122.6	4,131
	b Adj. by av. of current & past cost	7,687	78.2	9,830	5,064	104.0	4,869
5	Residential	31,754		33,905			
6	Total taxable, excl. public utilities						
	a Sum of 1a, 2, 3, 4a, & 5	57,388		65,503	22,706		23,836
	b Sum of 1b, 2, 3, 4b, & 5	57,388		70,050	22,706		24,957
7	Tax exempt	5,496	58.3	9,427	1,944	85.5	2,274
8	Steam railroads	12,247	58.3	21,007	3,264	85.5	3,818
9	Street railways	3,565	58.3	6,115	1,244	85.5	1,455
10	Pullman, express, etc.	24	58.3	41	250	85.5	292
11	Telephone	670	58.3	1,149	905	85.5	1,058
12	Telegraph	116	58.3	199	153	85.5	179
13	Shipping & canals						
	a Adj. by current cost	513*	58.3	880	969	122.6	790
	b Adj. by av. of current & past cost	513*	58.3	880	969	104.0	932
14	Electric light & power	1,604	58.3	2,751	1,196	85.5	1,399
15	Waterworks	299	58.3	513	17	85.5	20
16	Irrigation	427	58.3	732	24	85.5	28
17	Pipe lines	357	58.3	612	20	85.5	23
18	Total public utilities						
	a Sum of 8-12, 13a, 14-17	19,822		33,999	8,042		9,062
	b Sum of 8-12, 13b, 14-17	19,822		33,999	8,042		9,204
19	Total improvements						
	a Sum of 6a, 7, & 18a	82,706		108,929	32,692		35,172
	b Sum of 6b, 7, & 18b	82,706		113,476	32,692		36,435

* Book valuation and, therefore, adjusted by cost index.

Column 1

LINE 1: The estimate is for March 1 as obtained from the Bureau of Agricultural Economics.

LINE 2: Capital invested is reported in the *1919 Census of Mines and Quarries*. The value of real estate is obtained by multiplying capital invested by the ratio of real estate to it. The ratio is interpolated along a straight line between 1890 and 1922 (for the latter see the notes to Table IV 2, line 2, col. 2 and 5).

The value of improvements is obtained by multiplying the value of real estate by the ratio of improvements to it. The ratio is interpolated along a straight line between 1890 and 1922 (for the latter see the notes to Table IV 2, line 2, col. 2 and 5).

This value figure is for the end of 1919, and no data are available by which a figure for January 1, 1919 could be computed.

LINE 3: Capital invested is reported in the *1919 Census of Manufactures*. The value of improvements is obtained by multiplying capital invested by the ratio of improvements to it (Paul H. Douglas, *Theory of Wages*, Ch. 5, Table 4).

Here also the figure is for December 31, 1919 but there is some evidence that the estimate for the first of the year would not be much smaller. Chawner estimates expenditures for plant in 1919 as $815 million, and for equipment, $1,409 million. Fabricant estimates depreciation as $1,152 million, leaving a $1,072 million net increase in 1919 in the value of plant and equipment. It can be assumed therefore that the December 31, 1919 figure is representative of the situation at the beginning of the year (the error involved after converting the increase in the value of plant and equipment to 1929 prices amounts to less than 5 percent of the December 31, 1919 value).

LINE 4: The value of manufacturing improvements is used to interpolate the value of other industrial improvements between 1912 and 1922 (for the latter see the notes to Table IV 2, line 4, col. 4 and 5).

LINE 5: From the value of residential improvements in 1922 (see Table IV 2, line 5, col. 5) residential real estate construction, 1919-22, is subtracted, and to it residential real estate consumption, 1919-22, is added (see Part I, Table I 7, col. 1, and the notes to Table I 16, col. 1).

LINE 7: The total value of real estate and equipment is interpolated between 1912 and 1922 (see the notes to Table IV 2, line 7, and Table IV 3, line 6, for derivation of estimates for these years) by the value reported for property of states and of cities of 30,000 and over. The values of both state and city property in 1912 are reported in the *Census of Wealth, Debt, and Taxation, 1913*. The state property figures in 1918 and 1922 are from *Financial Statistics of States, 1919* and *1923*. Since the majority of the states report for fiscal years ending June 30 we have not made any further adjustment. The property figures for cities of 30,000 and over in 1918 and 1922 are from *Financial Statistics of Cities, 1918* and *1923* (no data are available for 1922).

The ratios of improvements and of equipment to total real estate and equipment are interpolated along a straight line between 1912 and 1922 (see the notes to Table IV 2, line 7, and Table IV 3, line 6) and applied to the estimated total for 1918 to yield the values of improvements and equipment.

LINE 8: The gross value of road and equipment for steam railroads and switching and terminal companies are both given in the *1918 Statistics of Railways*. The ratios of real estate to road and equipment and land to real estate are interpolated along a straight line between 1912 and 1922 (see the notes to Table IV 2, line 8, col. 4 and 5). By applying these ratios to the value of road and equipment, we get the values of improvements and of equipment.

Table IV 7 continued:

COLUMN 1 *(concl.)*

Total depreciation on road and equipment for both steam railroads and switching and terminal companies, also reported in the *1918 Statistics of Railways,* is divided into depreciation on road and on equipment by means of the 1920 figures for depreciation on equipment and total depreciation (*1938 Statistics of Railways*). The 1920 relation is assumed to apply in 1918.

LINE 9: Value of road and equipment at the end of 1917 is reported in the *Census of Electric Railways.* The ratios of real estate to road and equipment and of land to real estate are interpolated along a straight line between 1912 and 1922 (see the notes to Table IV 2, line 9, col. 3-5). By applying these ratios we get the values of improvements and of equipment at the end of 1917. To obtain the value of improvements, December 31, 1918 we add construction expenditures in 1918 as estimated by Lowell Chawner (*Construction Activity in the United States, 1915-1937*).

LINE 10: The value of plant and equipment is interpolated between 1912 and 1922 by gross revenues reported by the Pullman Company (*Statistical Abstract, 1923*). The ratios of real estate to plant and equipment and land to real estate are interpolated along a straight line between 1912 and 1922 (see the notes to Table IV 2, line 10, col. 3-5). By applying these ratios we get the values of improvements and of equipment.

LINE 11: Value of plant and equipment, December 31, 1917 is reported in the *1932 Census of Telephones.* For the procedure see the notes to line 9; for the sources see the notes to Table IV 2, line 11.

LINE 12: Value of plant and equipment, December 31, 1917 for telegraph companies is reported in the *1932 Census of Electric Light and Power Stations* and that for wireless companies in the *1917 Census of Telegraphs.* For the procedure see the notes to line 9; for the sources, see the notes to Table IV 2, line 12.

LINE 13: Value of vessels is interpolated between 1916 and 1922 by the gross tonnage reported (*1923 Annual Report,* Bureau of Navigation). On the basis of the value of vessels the value of improvements is derived by the procedure described in the notes to Table IV 2, line 13.

LINE 14: Value of plant and equipment, December 31, 1917 is reported in the *Census of Electric Light and Power Stations.* For the procedure see the notes to line 9; for the sources see the notes to Table IV 2, line 14.

LINES 15 AND 16: Value of capital is interpolated along a straight line between 1912 and 1922. See the notes to Table IV 2, lines 15 and 16, for the 1912 and 1922 figures and the procedure used to derive the values of improvements and of equipment.

LINE 17: The procedure is described in the notes to Table IV 2, line 17.

COLUMN 2

The price indexes are averages for the year; values are for the first of the year. So far as prices were moving upward during this period the figures in constant prices are underestimates.

LINES 1a AND 4a: Market price index. The sources and methods are given in the notes to Table IV 4, lines 3a and 4a.

LINES 1b AND 4b: Average of market and cost price indexes; see the notes to Table IV 4, lines 3b and 4b.

LINES 2, 3, 7-17: Index of prices underlying book values. The sources and methods are given in the notes to Table IV 4, line 5.

REPRODUCIBLE WEALTH

COLUMN 3

LINES 1-4, 7-17: Col. 1 divided by col. 2.

LINE 5: See the notes to col. 1, line 5; Table I 8, col. 1; and the notes to Table I 16, col. 6.

COLUMN 4

LINE 1: Estimate prepared by the Bureau of Agricultural Economics (*Income Parity for Agriculture,* Part II, Sec. 3, Washington, D. C., Aug. 1940). To allow for business use, it includes 40 percent of the value of automobiles.

LINE 2: The value of equipment is obtained by multiplying the value of other assets (capital invested minus real estate) by the ratio of equipment to it. For the derivation of the value see the notes to col. 1, line 2; for the ratio see the notes to Table IV 3, line 2, col. 3-5.

LINE 3: See the notes to col. 1, line 3. The ratio of equipment to capital invested is also from Douglas' *Theory of Wages.*

LINE 4: The value of real estate is derived by dividing the value of improvements (see the notes to col. 1, line 4) by the ratio of improvements to it. The ratio is interpolated along a straight line between 1912 and 1922 (see the notes to Table IV 2, line 4, col. 4 and 5). With value of real estate estimated the value of equipment is derived by the procedure described in the notes to Table IV 3, line 4.

LINES 7, 8, 10-17: See the notes to col. 1, lines 7, 8, 10-17.

LINE 9: See the notes to col. 1, line 9. To obtain the value of expenditures in 1918 the 1919 figure was extrapolated by the number of street railway cars built, the procedure used by George Terborgh (see *Federal Reserve Bulletin,* Sept. 1939).

COLUMN 5

LINES 1a, 4a, AND 13a: Market price index. The sources and methods are given in the notes to Table IV 4, line 6a.

LINES 1b, 4b, AND 13b: Average of market and cost price indexes; see the notes to Table IV 4, line 6b.

LINES 2, 3, 7-12, 14-17: Index of prices underlying book values. The sources and methods are given in the notes to Table IV 4, line 7.

COLUMN 6

LINES 1-4, 7-17: Col. 4 divided by col. 5.

Table IV 8

Value of Additions to Improvements and Equipment, Gross and Net Current Prices, 1919-1938 (millions of dollars)

	IMPROVE- MENTS Gross (1)	EQUIP- MENT Gross (2)	IMPROVE- MENTS & EQUIP- MENT Gross (3)	CONSUMP- TION OF IMPROVE- MENTS & EQUIP- MENT (4)	IMPROVE- MENTS & EQUIP- MENT Net (5)
1 Agriculture	3,650	11,067	14,717	17,254	−2,537
2 Mining & manufacturing	8,098	38,804	46,902	52,795	−5,893
3 Other industrial	12,455	30,787	43,242	29,639	13,603
4 Residential	50,414	...	50,414	42,281	8,133
5 Total taxable, excl. public utilities	74,617	80,658	155,275	141,969	13,306
6 Nonprofit institutions	6,841	...	...	...	...
7 Public[a]	20,352	...	...	...	...
8 Tax exempt	27,193	2,999	30,192	16,667	13,525
9 Steam railroads	5,582	5,350	10,932	...	...
10 Transit	1,170	1,169	2,339	...	...
11 Telephone	2,762	3,785	6,547	...	...
12 Electric light & power	5,011	4,630	9,641	...	...
13 Other public utilities[b]	3,000	1,463	4,463	...	...
14 Total public utilities	17,525	16,397	33,922	18,533	15,389
15 Total[a]	119,334	100,054	219,388	177,169	42,219

[a] Excludes construction of streets and roads, $18,684 million.
[b] Includes pipe lines, gas, and telegraph and cables.

Column 1

LINE 1: Sum of annual estimates of nonresidential construction (see the notes to Table I 7, col. 2).

LINES 2, 3, AND 6: 'Other private construction' (Table I 7, col. 2) minus agricultural construction (an unpublished series underlying the former) yields a total which is distributed among mining and manufacturing, other industrial, and nonprofit institutions. This distribution is based upon the percentage distribution of expenditures on plant for mining and manufacturing, commercial and miscellaneous, and buildings for nonprofit institutions (George Terborgh, 'Estimated Expenditures for New Durable Goods, 1919-1938', *Federal Reserve Bulletin,* Sept. 1939 and Feb. 1940). The series for mining and manufacturing, however, is adjusted to exclude mining development outlays.

'Other industrial' (line 3) covers all types of private property other than railroads, electric light and power, telephones, electric railways and buses, pipe lines, gas, telegraph and cables, mining and manufacturing, and agriculture. It therefore includes miscellaneous public utilities not estimated separately below.

LINE 4: Table I 7, col. 1 contains the annual estimates of which this item is the sum.

LINE 5: Sum of lines 1-4.

LINE 7: From annual estimates of total public construction (Table I 7, col. 5) the value of construction of streets and roads (Lowell J. Chawner, *Construction Activity in the United States* and the *Survey of Current Business,* June 1943 and June 1944), was deducted.

LINE 8: Sum of lines 6 and 7.

LINES 9-13: The allocation of the total public utility estimate (see the notes to line 14) to the minor public utility groups is based on the percentage distribution of Terborgh's estimates for those groups (see the notes to lines 2, 3, and 6 for the source of Terborgh's data).

LINE 14: Table I 7, col. 3 contains the annual estimates of which this item is the sum.

LINE 15: Sum of lines 5, 8, and 14.

COLUMN 2

LINE 1: Sum of annual estimates prepared by the BAE (*Income Parity for Agriculture*, Part II, Sec. 3). To allow for business use, it includes 40 percent of expenditures on automobiles.

LINES 2 AND 3: Total expenditures on mining and manufacturing and other industrial business equipment is the difference between total expenditures on equipment (the sum of annual estimates in Table I 6, col. 2) and expenditures on agriculture, public utility, and tax exempt equipment. Agricultural expenditures are from line 1; public utility and tax exempt expenditures, from lines 14 and 8, respectively. The residual is apportioned between the two groups by the percentage distribution of the similar total from Terborgh's data (see the notes to col. 1, lines 2, 3, and 6 for source).

LINE 5: Sum of lines 1-3.

LINE 8: Expenditures on equipment are derived for 1923-33 from the estimates of the value of equipment in the Notre Dame report (*A Study of the Physical Assets, Sometimes Called Wealth, of the United States*). Since the data are on a cost basis and no allowance is made for depreciation, according to that report, the increase from year to year reflects actual expenditures. From 1923 the estimate is extrapolated back to 1919 with expenditures on improvements as index; from 1933 it is extrapolated forward to 1938 by the same index.

LINES 9-13: The data are taken directly from Terborgh's tables (see the notes to col. 1, lines 2, 3, and 6 for source).

LINE 14: Sum of lines 9-13.

LINE 15: Sum of lines 5, 8, and 14.

COLUMN 3

Sum of col. 1 and 2.

COLUMN 4

For the coverage of these estimates and comparability with the data on expenditures see the notes to Table IV 9, col. 4.

LINE 1: Sum of annual estimates prepared by the BAE (*Income Parity for Agriculture*, Part II, Sec. 3 and 5). To allow for business use, it includes 40 percent of depreciation on automobiles.

LINES 2, 3, AND 14: The total for these groups, agriculture, and residential property is derived from the annual series (Table I 16, col. 1). The residual after deducting agriculture (line 1) and residential (line 4) is distributed among the three groups on the basis of the industrial distribution of depreciation and depletion charges, reported for 1919-35 in terms of accounting measures by Fabricant in *Capital Consumption and Adjustment*, Tables 17 and III, and estimated by similar methods for 1936-38. For their conversion to charges in 1929 prices see the notes to Table IV 9, col. 4. The annual data in 1929 prices are multiplied by Fabricant's price index (*ibid.*, Table 32, for 1919-35, and estimated by similar methods for 1936-38) to yield the current price series by which the total is distributed.

LINE 4: Sum of the annual data underlying Table I 16, col. 1.

Table IV 8 concluded:

COLUMN 4 (*concl.*)

LINE 5: Sum of lines 1-4.

LINE 8: Sum of the annual data in Table I 16, col. 2.

LINE 15: Sum of lines 5, 8, and 14.

COLUMN 5

Col. 3 minus col. 4.

TABLE IV 9

Value of Additions to Improvements and Equipment, Gross and Net
1929 Prices, 1919-1938 (millions of dollars)

	IMPROVE-MENTS Gross (1)	EQUIP-MENT Gross (2)	IMPROVE-MENTS & EQUIP-MENT Gross (3)	CONSUMP-TION OF IMPROVE-MENTS & EQUIP-MENT (4)	IMPROVE-MENTS & EQUIP-MENT Net (5)
1 Agriculture	3,666	11,091	14,757	17,603	−2,846
2 Mining & manufacturing	8,170	39,854	48,024	54,011	−5,987
3 Other industrial	12,673	31,830	44,503	30,652	13,851
4 Residential	52,255	...	52,255	45,478	6,777
5 Total taxable, excl. public utilities	76,764	82,775	159,539	147,744	11,795
6 Nonprofit institutions	7,003	...	...	...	...
7 Public[a]	20,586	...	...	...	...
8 Tax exempt[a]	27,589	3,050	30,639	17,213	13,426
9 Steam railroads	5,658	5,327	10,985	...	...
10 Transit	1,181	1,193	2,374	...	...
11 Telephone	2,799	3,946	6,745	...	...
12 Electric light & power	5,046	4,739	9,785	...	...
13 Other public utilities[b]	3,035	1,491	4,526	...	...
14 Total public utilities	17,719	16,696	34,415	19,476	14,939
15 Total[a]	122,072	102,521	224,593	184,433	40,160

[a] Excludes construction of streets and roads, $18,993 million.
[b] Includes pipe lines, gas, and telegraph and cables.

COLUMN 1

The preliminary totals for 1919-38 are the sum of the annual data converted to 1929 prices. The final estimates are then derived by the methods described for the current price data. For the methods and the sources of the annual data in current prices see the notes to Table IV 8, col. 1; for the price indexes, see the following notes.

LINES 1, 2, 3, AND 6: The price index is that implicit in 'other private construction' and is derived from Tables I 7 and I 8, col. 2.

LINE 4: The price index is derived from Tables I 7 and I 8, col. 1.

LINE 7: The price index is the Aberthaw index of construction costs (see the notes to Table I 8, col. 2 for source), assumed applicable to public building.

LINES 9-14: The price index is that implicit in public utility construction, and is derived from Tables I 7 and I 8, col. 3.

Column 2

Here also the preliminary totals for 1919-38 are the sum of the annual data converted to 1929 prices. The final estimates are then derived by the methods described for the current price data. For the methods and the sources of the annual data in current prices see the notes to Table IV 8, col. 2. The price index is Shaw's for producer durable goods, adjusted by minor groups to the 1929 base.

Column 3

Sum of col. 1 and 2.

Column 4

LINE 1: The annual series in current prices (see the notes to Table IV 8, col. 4, line 1 for source) is converted to 1929 prices by Fabricant's current price index for business capital goods (*Capital Consumption and Adjustment,* Table 32, for 1919-35, and estimated by similar methods for 1936-38).

LINES 2, 3, AND 14: Annual estimates of capital consumption for business use underlie the series in Table I 16, col. 6, but they include a series on agricultural capital consumption. To distribute the total for business use the residual after subtracting line 1 is used.

Accounting measures of depreciation and depletion, given by Fabricant for 1919-35 for mining and manufacturing, other industrial, and public utilities (*Capital Consumption and Adjustment*), are extrapolated to 1936-38 by *Statistics of Income* corporate data. The annual data are converted to 1929 prices by Fabricant's index of prices underlying depreciation charges (*op. cit.,* Table 35, and unpublished estimates for 1936-38 prepared by similar methods). The percentage distribution of the resultant totals for 1919-38 is used in apportioning total consumption among the industrial groups.

Line 3 includes forestry and fishing, service, finance and real estate, construction, trade, and miscellaneous. Differing in coverage from the expenditure data in that it excludes miscellaneous public utilities not estimated separately, it results in an overestimate of the net change in the value of improvements and equipment for this group. Line 14, therefore, suffers from the same lack of comparability between expenditures and consumption.

LINE 4: Sum of annual estimates underlying the series in Table I 16, col. 6.

LINE 5: Sum of lines 1-4.

LINE 8: Sum of annual estimates in Table I 16, col. 7. The data are not comparable with the expenditure estimates since they cover government property only. No estimates are available for consumption of other tax exempt property.

LINE 15: Sum of lines 5, 8, and 14.

Column 5

Col. 3 minus col. 4.

TABLE IV 10

Growth of Reproducible Wealth other than Household
Selected Dates, 1880-1939, 1929 Prices (millions of dollars)

		REAL ESTATE IMPROVEMENTS & EQUIPMENT (1)	(2)	INVENTORIES (3)	BALANCE OF FOREIGN CLAIMS (4)	TOTAL REPRODUCIBLE WEALTH (5)	(6)
		A	BASED ON	WEALTH	ESTIMATES		
1	June 1, 1880	32,190	31,685	11,399	−1,600	41,989	41,484
2	June 1, 1890	60,279	58,644	16,766	−4,800	72,245	70,610
3	June 1, 1900	88,485	87,922	20,963	−4,800	104,648	104,085
4	Dec. 31, 1912	154,397	156,644	29,710	−5,000	179,107	181,354
5	Dec. 31, 1922	158,100	168,423	42,515	5,000	205,615	215,938
		B	BASED ON CAPITAL	FORMATION	DATA		
6	Jan. 1, 1879	29,968		10,554	−1,700	38,822	
7	Jan. 1, 1889	51,157		16,188	−4,700	62,645	
8	Jan. 1, 1899	86,511		20,073	−5,500	101,084	
9	Jan. 1, 1909	132,064		26,063	−5,700	152,427	
10	Jan. 1, 1919	177,299		35,201	2,400	214,900	
11	Jan. 1, 1929	227,744		47,211	8,000	282,955	
12	Jan. 1, 1939	236,454		46,528	4,600	287,582	

COLUMN 1

LINES 1-5: Table IV 5, line 19, plus Table IV 6, line 18.

LINE 6: The value of real estate improvements and equipment is the difference between their estimated values on June 1, 1880 and the flow of each from January 1, 1879 to June 1, 1880, derived by applying to the flow for the decade 1879-88 (given in the form of annual averages in Table II 14, col. 2 and 5) the ratio of the output in 1879 plus one-half the output in 1880 to the total output in 1879-88. All data are in 1929 prices.

LINES 7-12: The sum of line 6 and the flow of producer durables and net construction (Table II 15, col. 6 and 7).

COLUMN 2

LINES 1-5: Table IV 5, line 38, plus Table IV 6, line 36.

COLUMN 3

LINE 1: The value of inventories on June 1, 1880, in current prices, was derived from the wealth data (*Estimated National Wealth,* Table 3). From the total for "Livestock, whether on or off farms, and farming tools and machinery" the value of agricultural equipment (Table IV 3) was subtracted to yield the value of livestock. The value of mining inventories had already been computed (Table IV 2). The Census of Wealth includes "three-quarters of the annual product of agriculture and manufactures and of the annual importation of foreign goods, assumed to be the average supply in the hands of producers or dealers". We reduced this figure one-third, assuming one-half the value of product to be the inventory figure. Finally, we took the value of specie as reported.

Each of these four components of inventories was then converted to 1929 prices. The price index for livestock is based on the weighted average of the price per head of milk cows, other cattle, hogs, sheep, horses, and mules. Averages of the January 1, 1880 and January 1, 1881 data were taken to represent June 1880. The price index for the mining and other commodity inventories is the BLS index of wholesale prices. The value of specie reported was divided into gold and silver on the basis of figures in the *Annual Report* of the Director of the Mint. The value of gold in 1929 prices is the same as in current prices. For silver the price index is based on the price per fine ounce in New York. The unallocable balance is assumed to be the same in 1929 prices as in current. The value of inventories on June 1, 1880, in 1929 prices, is the sum of the four items.

LINES 2-5: The sum of line 1 and the net change in inventories (Table II 15, col. 8), the annual averages for the decades used being those mentioned in Section 6 of the text.

LINE 6: For January 1, 1879 the value of inventories, in 1929 prices, was estimated by subtracting from the June 1, 1880 figure 1.5 times the annual average of the change in inventories for the 1879-88 decade (Table II 15, col. 8).

LINES 7-12: The sum of line 6 and the net change in inventories (Table II 15, col. 8).

COLUMN 4

Algebraic totals of foreign investments in the United States (—) and of United States investments abroad (+). The net balance is estimated in current prices, then converted to 1929 prices by the BLS wholesale price index. For the years beginning with 1919, the approximations to the net balance in current prices are based upon the estimates in the *United States in the World Economy* (Department of Commerce, Economic Series 23, Washington, D. C., 1943, especially Table 13, p. 123). The estimates in this publication for the end of 1919, 1930, 1933, and 1939 are shifted to the dates in Table IV 10 with the help of the annual balances on all capital transactions (*ibid.,* Table I, following p. 216), adjusted to check with the cumulated differences in the net balance of capital indebtedness. For the years prior to 1919, the approximations are based upon various estimates, chiefly those derived or cited in the Bullock, Williams, and Tucker study (*Review of Economic Statistics,* July 1919) as well as in Cleona Lewis, *America's Stake in International Investments* (Brookings Institution, 1938, especially Ch. XXI, pp. 439-56).

The figures on the net balance in current prices are (in billions of dollars): 1879 and 1880, 1.1; 1889 and 1890, 2.8; 1899 and 1900, 2.8; 1909, 3.9; 1912, 3.7; 1919, 3.4; 1922, 5.4; 1929, 8.0; 1939, 3.7. In deriving the figures for the years before 1899 American investment abroad was set roughly at $0.1 billion in 1879 and 1880 and at $0.2 billion in 1889 and 1890.

COLUMN 5

Sum of col. 1, 3, and 4.

COLUMN 6

LINES 1-5: Sum of col. 2, 3, and 4.

Table IV 11
Value of Real Estate Improvements and Equipment
Selected Dates, 1880-1939, 1929 Prices (millions of dollars)

	REAL ESTATE IMPROVEMENTS		EQUIPMENT		TOTAL	
	(1)	(2)	(3)	(4)	(5)	(6)
	A BASED ON WEALTH ESTIMATES					
1 June 1, 1880	27,480	27,059	4,710	4,626	32,190	31,685
2 June 1, 1890	48,642	47,109	11,637	11,535	60,279	58,644
3 June 1, 1900	68,510	67,595	19,975	20,327	88,485	87,922
4 Dec. 31, 1912	116,329	118,240	38,068	38,404	154,397	156,644
5 Dec. 31, 1922	117,405	127,899	40,695	40,524	158,100	168,423
	B BASED ON CAPITAL FORMATION DATA					
6 Jan. 1, 1879	25,766		4,202		29,968	
7 Jan. 1, 1889	42,470		8,687		51,157	
8 Jan. 1, 1899	73,866		12,645		86,511	
9 Jan. 1, 1909	109,052		23,012		132,064	
10 Jan. 1, 1919	140,725		36,574		177,299	
11 Jan. 1, 1929	175,164		52,580		227,744	
12 Jan. 1, 1939	180,864		55,590		236,454	

COLUMN 1

LINES 1-5: Table IV 5, line 19.

LINES 6-12: See the notes to Table IV 10, col. 1, lines 6-12.

COLUMN 2

LINES 1-5: Table IV 5, line 38.

COLUMN 3

LINES 1-5: Table IV 6, line 18.

LINES 6-12: See the notes to Table IV 10, col. 1, lines 6-12.

COLUMN 4

LINES 1-5: Table IV 6, line 36.

COLUMN 5

Sum of col. 1 and 3.

COLUMN 6

Sum of col. 2 and 4.

REPRODUCIBLE WEALTH   231

TABLE IV 12

Value of Real Estate Improvements and Equipment, by Industry
Selected Dates, 1880-1938, 1929 Prices (millions of dollars)

		JUNE 1			DECEMBER 31		
		1880	1890	1900	1912	1922	1938
		(1)	(2)	(3)	(4)	(5)	(6)
	A ADJUSTED BY CURRENT COST (FOR MARKET VALUATION) AND PAST COST (FOR BOOK VALUATION)						
1	Agriculture	5,533	7,486	9,975	15,815	14,627	8,631
2	Mining	421	834	1,626	3,184	3,825	
3	Manufacturing	1,827	5,019	8,957	18,657	30,242	
4	Mining & manufacturing	2,248	5,853	10,583	21,841	34,067	25,995
5	Steam railroads	8,266	14,307	19,236	27,794	26,056	
6	Street railways	264	746	3,202	8,372	6,608	
7	Pullman, express, etc.	65	140	203	218	542	
8	Telephone	34	142	867	2,058	2,687	
9	Telegraph	166	304	351	424	439	
10	Shipping & canals	579	835	1,225	2,332	1,893	
11	Electric light & power	0	141	804	3,729	5,092	
12	Waterworks	491	514	577	561	536	
13	Irrigation	63	137	230	699	817	
14	Pipe lines	25	96	337	695	743	
15	Other industrial	4,743	9,749	12,081	18,596	15,394	25,826
16	Residential	7,964	16,271	22,522	39,685	34,603	40,682
17	Tax exempt	1,749	3,558	6,292	11,578	13,996	25,127
18	Total	32,190	60,279	88,485	154,397	158,100	184,261
	Major categories						
19	Private industrial (1 + 4 + 15)	12,524	23,088	32,639	56,252	64,088	60,452
20	Residential (16)	7,964	16,271	22,522	39,685	34,603	40,682
20a	Total private (19 + 20)	20,488	39,359	55,161	95,937	98,691	101,134
21	Public utilities (5 through 14)	9,953	17,362	27,032	46,882	45,413	58,000
22	Tax exempt (17)	1,749	3,558	6,292	11,578	13,996	25,127
	Major business categories						
23	Agriculture (1)	5,533	7,486	9,975	15,815	14,627	8,631
24	Electric light & power (11)	0	141	804	3,729	5,092	
25	Mining & manufacturing (4)	2,248	5,853	10,583	21,841	34,067	25,995
26	Transportation (5, 6, 7, 10, & 14)	9,199	16,124	24,203	39,411	35,842	
27	Communication (8 & 9)	200	446	1,218	2,482	3,126	
28	Other industrial (12, 13, 15)	5,297	10,400	12,888	19,856	16,747	
29	Total	22,477	40,450	59,671	103,134	109,501	118,452

Table IV 12 concluded:

		JUNE 1			DECEMBER 31		
		1880	1890	1900	1912	1922	1938
		(1)	(2)	(3)	(4)	(5)	(6)

B ADJUSTED BY AN AVERAGE OF CURRENT AND PAST COST (FOR MARKET VALUATION) AND PAST COST (FOR BOOK VALUATION)

		(1)	(2)	(3)	(4)	(5)	(6)
1	Agriculture	5,374	7,108	9,839	16,264	16,846	11,575
2	Mining	421	834	1,626	3,184	3,825	
3	Manufacturing	1,827	5,019	8,957	18,657	30,242	
4	Mining & manufacturing	2,248	5,853	10,583	21,841	34,067	25,995
5	Steam railroads	8,266	14,307	19,236	27,794	26,056	
6	Street railways	264	746	3,202	8,372	6,608	
7	Pullman, express, etc.	65	140	203	218	542	
8	Telephone	34	142	867	2,058	2,687	
9	Telegraph	166	304	351	424	439	
10	Shipping & canals	570	826	1,261	2,376	1,874	
11	Electric light & power	0	141	804	3,729	5,092	
12	Waterworks	491	514	577	561	536	
13	Irrigation	63	137	230	699	817	
14	Pipe lines	25	96	337	695	743	
15	Other industrial	4,590	9,322	12,087	19,092	16,954	28,550
16	Residential	7,780	15,450	22,053	40,943	41,166	40,682
17	Tax exempt	1,749	3,558	6,292	11,578	13,996	25,127
18	Total	31,685	58,644	87,922	156,644	168,423	190,071

Major categories

19	Private industrial (1 + 4 + 15)	12,212	22,283	32,509	57,197	67,867	66,120
20	Residential (16)	7,780	15,450	22,053	40,943	41,166	40,682
20a	Total private (19 + 20)	19,992	37,733	54,562	98,140	109,033	106,802
21	Public utilities (5 through 14)	9,944	17,353	27,068	46,926	45,394	58,142
22	Tax exempt (17)	1,749	3,558	6,292	11,578	13,996	25,127

Major business categories

23	Agriculture (1)	5,374	7,108	9,839	16,264	16,846	11,575
24	Electric light & power (11)	0	141	804	3,729	5,092	
25	Mining & manufacturing (4)	2,248	5,853	10,583	21,841	34,067	25,995
26	Transportation (5, 6, 7, 10, & 14)	9,190	16,115	24,239	39,455	35,823	
27	Communication (8 & 9)	200	446	1,218	2,482	3,126	
28	Other industrial (12, 13, 15)	5,144	9,973	12,894	20,352	18,307	
29	Total	22,156	39,636	59,577	104,123	113,261	124,262

COLUMNS 1-5
LINES 1-18, Parts A & B: Sum of Tables IV 5 and IV 6, col. 1-5 for the respective industries.

COLUMN 6
LINES 1-18: Sum of Table IV 7, col. 3 and 6, and Table IV 9, col. 5 for the respective industries.

TABLE IV 13

Increase in Value of Real Estate Improvements and Equipment,
by Industry, Selected Dates, 1880-1939, 1929 Prices
(millions of dollars)

		June 1, 1880 to June 1, 1900 (1)	June 1, 1900 to Jan. 1, 1919 (2)	June 1, 1880 to Jan. 1, 1919 (3)	Jan. 1, 1919 to Jan. 1, 1939 (4)	June 1, 1880 to Jan. 1, 1939 (5)
	A Adjusted by Current Cost (for Market Valuation) and Past Cost (for Book Valuation)					
1	Agriculture	4,442	1,502	5,944	−2,846	3,098
2	Mining	1,205	2,504	3,709		
3	Manufacturing	7,130	18,895	26,025		
4	Mining & manufacturing	8,335	21,399	29,734	−5,987	23,747
5	Steam railroads	10,970	5,589	16,559		
6	Street railways	2,938	4,368	7,306		
7	Pullman, express, etc.	138	130	268		
8	Telephone	833	1,340	2,173		
9	Telegraph	185	27	212		
10	Shipping & canals	646	445	1,091		
11	Electric light & power	804	3,346	4,150		
12	Waterworks	86	−44	42		
13	Irrigation	167	530	697		
14	Pipe lines	312	298	610		
15	Other industrial	7,338	−106	7,232	13,851	21,083
16	Residential	14,558	11,383	25,941	6,777	32,718
17	Tax exempt	4,543	5,409	9,952	13,426	23,378
18	Total	56,295	55,616	111,911	40,160	152,071
	Major categories					
19	Private industrial (1 + 4 + 15)	20,115	22,795	42,910	5,018	47,928
20	Residential (16)	14,558	11,383	25,941	6,777	32,718
20a	Total private (19 + 20)	34,673	34,178	68,851	11,795	80,646
21	Public utilities (5 through 14)	17,079	16,029	33,108	14,939	48,047
22	Tax exempt (17)	4,543	5,409	9,952	13,426	23,378
	Major business categories					
23	Agriculture (1)	4,442	1,502	5,944	−2,846	3,098
24	Electric light & power (11)	804	3,346	4,150		
25	Mining & manufacturing (4)	8,335	21,399	29,734	−5,987	23,747
26	Transportation (5, 6, 7, 10, & 14)	15,004	10,830	25,834		
27	Communication (8 & 9)	1,018	1,367	2,385		
28	Other industrial (12, 13, 15)	7,591	380	7,971		
29	Total	37,194	38,824	76,018	19,957	95,975

Table IV 13 concluded:

		June 1, 1880 to June 1, 1900 (1)	June 1, 1900 to Jan. 1, 1919 (2)	June 1, 1880 to Jan. 1, 1919 (3)	Jan. 1, 1919 to Jan. 1, 1939 (4)	June 1, 1880 to Jan. 1, 1939 (5)
B	ADJUSTED BY AN AVERAGE OF CURRENT AND PAST COST (FOR MARKET VALUATION) AND PAST COST (FOR BOOK VALUATION)					
1	Agriculture	4,465	4,582	9,047	−2,846	6,201
2	Mining	1,205	2,504	3,709		
3	Manufacturing	7,130	18,895	26,025		
4	Mining & manufacturing	8,335	21,399	29,734	−5,987	23,747
5	Steam railroads	10,970	5,589	16,559		
6	Street railways	2,938	4,368	7,306		
7	Pullman, express, etc.	138	130	268		
8	Telephone	833	1,340	2,173		
9	Telegraph	185	27	212		
10	Shipping & canals	691	551	1,242		
11	Electric light & power	804	3,346	4,150		
12	Waterworks	86	−44	42		
13	Irrigation	167	530	697		
14	Pipe lines	312	298	610		
15	Other industrial	7,497	2,612	10,109	13,851	23,960
16	Residential	14,273	11,852	26,125	6,777	32,902
17	Tax exempt	4,543	5,409	9,952	13,426	23,378
18	Total	56,237	61,989	118,226	40,160	158,386
Major categories						
19	Private industrial (1 + 4 + 15)	20,297	28,593	48,890	5,018	53,908
20	Residential (16)	14,273	11,852	26,125	6,777	32,902
20a	Total private (10 + 20)	34,570	40,445	75,015	11,795	86,810
21	Public utilities (5 through 14)	17,124	16,135	33,259	14,939	48,198
22	Tax exempt (17)	4,543	5,409	9,952	13,426	23,378
Major business categories						
23	Agriculture (1)	4,465	4,582	9,047	−2,846	6,201
24	Electric light & power (11)	804	3,346	4,150		
25	Mining & manufacturing (4)	8,335	21,399	29,734	−5,987	23,747
26	Transportation (5, 6, 7, 10, & 14)	15,049	10,936	25,985		
27	Communication (8 & 9)	1,018	1,367	2,385		
28	Other industrial (12, 13, 15)	7,750	3,098	10,848		
29	Total	37,421	44,728	82,149	19,957	102,106

COLUMN 1
LINES 1-18, Parts A & B: Difference between col. 3 and col. 1 of Table IV 12 for the respective industries.

COLUMN 2
LINES 1-18: Difference between the sum of col. 3 and 6 of Table IV 7 and col. 3 of Table IV 12 for the respective industries.

COLUMN 3
Sum of col. 1 and 2.

COLUMN 4
LINES 1-18, 21: Table IV 9, col. 5 for the respective industries.

COLUMN 5
Sum of col. 3 and 4.

Index

Armed forces, services of, 22
ARNOLD, J. R., 192

BARGER, HAROLD, 8, 11, 34, 140n
BEAN, L. H., 91
BENEY, M. A., 156n
Budget studies
  city and state data, 124
  components, 125-6
  consumer groups covered, 123-4
  expenditures, 125, 126, 127
  income range, 123
  occupational or industrial affiliation, 123-4
  use in estimating services, 77
  see also Consumers' outlay
BULLOCK, C. J., 83, 112, 113, 229
BURNS, A. F., 91
Business use of passenger cars, 3, 4, 15, 17, 21, 24-5, 27, 28, 37, 75-6, 79, 102-3, 189

Canals, value of, 191
Capital consumption
  adjustment in, 17
  derivation of, 53, 80, 116-7
  effect on comparison of capital formation and increase in wealth, 197
  influence of assumed life period on, 197
  on construction, 80
  on government construction, 19
  on producer durable goods, 80
  on war construction, 17, 18, 19, 21
  ratio of to gross value, 80
Capital formation
  compared with wealth estimates, 193-9
  coverage, peacetime concept, 14, 85
  coverage, wartime concept, 14
  effect of bias in inventory changes on, 83
  gross, compared with original estimates, 17
  net, as share in net national product, 21
  net, compared with original estimates, 17
  private, compared with Dept. of Commerce estimates, 18
  proportion of changes in claims against foreign countries in, 83
  proportion of changes in inventories in, 83
CARSON, DANIEL, 120
CHAWNER, L. J., 15, 40, 42, 100, 205, 214, 221, 222, 224
Claims against foreign countries
  see Net changes in claims against foreign countries
Clothing, share in total outlay, 145-9
Consumer commodities
  adjustments in estimates, 3-4, 75-6
  compared with Dept. of Commerce estimates, 4-5
  compared with original estimates, 4
  compared with Shaw's estimates, 5
  Dept. of Commerce estimate as component of gross national product, 6
  price index for, 78
  value of, 3
  see also Flow of goods to consumers
Construction, new
  based on flow of construction materials, 15, 62, 65
  by industrial categories, 186
  by user categories, 15
  change in finished inventories of, 63-5
  compared with increase in real estate improvements, 193
  compared with original estimates, 15
  consumption of, 80
  cyclical movement in, 73
  derivation of, 40-1, 99-101, 116-7
  error in estimates of, 65, 85
  nonwar public, 18
  price indexes for, 41
  ratio to construction materials, 68-71

Construction, new—*Cont.*
   relation to maintenance and repairs, 71-2
   revisions in, 15
   transportation and distribution costs, 65
Construction wage index, 70
Consumer durable goods
   derivation of, 28-31, 95-6, 102-3
   see also Consumer commodities
Consumer goods
   see Flow of goods to consumers
Consumers' outlay
   adjustment in 1914 estimate, 156-7
   allocation to commodities or services, 127, 158-9
   appraisal of sample data, 169-79
   change in service shares, 137-8, 141, 157, 169
   components, 125-6
   extrapolation to 1914 of state sample data for 1918, 155-6
   for all urban consumers, 134, 136-7
   for low income urban consumers, 123-34, 136-7
   for rural farm consumers, 134, 136-7
   for rural nonfarm consumers, 134, 136-7
   imputed values included in, 135
   percentage distribution, 126
   service share compared with Lough's, 157
   service share for all consumers, 138-40
   service share for low income and all income groups compared, 136-7
   service share in state samples
     median, 129
     median and mean changes in, 129
     per year change in, 127-8
   share of 'other' services in, 133
   share of rent in, 133
   total in budget studies, 124-5
   see also Flow of goods to consumers

Depletion, 196-7
Depreciation, 192, 193, 195
   see also Capital consumption
Distribution costs
   see Transportation and distribution costs

DOANE, R. R., 204, 205
DOUGLAS, PAUL, 204, 205, 214, 216, 221, 223

ENGLE, N. H., 110
Equipment, value of
   additions to, current prices, 224-6
   additions to, 1929 prices, 226-7
   by industry, 231-4
   category of wealth, 189
   derivation of, 213-5
   in constant prices, 219, 220-3
Error in
   construction, 65
   flow of goods to consumers, 65, 85
   national product, 85
   net change in claims against foreign countries, 83, 85
   net change in inventories, 83, 85
   producer durable goods, 65, 85
   value of services, 145
   wealth valuation, 196
Establishments, small, 59, 60

FABRICANT, SOLOMON, 17, 53, 101, 145n, 191n, 197, 205, 225, 227
Fire losses, 197
Flow of commodities at producers' prices
   in constant prices, 62
   raised to flow at final cost, 62
   shortages in, 60
   understatement in 1869 Census, 59, 60-2
Flow of goods at final cost, 62
   see also Construction, new, Flow of goods to consumers, *and* Producer durable goods
Flow of goods to consumers
   adjustment for business use of passenger cars, 75-6
   change in finished inventories, 63-5
   compared with original estimates, 12-3
   compared with other estimates, 13
   Dept. of Commerce estimate, 12
   derivation, 12
   error in estimates, 65, 85
   ratio of services to, 77, 123
   share in net national product, 21
   stocks in households, 185-6

INDEX

transportation and distribution costs, 65
under peace- and wartime concepts, 14
Food, share in total outlay, 145-9

Government
  assets, 19
  expenditures, 23
  inventories, 85
  manufacturing establishments, 59, 60
  savings, 87

Hand trades and custom establishments, 59, 61

Income
  originating in commodity production, 65
  originating in construction, 69-71
  originating in transportation and trade, 65
Inventories
  see Net changes in inventories

Land, value of
  basis of valuation, 188-9
  derivation of, 201
  inclusion of improvements in, 189, 195
Lend-Lease, 51
LOUGH, W. H., 34, 104, 134, 140n, 148, 157

Maintenance and minor repairs, 15, 63, 71-2
Manufacturing depreciation, 192
MARTIN, R. F., 69, 70, 86, 87, 89, 117
Motor vehicles, value of, 189

National income
  see National product, net
National product
  concepts, 3, 13
  see also National product, gross, *and* National product, net
National product, gross
  compared with Dept. of Commerce estimates, 21-3
  compared with original estimates, 21
  compared with production indexes, 88-90
  Dept. of Commerce estimate, 6-7, 13
  error in, 85
  fluctuations in, 88-9
  peacetime concept, 14, 19, 21, 22, 85
  share of changes in claims against foreign countries, 83
  share of changes in inventories, 83
  wartime concept, 14, 19
National product, net
  allocation of, 9
  apportionment by final product, 21
  basis of decade estimates, 87
  compared with Dept. of Commerce estimates, 21-3
  compared with Martin's estimates, 86
  compared with original estimates, 21
  effect of bias in inventory changes on, 83
  error in, 85
  final product approach to, 8
  in 1929 prices, 21
  income flow approach to, 7, 8, 19, 87
  peacetime concept, 13, 14, 19, 23, 85
  reconciliation of estimates, 9, 13
  reliability of estimates, 8
  share of changes in claims against foreign countries, 83
  share of changes in inventories, 83
  use as controlling total, 7, 19
  wartime concept, 14, 19, 23
Net changes in claims against foreign countries
  and wealth estimates, 186
  derivation of, 49, 50, 113-4
  error in, 83, 85
  share in capital formation, 83
  share in national product, 83
  trend in, 83
Net changes in inventories
  and wealth estimates, 186
  derivation of, 46-9, 50, 108-12
  error in, 83, 85
  finished, 62, 63-5
  government, 14
  procedure used in estimating, 82
  ratio to total activity, 82
  share in capital formation, 83
  share in national product, 83

Passenger cars
  see Business use of passenger cars
PEARSON, F. A., 88
Perishable commodities
  derivation of, 24-6, 90-2
  see also Flow of goods to consumers
PERSONS, W. M., 88n, 109
Price index
  book value, 191, 196, 216-7
  construction, 101
  consumer durable goods, 29, 96
  current value, 191, 196, 216-7
  perishable goods, 25, 92
  producer durable goods, 37, 98
  rent, 77, 138
  semidurable goods, 27, 94
  services, 105
Producer durable goods
  adjustments, 15, 76
  by industrial categories, 186
  change in finished inventories, 63-5
  compared with increase in equipment, 193
  compared with original estimates, 15-6
  consumption, 80
  derivation of, 36-9, 97-8, 102-3, 116-7
  error in, 65, 85
  transportation and distribution costs, 65
Production
  compared with gross national product, 88-90
  Day-Persons index, 88-9
  Warren-Pearson index, 88-9
Public utility depreciation, 193

Quality changes, 77-8

Real estate improvements
  additions to
    constant prices, 226-7
    current prices, 224-6
  by industry, 231-4
  derivation of, 202-13
  exclusion of land, 188
  in constant prices, 218, 220-3
  inclusion in land values, 189, 195
Real estate, taxable, valuation basis, 191
Real estate, value of, 72

Rent
  appraisal of sample data, 169-79
  imputed, 11, 13, 135
  share for all consumers, 138-40
  share in consumers' outlay, 133
  shares for low income and all income groups, 136-7
RICE, F. R., 134n, 157n
RIGGLEMAN, J. R., 117

Savings of enterprises, 86
SCHELL, E. D., 134n, 157n
Semidurable commodities
  derivation of, 27-8, 93-4
  see also Flow of goods to consumers
Services not embodied in new commodities
  alternative estimate, 11
  appraisal of sample data, 169-79
  as a residual, 7, 9, 76-7
  check on estimates, 145
  compared with original estimates, 10-1
  compared with other estimates, 11
  comparison of share in consumers' outlay with Lough's, 157
  conversion to constant prices, 141
  Dept. of Commerce estimate, 6, 11
  derivation of, 32-4, 104-5, 141
  imputed values included in, 135
  in 1929 prices, 77
  median and mean changes in share of consumers' outlay, 129
  per year change in share of consumers' outlay, 127-8
  price index, 78
  relation to income payments, 87
  share in consumers' outlay, state samples, 127, 129
  share in flow of goods to consumers, 77, 78, 123
  share in net national product, 21-79
  share of all urban consumers, 134, 136-7, 138-40
  share of low income urban consumers, 123-34, 136-7
  share of rural farm consumers, 134, 136-7
  share of rural nonfarm consumers, 134, 136-7

INDEX 239

Services other than rent
  appraisal of sample data, 169-79
  price index, 77
  share in consumers' outlay, 133
  share for all consumers, 138-40
  shares for low income and all income groups, 136-7
SHAVELL, HENRY, 25, 29, 33, 37, 44
SHAW, W. H., 3, 4, 5, 7, 8, 11, 13, 25, 27, 28, 32, 34, 37, 59, 60, 61, 62, 63n, 75, 91, 92, 93, 95, 97, 99, 102, 145, 147, 148, 216, 227
Shipping, valuation basis, 191
SNYDER, CARL, 105, 138n
SPLAWN, WALTER, 213
STRAUSS, FREDERICK, 91
Streets and roads, 187, 193-5

Tax exempt property, valuation basis, 191
Taxes, direct, 23
TERBORGH, GEORGE, 223, 224, 225
THOMPSON, W. S., 107
Transportation and distribution costs, 62, 63, 65-8
TUCKER, R. S., 83, 112, 113, 229

U. S. Navy, 185, 187-8, 195

VIAL, E. E., 91

WALKER, F. A., 60n
WARBURTON, CLARK, 8

War goods
  changes in prices, 23
  consumption, 14
  derivation of, 42-5
  inclusion in national product, 19, 23
  under peacetime concept, 13-4, 19
  under wartime concept, 14, 19
WARREN, G. F., 88
Wealth
  allocation by type, 189-90
  compared with capital formation, 193-9
  conversion to common price basis, 191-2
  definition, 185
  derivation of, 228-30
  distributed on basis of ownership, 190
  distributed on basis of use, 190
  errors in, 196
  gross or net, 192-3
  household commodity stocks, 185-6
  increase in, 185
  industrial distribution, 186, 190
  omissions from, 187-8
  reproducible, 188, 189
  valuation, 191-2, 195-6
WHELPTON, P. K., 107
WILLCOX, W. F., 60n
WILLIAMS, F. M., 123n, 134n, 157n
WILLIAMS, J. H., 83, 112, 113, 229

ZIMMERMAN, C. C., 123n

DATE DUE	
APR 0 1 1992	
NOV 2 5 1997	
JAN 2 9 1998	
MAR 1 7 1999	
OCT 2 8 2000	
DEC 1 6 2000	